The
Autobiography
of
Daniel J. Isengart

PUBLISHED, 2013, BY
OUTPOST19, SAN FRANCISCO

COVER PHOTO:
RUSSEL GERA

OUTPOST19 | SAN FRANCISCO
OUTPOST19.COM

Noterdaeme, Filip
    The Autobiography of Daniel J. Isengart/
    Filip Noterdaeme
    ISBN 9781937402488 (pbk)
    ISBN 9781937402518 (ebk)

Library of Congress Control Number:
    2012923466

july 2013

OUTPOST
19

PROVOCATIVE READING
SAN FRANCISCO
NEW YORK
OUTPOST19.COM

"In his introduction to her collected works, Truman Capote said of the writer Jane Bowles that her dialogue 'sounds, or sounds to me, as though it has been translated into English from some delightful combination of other tongues.' The same could be said of the intimate, witty and wry memoirish prose of the Belgian artist and now author Filip Noterdaeme. Technically a novel, THE AUTOBIOGRAPHY OF DANIEL J. ISENGART traces the paths of its two expat heroes Filip and Daniel from their original countries of Belgium and Germany and fuses their destinies as lovers and partners in aesthetic crime and delirious invention in the clubs and pop-up galleries of New York. It is a portrait of a vanishing but never quite vanquished world: of conceptualists, art dealers, performance artists, patrons, phonies, freaks, punks, drag queens, you name it. Part bildungsroman (both come of age together as rather disabused but unbeatable believers in themselves and each other) and part picaresque (taking us to after parties, rich people's happenings, and seedy Lower East Side burlesques), THE AUTOBIOGRAPHY is a mixed-media distillation of charm and spunk and, maybe best of all, gossip."

— Edmund White

Foreword

Perhaps as you are reading this, Filip Noterdaeme is sitting at his table in Brooklyn, gazing over a dish of perfectly cooked asparagus, into the eyes of his lover and artistic co-conspirator Daniel J. Isengart. No matter what else may be happening, they are having a wonderful meal. Daniel is a wonderful cook and a wonderful singer. Filip is a wonderful artist and a wonderful eater, and no matter what else might be wrong, they are never going to have a bad meal or ever not be in love. This is what makes Filip Noterdaeme and Daniel J. Isengart different from you and me.

In the early years of the 20th century, there was another household, in Paris, where food and art, too, were very important. This was the home of Gertrude Stein and her lover and artistic co-conspirator Alice B. Toklas. They were very serious about art, very serious about ideas, and they were very, very serious about food. No matter what else was going on, they would always have wonderful meals, even when they were poor during the war, and no matter what, they would always be in love. In 1933, Stein was very obscure in the greater world but a huge presence among the Paris avant-garde. She wrote THE AUTOBIOGRAPHY OF ALICE B. TOKLAS as an account of their life there between the two World Wars. Written by Stein from Toklas's point of view, Stein could go into great detail about her own work under the guise of someone who knew, loved and understood her work. She wrote this book to make money, and it was her only commercially successful book. It made her famous in the real world. It worked.

THE AUTOBIOGRAPHY OF DANIEL J. ISENGART is a story of what life was like in NYC in the 1990's and 2000's for kids who came to NY, wanting to be artists. It is not a queer JUST KIDS although you could read it like that and some people will because that is the world we live in now, mediated always by something that is either derived from or based on something we have seen before. So let's say that in a way THE AUTOBIOGRAPHY OF DANIEL J. ISENGART is like Patti Smith's book, that is, if you are queer, European, a dandy, educationally and socially privileged, obsessed with art and the history of art, long to find your place in that lineage and only eat delicious, well-prepared food even when you are poor and just scraping by.

Filip Noterdaeme and Daniel J. Isengart came to New York respectively at the end of the 1980's and beginning of the 1990's, a bleak time for artists who were seekers, but of course they did not know that. They were romantics and fierce about art. They were willing to gamble everything on their artistic development at a time when the idea of artistic development still existed – pre-internet, pre-art school stars, pre-American Idol, in the midst of the AIDS epidemic, before people believed that the AIDS epidemic was over or that it was just an illness you needed a prescription for. The word queer was still lower case and not yet co-opted as a marketing and lifestyle strategy. Filip and Daniel were privileged in many ways and poor in most of the ways that counted at the end of the

20th century, meaning they had to work to pay their rent yet were still focused on securing their place in the history of art. Just a few short years before their arrival in New York, seven out of ten in the downtown art scene had died or were dying of AIDS or just dying, and those who hadn't died were very sad, very angry and very traumatized. If they had arrived a decade earlier, they would have met Jack Smith and Jackie Curtis and Margot Howard-Howard and Peter Hujar and Paul Thek and Keith Haring and Robert Mapplethorpe and Brian Damage and John Sex and Hannah Wilke and Cookie Mueller, and, well, the list of those who died just goes on and on. Instead, they arrived at the same time as a new generation of perfectly nice middleclass kids who wanted to be dark, edgy and dangerous artists. It was the beginning of expectation, the beginning of the professionalization of the arts, which deeply affected the artistic community.

Originally, at least in my lifetime, artistic community was a place where you got together to talk about art and life, about making art and living life, and talk about the ideas around art and life. What replaced it is a simulacrum of artistic community where people talk about how to get grants and where to get grants. Once, at a dinner party at my house, a couple of years ago, Filip Noterdaeme met my neighbor, the octegenarian painter KC Rowling, who had just lost his lover of 60 years, the painter and sculptor Malcolm Anderson. Filip was very moved listening to KC's story of love and loss, of a world before gay identity, a world where artists stopped showing their work publicly because of their artistic integrity, a world where young artists worked as night guards at The Metropolitan Museum in order to draw from the masters, a world where very young artists became very old artists. It inspired him to write his own story.

What you are about to read here is much more than a personal history. It is a courageous critique of the politics of art, something that Filip Noterdaeme has committed himself to ever since he hit Manhattan at age 22. By naming names and saying what he thinks, he exposes an art world where not only the Emperor is not wearing any clothes but neither is anyone in his court. It is a funny, lovely, delicate and sturdy little book that captures an ephemeral, tragic and undiscovered history just before the world changed forever. I was the first person to read it and I was very amused and very excited by the fact that Filip Noterdaeme, like Stein, could write in great detail about the ideas behind his work.

Filip Noterdaeme is a conceptualist. You know he is a good conceptualist because he was thrown out of his Master of Fine Arts program at City University of New York because of an idea. No one has ever gotten thrown out of art school for being mediocre. Filip got thrown out of art school because he was exhibiting the same brilliant, sly articulation that makes him a powerful artist today, and a threat to the art establishment.

The book is also about Filip Noterdaeme's antidote to the self-serving cesspool of the contemporary art world: individuality, integrity and respect. Real, deep-down respect for everyone he comes in contact with during those long days he spends at the desk of his Homeless Museum of Art. Here, the museum director is always in, always ready to listen and speak to the public. Always ready to embrace the space between art and life. His is a metaphysical act, and his public critique of the corrupt and phony art world is eloquent, lucid, witty and to be reckoned with. He speaks truth to power, like the prince who exchanged his royal robes for a pauper's rags, and that takes real guts.

There will always be artists who live for the high bitter romance of Art. They are seekers, and they have lived in all eras. They are romantic and visionary, uncompromising and brave. Filip Noterdaeme has seized the bull of his personal history by the horns, pulled his lover Daniel J. Isengart up behind him and they are riding away into the sunset. No doubt they will soon have a delicious meal.

Meanwhile, I am wondering who will play me in the movie. You see, I am very 20th Century.

— Penny Arcade
London, December 7, 2012

Publisher's note

The unique syntax, punctuation and capitalization used by Filip Noterdaeme in THE AUTOBIOGRAPHY OF DANIEL J. ISENGART are in meticulous homage. We encourage readers to compare the work at hand with Gertrude Stein's THE AUTOBIOGRAPHY OF ALICE B. TOKLAS.

OUTPOST19

I

Before I Came to New York

I was born in Munich, Germany and grew up in Paris, France. I have in consequence always preferred living in a moderate climate but it is difficult, in America or even on the continent of Europe, to find a moderate climate and live in it. My mother's father was a professor, he came to Bavaria in '39, he married my grandmother who was very fond of literature. She was the daughter of a fur merchant. My mother was and is a charismatic ambitious woman named Ulla.

My father came of germanic czech stock. His german father was a romantic and artistic but his family convinced him to pursue a military career. His czech wife, my grandmother, left him shortly after giving birth to my father and his younger sister when he began to sympathize with the Nazis and raised her two children by herself, but the war being over, she was expelled from her home country for having been married to a german and sent to Bavaria where she remarried and led the life of a conservative well-to-do garment retailer.

I myself have had no liking for violence and have always enjoyed the pleasures of singing and cooking. I am fond of kitchenware, desserts, books, scarves, cardigans and even cologne and lip balm. I like a man's suit but I like it worn by a woman.

I led in my childhood and youth the sheltered existence of my class and kind, first in Paris and then in Munich. I had some early experiences as a dancer but none were very serious. When I was about nine years of age I was very fond of Mozart. I felt that The Magic Flute should have a sequel and I decided that I would write it. I received the opera score from my grandparents as a gift and then, when I felt my inadequacy, rather blushed for myself and did not pursue the idea. Perhaps at that time I did not feel skilled enough to study an opera score, at any rate it is now in the basement of my parents' house in Munich.

Up to my seventeenth year I was seriously interested in singing and dancing. I studied and practiced assiduously but shortly then it seemed futile, I lacked the discipline to become really proficient and there was no teacher who inspired me to work really hard. In the sculpture Scented Candle Descending a Staircase Filip Noterdaeme has created a very good image of me as I was at that time.

From then on for about four years I was biding my time. I led a fairly uninteresting life, I had no inspiration, much boredom many worries, my life was miserably empty and I suffered but did not know how to find a way out of it. This brings me to spring break of '92 which had as a consequence that Harry Heissmann a fellow student at the Academy of Fine Arts in Munich went and came back from a trip abroad saying Daniel, New York is where you belong, and this led to a complete change in my life.

I was at this time living by myself. I lived quietly and took things quietly, although I felt them deeply. The one thing I liked to do was to go out dancing and one night there was Patricia Laval, another student from the academy, and I was dancing and on fire. Why don't you, she said, live the way you dance. I remember that once when I was still very young my mother led a little neighbor friend into my room, I was occupied with a drawing, the little neighbor friend began to make a terrible scene. Let me finish my drawing first, said I, and calmly went back to drawing. One of my mother's favorite literary quotes I always remember, Mensch, werde wesentlich, man, become your essence. She also told me that a cook should never take any shortcuts in his creation of a meal, if there is a cook there are insofar as there is a cook no shortcuts.

As I was saying I was living by myself but there was in my mind a growing desire for change. Harry Heissmann's return from a trip to New York followed by his suggestion that perhaps I belong there made the difference.

Harry Heissmann brought me several gifts from New York, an invitation card for a party at the Roxy, a Wet Paint sign and a subway token, the first New York things I owned. He also told me many stories of life in New York. I went to visit my parents who were living in Barcelona at the time and told them I would leave the academy and Europe and become a cabaret entertainer in New York. My parents were very disturbed by this, after all there had been at that time a great deal of talk about New York being a very dangerous city. Within a few months I dissolved my household in Munich and moved to New York. It was only a few years later when I got to perform at Bar d'O with Joey Arias who had reinvented the art of cabaret and there I met Filip Noterdaeme. I was impressed by his tight white T-shirt with the word Dreamer printed across the chest. I may say that only three times in my life have I met a genius and each time a bell within me rang and I was not mistaken, and I may say that in neither of the three cases was it ever necessary for anybody else to tell me so as I recognized the quality in each of them instantly and on my own. The three people of whom I wish to speak are Filip Noterdaeme, Joey Arias and Meow Meow. I have met many talented people, I have met some brilliant people but I have only known three first class geniuses and in each case on sight within me something rang. In no one of the three cases have I been mistaken. In this way my new full life began.

II
My Arrival in New York

This was the year 1993. Filip Noterdaeme was just finishing his thesis on Gertrude Stein and Paul Celan and he was deep in the Diaries of Marcellus Wasbending-Ttum, his fictional illustrated diary. Tommy Tune was directing the Will Roger Follies on Broadway, Penny Arcade caused a sensation at the Village Gate with her show Bitch! Dyke! Faghag! Whore! and Quentin Crisp could be seen as Queen Elizabeth in the film version of Virginia Woolf's Orlando. I was on my way to New York.

I went to the academy one last time to tell my professor I was leaving Munich forever and he said he thought I would have done rather well as an interior designer. But not at all I said, you have no idea how happy I am to leave. I have so much inertia and so little initiative that very possibly if I had not decided to quit I would have, well, not taken to the practice of interior design but at any rate to interior decoration and you don't know how little I care for interior decoration, and how all interior design bores me. The professor was completely taken aback and that was the end of my academic education.

On the day of my departure from Munich to New York a great many friends came to the airport to bid me farewell. It was a very emotional moment. I believe it was the very kind steward at the check-in counter who took notice and action because when I was shown my seat on the plane I realized I had been upgraded to business class. Something similar had happened to me once before when I was only 10 years old. I had been invited by a french family to spend the summer with them in the south of France, and my parents put me on a plane. It was my first time on a plane and as I said I was 10 years old but I believe I looked quite a bit younger to the Air France stewardesses who took pity on this little boy all by himself and kindly sat me in first class.

In any case, on that long flight from Munich to New York, I had in my pocket a student visa for the Ballet Arts Dance School and the keys to an apartment on the Upper West Side I was going to sublet from Mary Vivien. I must tell a little about Mary Vivien.

She was from California and had lived much of her life as a dancer in New York before moving to Munich where she taught german ballerinas the roots of black dance. She had kept a rental apartment at 375 West 75th Street in New York and sublet it illegally to a dancer but there was something about this dancer that had made her nervous. I do not know what happened. In any case when she heard that I was going to move to New York and looking for a place to stay she had an idea.

Mary Vivien had her opinions, she did not for instance trust white people all that easily. And so she did not then and went around asking about me, not just anyone but every black person in Munich that we both knew. She talked to my black ballet teacher and to my black vocal coach and then she talked to Bao the black cook I was working with at an italian restaurant named Tiramisu. Can I trust him she asked and they all said, yes you can. And so this, one of the luckiest happenstances of my life took place around this period when Mary Vivien decided to get rid of the dancer who was staying at her apartment and make it available for me to sublet. She gave me the keys and said, Daniel, she said to me, the landlord must not under any circumstances find out that I am not presently living in the apartment. If anybody asks, she said, you tell them you are my roommate and that I am at work. I promised I would.

And so I arrived at my new home at 375 West 75th Street on the Upper West Side of Manhattan one late evening and it was the beginning of my life in New York. There are a great many things that happened since then but now I must tell what I saw that first evening.

The apartment was a one bedroom on the top floor of a run-down brownstone building. It was poorly furnished and a bit untidy in the way that was typical for the Upper West Side in those days. As welcoming gifts, the dancer had left a container of old chinese takeout food in the refrigerator and a half-empty bottle of vodka in the freezer. There was a dead water bug on the bedroom floor. I put down my suitcase, disposed of the water bug, the takeout and also the vodka and went around the corner to Fairway Market to buy my first meal in the new world. This was the beginning of my passion for late night grocery shopping which of course is not done anywhere in Europe. At Fairway I wondered about the disorderly heaps of vegetables and sawdust on the floor. Surely, I said to myself, this is a food store for poor people. It must be said that my first impression of the Upper West Side was also rather dismal. I thought it was a very poorly maintained and possibly very dangerous neighborhood. Indeed I felt very much like an adventurer being there.

Later much later someone explained to me that Fairway was considered one of the better food stores around and that the Upper West Side was one of New York's most desirable neighborhoods, for married couples with children in any case. That night at Fairway I bought two things I had never eaten before, chinese cold sesame noodles and israeli hummus. It was a very odd combination.

Having heard of cockroaches' preference for coming out at night and traveling along the walls I moved Mary's futon into the center of the living room. It was a very unnerving night. I kept waking up from the sound of car alarms, a sound I had never heard before.

It was not until the next morning that I inspected the apartment very closely. I have always maintained that a lived-in interior must be functional and orderly and just pleasant enough. I decided that some changes would have to be made. I began by carrying much of the old and shabby furniture down to the street where it was soon picked up by a couple of homeless men. The next thing I did was gather all of Mary Vivien's personal belongings and put them away in one of the closets. I locked the closet door and only reopened it once in the four years I lived at 375 West 75th Street but more of that a little later. Then I got down on my hands and knees and thoroughly cleaned and disinfected the entire apartment. The kitchen was a problem. The cupboards were encrusted with grime and there were dead insects in the cracks. There was nothing else to do than rip out the cupboards and replace them with open shelves. All this I did quite resolutely and without any hesitation. At last I painted the entire apartment Richard Meier white.

It was not until three years later that Mary Vivien

came to New York for a visit. When she came by 375 West 75th Street she did not believe her eyes at the changes I had made. This, she said to me, is the first time anybody has ever made something out of this place, including myself. As a matter of fact it made her not a little angry to see that for all these years she had had an apartment in New York that could be made beautiful. But I am running far ahead of those early days in New York.

Every month, I deposited the rent in Mary Vivien's bank account. I also collected her mail and forwarded it to her address in Germany. When someone asked about her I pretended that she was living with me at 375 West 75th Street. Usually no one asked. Then the incident with the burglary happened.

It was a lovely autumn night and I came home late to find the apartment door broken and unhinged and the place in great disarray. Naturally, there had not been a great deal of valuable things to steal, but gone was my collection of music records and my stereo system and my old Yashica camera.

Of course the apartment door had to be replaced and I had to call the landlord and pretend that I was Mary Vivien's roommate and that she was at work. He said he would have to come by and look at the damage. I got very nervous at the thought of him seeing the apartment all white with no sign of black Mary. I unlocked the closet where I had put away all of Mary Vivien's belongings and nervously grudgingly redecorated the apartment with her girlie things. It did look convincing but perhaps not convincing enough and so I called upon my friend Nicole, an actress from South Africa who lived a few blocks down on 72nd Street, to borrow some more girlie clothes and girlie

9

things. She was rather amused and said, why certainly with pleasure. With her help I made the apartment look like Mary Vivien was living there, everywhere. I even put a second toothbrush and a hairbrush full of long black hair in the bathroom. The landlord arrived, big and imposing. Where is Miss Vivien he said. She's at work, I said. He inspected the apartment a little bit and, seeming satisfied with what he saw, left again, promising to have a new apartment door installed soon. One week later two workmen arrived with a door but evidently neither of them was very good at installing it and I yelled at them. I was beside myself by then, having not been able to lock the apartment for so long even though my few valuable belongings had already been stolen. Oh yes, said they nodding their heads, certainly sir we understand very well. But you see, said they, this door they gave us is the wrong door. In any case it took another week before I was able to lock the apartment again and it was an ordeal. Now that I am living at 172 Clinton Street with Filip Noterdaeme, he and I always have an argument because he does not care to lock the door at night.

During my first year in New York, everything and nothing happened. I took dance classes every day, one after another, and one day I went to a ballet class taught by Evee Lynn. She was by far the most imposing teacher at Ballet Arts. I had often seen her walking about with a black cane, always commenting on everything to anybody. She was tall, her hair was jet-black and cut short and her rather big expressive eyes were always made up with heavy black eyeliner that made one think of oriental masks. I say she looked oriental but she was european. She always wore black and was very fond of jewelry. She was very popular among japanese ballet students accustomed to strictness and obedience.

Evee Lynn was born in Vienna, Austria, of a very respectable lyricist, Bruno Hardt-Warden, and a very disrespectable barmaid who gave her away when she was 2 years old. She always says she never forgave her mother for giving her away, she has a horror of what she calls unreliable people. She had thus grown up in an orphanage and foster care and eventually was sent to Tatjana Gsovsky's ballet school in Berlin where she was trained in the russian style and became a ballerina. In 1944 she was cast as the lead in Gottfried von Einem's ballet Turandot and performed it in Dresden. She was then 17 years of age and as she always says, it was a big deal because Joseph Goebbels was in the audience. After the war she fled to Vienna where she worked as an exotic dancer at the Casanova Bar, the same nightclub that Carol Reed so effectively used as a backdrop in The Third Man. There she met an american lieutenant who married her and brought her to the States. The marriage lasted two weeks and now over 50 years later I was taking ballet class with her almost every day. Years later in 2002 I was invited to perform my cabaret show at the Casanova bar in Vienna which still looked exactly like in The Third Man.

Evee Lynn was an excellent teacher. I was very surprised, having had a very different impression of her, taking her class for the first time, finding her to be incredibly funny and witty. There is, she often said, only one way to do ballet right so why don't you do it right just this once even if it is the only time you ever do something right in your life. This of course terrified many of the students and amused me to no end. She also had the bad habit of cursing out poor Dimitri the russian pianist who played for her class. Sometimes, she showed off her countless rings and bracelets and explained which were real and which were fake. One must, she said, know the real from the fake in life. Another thing Evee Lynn liked to say was, in life what you must do is give and give and then give some more and then you are on your deathbed and somebody will come and say you did not give enough. Later after she retired there were times when we fought vehemently and did not talk for months, like at the time when she argued that the world was permanently conspiring against her, or when she had asked me to clean her little studio apartment on West 57th Street and get rid of clutter while she was in the hospital getting a hip replacement. I was perhaps a little too eager at it and it became a problem when she was released from the hospital and found her apartment very clean and orderly but all her Norma Kamali suits and Calvin Klein jeans missing. And it is true, I had gotten rid of a lot of her clothes, they had been spilling out of every closet covered in dust and looking like they had not been worn in many many years. I of course knew that Evee Lynn had long stopped dressing up, preferring to wear pajamas and sweat pants and this perhaps made me feel justified in clearing away her old clothes. The story of the Norma Kamali suits however nearly ended our friendship. Evee Lynn has since forgiven me but every now and then when we have an argument she laments about how much money those vintage Norma Kamali suits had been worth and how could I just throw them away.

After her hip replacement operation Evee became a recluse. In those days she preferred talking about walking to walking and insisted that the hip operation had not been a success. How I miss walking, she always said, I used to love taking long walks and let my mind wander. She hardly ever left her home any more and her life became all about the four T's, telephone, tempest, tedium and television. Her building's superintendent and I were by then her only contact to the outside world. Sometimes there were anxiety attacks that brought back memories of the bombing of Berlin that she had lived through in 1945 and preferred not to talk about. She had in her dancing years hoped to become the next Leslie Caron and achieve superstardom but it had not happened. The talent was there, oh it was, Evee used to say, but her malady had been stronger. There had been two years in a mental institution and electroshock treatments and later a position as ballet mistress with Dance Theatre of Harlem. Having worked tirelessly all her life she was prepared for old age financially but not physically or emotionally. Do yourself a favor she often said to me, kill yourself when you're 60. I am still trying to convince her to write her memoirs.

In those early New York years I was earning my living as a waiter. My first job was waiting tables at Café Ravel on West 74th Street, the only place on the Upper West Side that would hire me without a work permit. It was not until years later that I received a work permit and became what americans call a resident alien of extraordinary ability. The funny thing about Café Ravel was how it was owned by israelis who had a lot of experience in the garment industry but none in the restaurant industry and so there was much trial and error with american italian food prepared by brazilian cooks and viennese pastries being ordered from an industrial american bakery. It was at Café Ravel that I first met and worked with Abi Maryan, a french actress who later became a real estate agent and told me how great a change this had made in her life. Daniel, she said simply, I will never be poor again. There was a fair sprinkling of americans among the staff, closeted Nick from New Jersey and blonde Gwendolyn the dancer who told me all about american life without health insurance. But what will you do if you have an accident and break a leg, I said. I cry, she said with a sad smile. Then there was Tiffany the red-haired hostess with whom I sometimes went out after work, usually to Webster Hall in the East Village where we delighted in dancing among gay voguers. Strangely enough it was only very much later that I found out that she was a heroin addict. It was a rather dramatic little episode. I don't know what happened but she ran into trouble with columbian drug dealers and was afraid to go home. I let her stay at 375 West 75th Street for the night and the next morning she took a bus to Florida to go to rehab and this made a great change in her life.

One day Sita Mani, an indian dance student at Ballet Arts told me, you really ought to quit working at the café and become a cater waiter like me. That way, she said, you could work less and still earn enough to live on if you live quietly. It was only a little later that I, having acquired a waiter's tuxedo and learned about the american way to do french service began working at cocktail parties and banquets in museums and other places.

Most performers and actors in New York in those days worked as cater waiters when they were not acting in film or theater, and most of them hardly ever found work in film or theater. In those years I met hundreds of young and not so young actors but only one of them as far as I know ever became known as an actor. That was Aasif

Mandvi. He was one of the obnoxious types who always draw attention to themselves and this, his talent for standing out among all the other actors, made his career in film and theater.

The most pleasant catering company to work for was Glorious Food. It was owned by Sean Driscoll who had worked and worked and worked and as they say had rewritten the book on how to do catering in New York. But what a great book the real story of what goes on behind the scenes in the catering world would be. Maybe one day somebody will write it. I remember so well a large dinner event in Mobile, Alabama. Glorious Food had arranged for an old chartered plane to fly the entire staff to Mobile to properly attend to the rich white gala guests and after dinner there was a private concert by James Brown. It was very exciting. James Brown sang Living in America and he was a devil in rhythm, I could not cease looking at him. I also remember the ladies among the guests frankly openly hitting on the black waiters among us.

Sometimes during those years I was booked to serve lunches and dinners in the homes of wealthy people. On one occasion, I was sent to the home of Ronald and Jo Carol Lauder for a ladies' luncheon. I remember being very impressed with their art collection. There were Picassos in the parlor and early american cookie jars in the kitchen and a beautiful white eggshell table by Marcel Broodthaers in the living room. Then there was the blue Yves Klein with a sea sponge in the dining room. The dining room had been set up with several round tables and it was tight. We were serving risotto and I was in charge of shaving white truffles on everybody's plate. The truffle I had been given was as big as a baby's fist and crumbled into pieces when I tried to shave it over Jo Carol's plate. Then I stood at attention with my back to the Yves Klein and suddenly felt something brushing against my shoulder. I had leaned back too far and touched the little blue sea sponge on the painting and it looked like it might fall off at any moment and I nearly fainted.

Feast and Fêtes, Daniel Boulud's catering company was a different story altogether. It was essentially french and therefore essentially disorganized and difficult to work for. But in spite of all this it must be said that french Daniel knew how to make a very good lamb ragout, except that one time at his own birthday dinner party at the Dakota when it was too salty and had to be sent back to the kitchen. Then there were the creations of pastry chef Francois Payard. How well I remember the dainty little chocolate domes filled with pistachio mousse and a crunchy wafer he had prepared for a New York City Ballet gala. Being that after the dinner there were many extra desserts lined up on tables in the back of the kitchen I freely indulged and ate about 5 of them, one after another. Later François Payard opened his own pastry shop and sadly gradually lost his touch.

I always say that working as a cater waiter gives one the feeling that life is one half party and one half cleanup. I did it for several years until I could not bear it any longer and began looking for other ways to make a living. When I found the opportunity to work as a personal chef I gladly took it and threw away my waiter's tuxedo. I was very pleased with myself when I did. Over the years I have cooked lunches and dinners for a great many different kinds of people. I have been lucky in finding good clients, though some had weaknesses in other ways. Filip Noterdaeme likes to remind me that if they did not have such faults, they would not be able to afford me. But I am once more running ahead of my bread and butter days in New York.

It was at about that time Evee Lynn introduced me to Dieter Riesle, a retired german ballet dancer. Evee Lynn was always delighted when Dieter Riesle came to her class because he knew ballet very well and it pleased her a great deal to have someone in class who did. In any case she told Dieter Riesle to help me with my technique and he did, in bed.

Dieter Riesle looked rather like a classic german with blond hair, steel blue eyes and sturdy german legs. He was the son of a criminal investigator and had the ruthless inquisitive eyes that of course are a characteristic of criminal investigators. To be sure he always laughed mockingly at someone or something, and this was difficult. We saw a great deal of each other for some time and then I met Carlos from Puerto Rico, entirely a different type. Carlos was sweet and caring and he and I had a very pleasant guilty one night stand. Dieter Riesle of course guessed right away that something had happened between me and Carlos and said, suit yourself, but this is not working for me. And broke up with me. I felt bad for a while. Dieter Riesle went on to study criminal justice like his father, and also acting. These combined skills later enabled him to play german soldiers in Hollywood movies every now and then and once, years later, with much amusement and surprise I saw his picture in a beer ad posted inside many a Long Island Railroad train. But to get back to my early adventures in New York.

I became involved in many a strange story and once

let a homeless schizophrenic woman spend the night at 375 West 75th Street. This is the story.

It was a cold December afternoon and I was standing on a street corner on the Upper West Side taking snapshots of the neighborhood to send home to my parents when suddenly a woman with wild salt and pepper hair and manic little black eyes began talking to me. Are you a fashion photographer, she said. I laughed and said, no. Nevertheless, she said, I should like to hire you to take pictures at a benefit with Jenny Shimizu that I am going to produce at the Henri Bendel department store on Fifth Avenue. She did not look like a homeless schizophrenic woman to me but of course I had never seen a homeless schizophrenic woman before so how could I have recognized one. Her name was Katharina Mani. It is difficult to explain how it all happened but Katharina Mani ended up with me at 375 West 75th Street, talking to me at great length about minimalist sculpture, Joseph Beuys, Nouvelle Vague movies and her teenage daughter. The unsettling thing was that she kept falling asleep in the middle of her own sentences. I politely offered her to stay for the night. She gladly accepted. She slept in the bedroom and I spent a very nervous night on the futon in the living room worrying a great deal about my strange guest.

In the morning Katharina Mani said she had to make some phone calls. There was no way to say no and so I showed her the phone and then sat listening and watching her calling one person after another. There seemed to be no end to the phone numbers she had memorized. Clearly no one seemed particularly interested in talking to her and she began yelling at people on the other line. I noticed with great astonishment how she told everybody that she was calling from her new office on West 75th street. When Katharina finally left I was in quite a state and did not answer my phone or doorbell for many weeks afterwards.

It was not until a year later that I saw Katharina Mani again. It was in the lobby of the Museum of Modern Art. She talked to me with her characteristic brilliant way of telling lies to get what she wanted but I politely refused to pay for her admission, much to the relief of the clerks who looked on, nervously. Clearly, she was well known and feared among them. I have not seen Katharina Mani since then and do not know what happened to her.

It was at about that time that I did my first solo show, Mind and Matter, at a little cabaret for beginners, the Duplex in the West Village. It was a tormenting process.

I did not know any cabaret pianists and so I hired Joe Cross, one of the accompanists from Ballet Arts. He was a tall sentimental man from Texas with a big red nose and a strong liking for whiskey. I put together a very varied program of german kabarett couplets, french chansons, american show tunes and jazz standards. Some people thought perhaps it was a little too varied. There was also the absolute necessity of including a literary quote in the show. I was at the time reading A Stone Boat by Andrew Solomon, a most charming little novel about a tormented pianist's jet set life and his dignified mother's death of cancer. There was a very elegant little paragraph in it that said how much had been made of the insecurities and anxieties of men with strong exteriors and how too little had been said of the devastating strength of those who had the mannerisms of delicacy. I liked this paragraph immensely and decided to contact Andrew Solomon and ask for his permission to recite it in my show. He kindly obliged. He was a charming young man with the complicated life of the independently wealthy. It is a remarkable little assumption among americans that independent wealth makes life easy but in Andrew Solomon's case, life has always been so much more complicated and he later wrote about it extensively in his atlas of depression, The Noonday Demon.

Mind and Matter opened and everybody came. I performed without much difficulty and I was encouraged. The show ran for several nights and gave me my first taste of the comedy and misery of cabaret life. On closing night something got into Joe Cross and he began playing freestyle jazz to my singing. After the show I told him in no uncertain terms to never do anything of the kind again. This made him very nervous and insecure. It was only a couple of days later that he nearly cut off his thumb when he tried to open a can with a kitchen knife. In short he fell on hard times and I had to find another pianist to work with.

Then something strange happened. Feast and Fêtes called and asked me to work at a large party at a townhouse on West 10th Street. I put on my waiter's tuxedo and arrived at the address ready to work. I was sorting through cutlery in the kitchen when I suddenly heard someone calling out my name in surprise. I turned around and there was Andrew Solomon. As it turned out it was his townhouse and his party. Daniel, he said to me with great embarrassment, I tried to call you all week to invite you to the party but your answering machine did not pick up and it was impossible to leave a message. This was true, my answering machine had in fact broken down just the week before and I had not had the time to replace it. This was in the days before everybody had a cell phone. Andrew Solomon showed me his to-do list and there was my name on top with my phone number. It was rather embarrassing for both of us but there was nothing either of us could do. He had to play host to his numerous famous guests and I had to serve champagne, caviar and blinis.

And now I must tell of how I became a personal chef.

Eric Ellenbogen was a rich media executive from Los Angeles. There was something about him that reminded me of Jerry Seinfeld the comedian and since the two have in fact known each other for a long time it has never been quite clear to me who modeled himself after the other. It was Eric Ellenbogen who had hosted the birthday dinner for Daniel Boulud at the Dakota where the lamb ragout had to be sent back. Later he had sometimes called upon me to wait on his guests during his small Wednesday dinner parties.

Eric Ellenbogen had a personal chef from Venezuela, Pedro, who looked very sexy in his checkered pants and chef's whites. Pedro was always horny and sometimes he and I made out in the kitchen between serving courses. I also remember a frequent dinner guest who had perfected the technique of dominating every gathering with her loud voice and crass ways. Once during a cocktail hour, when no one seemed to pay any particular attention to her for a moment, she promptly managed to choke on a shrimp and began gesticulating wildly towards everyone and pointing at her throat. Naturally everybody jumped to attention at once and one of the guests readily administered the Heimlich maneuver whereupon she promptly ejected the shrimp from her larynx. It sailed through the air and landed on the dining room floor. Everybody was relieved and sat down and I picked up the shrimp. It was only under such circumstances that anybody could see the danger of not letting this dinner guest have everybody's full attention, which was then resignedly restored to her by all for the rest of the evening.

It was during that spring that Eric Ellenbogen asked me for a meeting. His secretary led me to his office that had a very nice view over Central Park and after I sat down Eric Ellenbogen said, Daniel, my new house in East Hampton is ready to receive. Ah, I said. Yes, said he, and I wonder if you would be interested in spending your summer weekends there and do the food service for me and my friends. All you would have to do, he said, is buy prepared foods at the Barefoot Contessa shop and arrange and serve it on platters, in short a very casual affair. I told him that buying prepared foods did not interest me, not for myself nor for others, and would he consider hiring me to do the cooking myself. Eric Ellenbogen was interested. Do you, he said, know how to make a soufflé. I do, I said. Show me, he said. I did and he hired me for the summer.

The beginnings of my life as a personal chef are rather funny. Eric Ellenbogen was a very gracious and generous host and his house was very much an open house. There were many bedrooms and most of them were always occupied. Cary Davis, who had not yet met his future husband John McGinn, was always there, and quiet David Steward and aggressive Berkley Bowen, and all of them were at the time single and very keen on finding a companion if not for life then at least for the summer. In short many people came to visit and when it became known that Eric Ellenbogen had a full-time chef many more came. I remember one young couple that lived nearby and liked to drop in on Sundays around brunch time as if by coincidence and joining everyone at the table and helping themselves to everything and asking for fried eggs and pancakes. Then one late Sunday morning, everybody was out and about and I was busy preparing lunch, the couple came into the kitchen and sat down. They looked around a bit and finally said, well how about some pancakes. I'm afraid the restaurant is closed right now, I said. At this they blushed furiously and left. Later Martha the columbian housekeeper told Eric Ellenbogen everything about the couple and the pancake order and he was in full agreement with my reaction. We did not see much of the couple after this.

Another thing that used to annoy me dreadfully was the phone. There was a phone in every room of the house but for some reason everybody thought it would be so much more convenient if it was me who picked it up each time it rang and take down messages for everyone and post them on the small blackboard next to the refrigerator. I was less than pleased because I always had my hands full preparing three meals a day for sometimes more than 20 people. It was on one such occasion that I got particularly annoyed with Ross Bleckner. He was a frequent caller, never saying hello, never saying his name, only barking, is Cary there. Very evidently he wanted Cary Davis to buy one of his paintings. One day after he had called once again and barked at me on the phone in a particularly rude way I wrote on the message board, Ross Rude called, and everybody in the house instantly knew whom I meant, even aggressive Berkley Bowen who could be just as rude as Ross Bleckner.

One day one of the lunch guests came into the kitchen and said, I am a reporter from Tina Brown's new magazine, Talk. Ah, I said. Yes, he said, and I am doing research for an article about people like you and would you let me interview you. Yes, I said, later. At that moment young Chris Mooney, Eric Ellenbogen's new companion, came storming into the kitchen and said excitedly, Daniel you are going to become so famous after the article comes out, and is there any chicken left from last night's dinner.

When lunch service was over, the reporter and I sat down and he said, you see, I am wondering how you manage to do all this work all by yourself, with so many people to take care of and everybody always asking for something. Yes, I said, it is hard work. Isn't it sometimes getting too much, he said. No, I said, I can handle it, but one needs to set boundaries. Yes yes I understand perfectly now, he said.

A few weeks later, the article came out. It was not at all what the reporter had told me it would be, it was all about servants who did not behave the way the reporter thought servants should behave. I of course was not born a servant and have never behaved like one but I was an excellent chef and Eric Ellenbogen and Cary Davis knew it, even Berkley Bowen knew it. In any case Talk magazine folded a year later and the writer got hired to write for the Style Section of The New York Times, in other words he continued reporting in the fashion of the boulevard press. His name was Bob Morris.

Another person from that period who also got hired by The New York Times a little later was Philip Galanes.

He was a frequent lunch guest at Eric Ellenbogen's house and had not yet begun to dabble in writing or interior design, he was at the time still a white collar lawyer. I remember one Sunday where everybody was sitting at the kitchen table eating vichyssoise and there was Philip Galanes talking to a young couple about which school they should send their young son to. Don't, he said, send him to a local public school, what good could possibly come from your son growing up with children from poor families, surely he will never have anything to do with them later in his life. Like I said he was later hired by The New York Times. For some reason best known to the editors of that paper he appeared to be just the right person to answer questions on how to solve an awkward social situation and he became known as the writer of the Social Q's column.

In the meanwhile Mary Vivien, having spent enough years in Munich decided to move back to New York and I had to find a new home for myself. I moved into a small studio on the second floor at 971 Amsterdam Avenue. The place was much smaller than 375 West 75th Street and the rent was much higher but I was relieved to finally have my name on the lease and not having to pretend to be just a roommate any longer. There was always a smell of roast chicken in the studio because of the dominican bodega on the ground floor but it was clean and renovated and I never saw a cockroach or water bug, with the exception of the one night when Filip Noterdaeme spent the night there with me but that was not until 2 years after I had moved in.

The interesting thing about the studio was how one could see everything that went on in the studio across the narrow backyard. It was occupied by a young man that I got to know fairly well just by seeing him move about day and night. It was usually around 11 pm that he liked to masturbate in front of his television screen and it was very surprising to see him use a sock to do it. One day however, years later, it occurred to me to use a sock but it was not on myself, it was on Filip Noterdaeme and we were neither in bed or in front of a television screen, we were seated on a plane.

It was in those days that I for the first and only time in my life enjoyed frequenting the same bar night after night, the Saints, a little gay bar only three blocks away from my studio. It was very popular with young Columbia University students and sometimes I took one of them home with me for a brief affair, it was so convenient that way when you were single and living nearby.

It was during that period that I decided that I should start my own Christmas cookie business. I had always been fond of baking and seeing that viennese and german Christmas cookies were hard to come by in New York I began preparing and selling them, thousands of them, from my little home kitchen. I worked tirelessly. There was the baking and glazing and then the packaging in hand-painted boxes and the delivery on my bicycle. It was good experience but after one very busy tiring Christmas season I was ready for a life without cookies again. But Daniel, some american friends said to me, quite simply all you have to do is hire workers to do it all for you and pay them as little as possible. This did not interest me.

Sidney Meier, the manager of Don't Tell Mama, an old little cabaret in midtown called. Sidney Meier was himself a cabaret performer but after many years of trying for success he was reduced to giving a lecture to every performer who ever wanted to play at Don't Tell Mama. It is a pity that the public never saw him deliver this lecture, sitting at his desk in his little office in the back of the cabaret. It was a most excellent performance and famous among cabaret singers who had played at Don't Tell Mama. It lasted about half an hour and one was well advised to not interrupt him lest he might have to start again from the top. I sat and listened and said, I understand, you mean to say that the cabaret life is all about comedy and misery.

I asked Evee Lynn if she could recommend a pianist. Find someone who knows how to keep time, was her advice. I hired David Lamarche, the musical director of Dance Theatre of Harlem. He was a disciplined patiently kind man from Rhode Island. We got along rather well and our collaboration lasted several years. Later he became a principal conductor at American Ballet Theater.

It was in those days that it occurred to me that maybe I should have my own piano. I found a used Wurlitzer piano at a thrift shop and had it delivered to my little studio. There it stood large and imposing and as it turned out completely useless. No pianist ever wanted to rehearse in my little studio and I, having learned to play the piano in my youth in Germany but having been anything but ardent at it rarely sat down to play it. The only pieces I still remembered were Eric Satie's Gymnopédies and Mozart's Fantasie in C minor.

My shows at Don't tell Mama had come and gone and now I was booked to perform my new one man show, Kulturshock, at a very popular little cabaret in Greenwich Village called Eighty-Eight's. One day in the spring Erv Raible the owner asked me to come to the cabaret for a publicity shot with all the other performers that were going to be presented that season. The photographer positioned all of us on the staircase for the group photo and behind me stood a tall handsome american. This was Douglas Ladnier. He whispered little things into my ear and I had never heard such a seductive baritone voice, on the radio yes, but not whispered into my ear. I came away with a rather clear idea of his intentions. Naturally I was all for it.

I delighted in Douglas Ladnier's american enthusiasm and explanation of all things musical and erotic. He had had a great deal of adventure while touring the world with the Chippendales and now he was aiming for stardom on Broadway. To be sure we often sat in cafés with his american musical theater friends and I used to wonder if I could ever become one of them.

Douglas Ladnier broke up with me after three months and there was something not quite right in the way he did it. Oddly enough this past year we have gotten to be very fond of each other again. He is very much interested in my performances. It began with my show The Importance of Being Elvis just a year ago. He was convinced that I should sing A little Less Conversation and told me that his mother in her youth had known Elvis and spent time with him at Graceland. Much to his regret and in spite of being a blue-eyed, black-haired, handsome tall all-american heartthrob he cannot claim to be Elvis Presley's illegitimate son.

As soon as Kulturshock closed at Eighty-Eight's I was cast as a chorus member of a late night cabaret show with Joey Arias and Raven O. It was to be presented at the Kit Kat Club on Broadway where a new production of Cabaret the musical was about to open with Alan Cumming in the role of the Emcee.

I had first heard about Joey Arias in 1994 when everyone was talking about Strange Fruit, his homage to Billie Holiday. Tickets to the show were expensive and I begged some visiting friends from Germany to take me to see it. They did and I met my first genius. It was an even more wonderful show than I had expected. Joey Arias picked me among all the other male audience members and instructed me to hold his microphone between my legs. Seeing Joey Arias perform for the first time was, as I always say, the beginning of my understanding of mixing the frivolous with the profound in cabaret. Hitherto I had been concerned with earnestness and expression. Joey Arias's performance taught me to see the importance of style and artifice. And now, three years later, we were rehearsing together for the late night cabaret at the Kit Kat Club. The director was a retired dancer who had never directed a show before. I could not understand why he had been put in charge of directing the show.

Then after several weeks of rehearsals Cabaret premiered and everybody applauded Alan Cumming and then our cabaret performance began. No sooner had it commenced that everything went wrong. It began with Joey Arias's entrance. The director had promised him a dramatic entrance from the ceiling but all Joey got was an unbecoming harness and a rope and it was anything but safe. Then Joey started singing and his clip-on microphone wasn't working properly, nobody could hear him in the big theater. Joey signaled for the music to stop, coolly seized the little microphone and declared in his best Billie Holiday voice, this is the smallest penis I have ever seen. Everybody gasped. Then Raven O made an imperial entrance. He was a devilish elf, no one could cease looking at him. He furiously threw his red fur coat on the floor and started singing Night and Day all the while prancing around the stage like a tiger in a cage when suddenly the CD with his back-up track started skipping. Later some of the male dancers, thoroughly occupied with their costumes and make-up missed their cues. And so opening night turned into a closing night. Our late night cabaret show was never put up again, not once, but for all that it was the beginning of my friendship with Joey Arias.

It was at about this time that I began studying with vocal coach Larry Woodard. I must tell a little about Larry.

Larry Woodard was a large man in his fifties with a tender heart. He came from classical and gospel music but was also known to perform in cabarets. His favorite song was Wien, Wien Nur Du Allein. I had never seen a black man sing a viennese folk song before but it must be said Larry Woodard did it so much better than anybody else. His apartment on the Upper West Side was a most uncomfortable place to visit. The living room floor was covered with piles and piles of things and bags with more things and it was impossible to cross the room without stepping on at least a few of them. Once one had made one's way to the nook of the grand piano in the corner one had exactly one square foot to stand on. Of course one behaved as if this was all perfectly normal.

This story reminds me of Elisabeth Craine, a very sweet old lady who used to live below Mary Vivien's apartment at 375 West 75th Street. Whenever one visited her one had to pretend to not see any of the cockroaches everywhere. I remember once even finding one in the sugar bowl. Elisabeth never minded them and used to sometimes say with a twinkle in her eye, do you see any cockroaches here Daniel, and I would always reply, of course not, Elisabeth.

During our vocal lessons Larry Woodard sometimes said to me, hold on you just did a battleism don't do a battleism. What's a battleism I said. It's what Kathleen Battle does to Mozart, said he, she always tries to but I never let her because Mozart is Mozart and gospel is gospel and she and I always argue about it until she promises to never do it again but then she does it again anyway.

It was Larry Woodard who recommended Christopher Martin as the pianist for Tender is the Night, my first all-american cabaret show that I was planning to bring to a little cabaret in midtown, Danny's Skylight Room. We began rehearsals and there was something not quite right yet not quite wrong about Christopher Martin's playing and it made me wonder about Larry's judgment.

Christopher Martin had an agreement with a jewish nursing home to give little concerts for the elderly. He did this once every week. I decided to come along and see what it was all about. There was excitement among the old ladies when we arrived. Please, please, they called out to him, you must sing Hello Dolly. Later he sang a song nobody knew, it was all about his love for Jesus. A very dignified old man came up to him and politely asked about the song. That, Christopher Martin said proudly, is a song I wrote myself.

Then came the opening night of Tender is the Night. After the show Larry Woodard put his hand on my shoulder and whispered, I am so sorry Daniel, I should never have recommended Christopher. But you see, he said, I thought he was going to be as good a pianist as he is a singer.

It was at about that time that Joey Arias invited me to do a guest appearance at Bar d'O.

Bar d'O was a small cabaret in Greenwich Village that belonged to a french swiss, Jean-Marc Houmard. There Joey Arias had commenced singing jazz standards in fetish attire and this outfit later so well known on Madonna was the delight of downtown celebrities and hip tourists from Europe and Japan. Everybody went to Bar d'O once a week, at least, and usually everybody went on Tuesdays when Joey Arias was performing with Raven O and the divinely comical Sherry Vine.

And so one Tuesday night I went to Bar d'O and sang a duet with Joey and a little solo number, The Best Is Yet to Come. After my performance a handsome young man in a tight white T-shirt with the word Dreamer printed on it came up to me and introduced himself. This was Filip Noterdaeme.

Filip Noterdaeme immediately began to ask me many questions, where are you from, where do you live, where else are you performing. I told him about Tender is the Night, my show of american standards at Danny's Skylight Room. Why don't you, he said, sing european chansons, surely there is an audience for that here in New York. Oh really, I replied, where then has everybody been in the last two years when I did sing european chansons to almost empty houses. Well, he said, I am here now, and at that a bell within me rang.

The next week Filip Noterdaeme came to see Tender is the Night with his long-time friend Terry Brown Jr. He was a conservative republican homosexual who delighted in good company, especially the company of good-looking young men. He was not a literary type. One of his favorite places to go to was the Gaiety in Times Square. Everybody went to the Gaiety in those days. It has long been closed now but I remember how Filip Noterdaeme whenever he talked to Terry Brown Jr. on the phone always used to tease him by saying, we must go back to the Ballet, which was their code word for the Gaiety. Terry Brown Jr. was also a passionate cabaret aficionado who had known the incomparable Hildegarde and made his fortune as an interior decorator for Leona Helmsley and Lena Horne, caring little for the former and much for the latter.

Terry Brown Jr. was a delightful audience member, always polite always applauding. How well I remember hearing him gasp with delight that night at Danny's Skylight Room when I sang the title song of the show. After the show we all went out for drinks and Terry Brown Jr. said that Tender is the Night was his favorite song and Filip Noterdaeme said, but really the pianist played like an elephant.

The year was 1999. Each of us two had lived through the Nineties rather humbly and trying to sort out his life. Filip Noterdaeme had been working as an extra at the Metropolitan Opera and as an educator at the Metropolitan Museum and as a gallery lecturer at the Guggenheim Museum and therefore felt very much at home in opera houses and museums and knew about everything that went on behind the scenes in both of them. He had not been making art most of that time. Instead he had been looking hard at art and at people looking at art. Later, when he began making art again and created the Homeless Museum, the theatricality of all things, the deliberate glimpse through the fabric of the museum world became a fleeting refraction in all of his creations and a constant undercurrent in most of his works.

It was only a little later that Filip Noterdaeme and I had our first dinner together. He chose a restaurant he had recently discovered on Cornelia Street in Greenwich Village. It was called Home and Filip Noterdaeme was rather fond of its homestyle american food. I told him about my cooking, my cooking at home and in other people's homes. Filip Noterdaeme was very interested. It was not until a couple years later, at a very strange dinner at WD-50 that I realized that Filip Noterdaeme took nothing more seriously than food, that in fact food was the only thing he could not help but always take very seriously. We were having the acclaimed tasting menu and there was a trompe l'oeil sunny side up egg made of coconut and carrot juices and I also remember a course of fried mayonnaise cubes and Filip Noterdaeme, not in the least amused, kept whispering, where is the food.

It was only a couple of weeks after our dinner at Home that Filip Noterdaeme finally asked me to come home with him for the first time. It was after a very dull birthday dinner at an indian restaurant in the East Village. Earlier in the day Filip Noterdaeme had had his hair cut very short, and he arrived wearing a baseball cap. What is this, I said. What is what, he said. Let me see your hair, I said. He let me see. You look like a soldier, said I sternly. Then my face softening I added, all the same you are still you and the hair will grow back. Then everybody ate chutney and rice and sang happy birthday. We didn't linger and left the party together. We both knew it was an important night but felt a bit shy about it and so we went for a stroll through the neighborhood and then sat down for a drink at a gay bar called Flamingo East and only then did Filip Noterdaeme finally ask me if I wanted to come home with him. I said, yes.

My memory of our first night together is very vivid. There are a great many things to tell of what was happening then and what had happened before, which led up to then, but now I must describe what I saw.

Filip Noterdaeme's rental apartment occupied the entire top floor of an old brownstone at 172 Clinton Street in Brooklyn Heights and consisted then as it does now of a large living room with an open kitchen, a small bathroom, and two bedrooms. The ceilings were slanted and it was cozy. The view from the window in Filip Noterdaeme's bedroom, the smaller of the two, was an interesting one. One could see the tops of trees and the torch of the Statue of Liberty in the distance. I had never visited the Statue of Liberty but I was familiar with The New Colossus sonnet by Emma Lazarus because I had once sung a parody of it in 1994 in an Off Broadway show. The show was Stonewall Night Variations by Tina Landau and Ricky Ian Gordon and I had played an angel leading a martyred drag queen into heaven. I cannot quite remember the lyrics but it went something like Bring me your tired old queens, your dirty young fags, your horny masses yearning to be free. But to get back to that first night Filip Noterdaeme and I spent together.

There were a number of paintings hanging in the apartment and I asked, which one is by you. He pointed at a very strange painting above the bedroom door that showed the groin of a reclining female nude with a smoking pipe protruding from the vagina. This, he said, is the

35

painting that got me expelled from art school. He added, I call it the Pussy Painting and, do you like it. I said, it certainly is good product placement. Filip Noterdaeme laughed. Then he explained how the Pussy Painting was a fusion of two famous paintings, Courbet's L'origine du monde and Magritte's La trahison des images, and the only self-portrait he had kept from his art school days. It was enormously interesting but that night I must admit I was more interested in Filip Noterdaeme's groin. As I said it was our first night together and a rather important one as we needed to figure out if we were sexually compatible. We were.

I soon became a habitual visitor at 172 Clinton Street and Filip Noterdaeme introduced me to his roommate, blond pale white-skinned Nick Wilkinson, who had moved in two years earlier. I must tell a little about Nick.

He had grown up in Tucson, Texas and was originally from Long Island. He had early in his life developed an abiding interest in computers. When he moved in with Filip Noterdaeme, he was eighteen years old, overweight and a student at Brooklyn Poly. Under the influence of Filip Noterdaeme he soon underwent a radical transformation. It was Filip Noterdaeme who taught Nick how to live and eat well. Together they worked out a series of experiments in hair dying and Nick went from blond to strawberry blond and champagne blond and there were all not the same, naturally. In short, Filip Noterdaeme became a bit of a father figure for Nick Wilkinson. Once he took him to Bar d'O where Nick, standing very close to Filip Noterdaeme nervously asked, who are all these creatures. They are drag queens, answered Filip Noterdaeme. Nick was overcome. He had never seen drag queens before, one drag queen yes but not drag queens. It was on that night too that Raven O, just a little on the edge, and to everyone's astonishment persisted in throwing out a young woman who had been talking during one of his songs. He sent her away with the rather clear advice to grow up.

Nick Wilkinson had an astonishing intelligence and wit that always gave one an extraordinary pleasure when one saw him for some time. By the time I met him he had given up college and junk food, joined a gym and begun working for Saatchi & Saatchi. Having grown up with, as he always said, an evil stepmother he at first regarded me with a little suspicion but he soon came to see me as a good stepmother.

It was at about that time that Filip Noterdaeme and I had dinner at Blue Ribbon Bakery with Luis Moreno. At one moment I went to get something from the bar and it was then that Luis made his famous remark about me to Filip Noterdaeme, telling him that I was a keeper. When I came back Filip Noterdaeme leaned forward and said to me, guess what. What, I said. Luis says you are a keeper, he said.

A few weeks later Filip Noterdaeme spent the night with me at my little studio at 971 Amsterdam Avenue. We had already been asleep for a while when I suddenly woke up with a start. I woke up with a start and looked and there was a water bug crawling over sleeping Filip Noterdaeme's back. I did not believe that I would be fast enough but I was, fast enough to catch and kill it. I was very pleased with myself for having done so and in the following weeks kept reminding Filip Noterdaeme of how I had slayed the dragon to save him. One month later, I moved out of 971 Amsterdam Avenue and in with Filip Noterdaeme at 172

Clinton Street.

And now I will tell you how a belgian and a german happened to form a creative bond of which the New York art world at that time understood nothing.

III
Filip Noterdaeme in New York
1987 – 1999

During Filip Noterdaeme's two years at the flemish academy, Sint Lukas, Brussels, 1985-1987, he became friendly with Marie-Puck Broodthaers. She was the daughter of Marcel Broodthaers, his favorite belgian artist. He often visited her at her gallery on the rue Ravenstein. One day Marie-Puck showed him drawings by a belgian artist named Jacques Charlier. He bought one of them at a pretty high price. It was a wonderfully grotesque drawing that likened belgian artists to slaves in the former belgian colony of Congo.

The following year Filip Noterdaeme's father was nominated belgian ambassador to the United Nations in New York and Filip Noterdaeme decided to move to America with his parents. However his father and mother being incapacitated and held back in Belgium for a time, he went ahead all by himself. Of course no one was as tactless as to ask why Ambassador Noterdaeme kept postponing his move to New York but there were rumors and so it was of the utmost importance that Filip Noterdaeme put up a front for everyone.

When he traveled to the United States he brought with him the Charlier drawing, the first Charlier to cross the Atlantic. He flew first class on Sabena, the belgian national airline. Filip Noterdaeme's father being a high-ranking diplomat the entire family always flew Sabena on state expenses. At John F. Kennedy airport there was a driver waiting for him at the gate with a sign that said Mister Filip. This was Raj the indian driver of the belgian mission and he had been sent to pick up Filip Noterdaeme and drive him to the belgian embassy at 1 Beekman Place where he and his parents were to reside.

On that first evening after Raj the driver had dropped him off at 1 Beekman Place Filip Noterdaeme wandered through the unfurnished empty rooms of the large embassy duplex and up and down the grand spiraling staircase. It was an uninvitingly dark and desolate place with a lovely view of the East River. There had been some resentment from the former Ambassador about Filip Noterdaeme's father taking her place, it had something to do with her being a walloon and he a fleming, in other words it was a case of traditional belgian rivalry, and she had left the apartment in a bad state.

The refrigerator in the kitchen was empty but for an Entenmann's pound cake that Raj the driver had bought as a welcoming gift. It was Filip Noterdaeme's first meal in America.

The next day he received a note from Gaston Van Duysen saying, Dear Filip, I am in town, please join me for tea at the Swiss Hotel on Park Avenue. Gaston Van Duysen was a belgian diplomat and had been a frequent guest at the Noterdaeme household when they were living in Geneva. Filip Noterdaeme asked one of the doormen of 1 Beekman Place for directions, everything in New York was new and confusing to him. There were avenues with names and avenues with numbers and streets without names and a Park Avenue without a park and when he finally found the Swiss Hotel it did not appear swiss to him in the least. A bellhop showed him to the salon de thé where Gaston Van Duysen was already seated, waiting. Gaston Van Duysen jumped up and greeted Filip Noterdaeme with the greatest delight. They sat down and ordered tea and Filip Noterdaeme confessed that he was terribly nervous about being in New York. Gaston Van Duysen, wearing a colorful necktie and italian patent leather shoes just like he always had in Geneva told him, I perfectly understand how you feel but you must know that I am quite jealous of you, je suis jaloux de toi. Oh, to be young and live in New York, he said.

Filip Noterdaeme found living alone in the empty grandeur of the embassy during those first months rather strange. Every time he came home he had to greet first the doorman, then the elevator man and once he entered the duplex there was nothing but the big red Pepsi-Cola neon sign across the East River to look at. His neighbors he met in the mahogany-paneled elevator or sometimes in the communal pool on the lower level. In the elevator they looked distinguished in conservative clothes and said how do you do and in the pool they looked sallow in jersey swimsuits and ignored one another. One of his neighbors was fashion designer Arnold Scaasi who occupied a duplex on the third floor with his companion and two lovely dachshunds.

A little later when Filip Noterdaeme was just beginning knowing New York he went to see a performance of a belgian modern dance troupe at the Brooklyn Academy of Music. He does not remember the name of the troupe but he remembers being enormously interested in what they were doing, interested in their movements and interested in the male dancers. After the show he went backstage to give his compatriotic compliments and the choreographer introduced him to everybody. The choreographer told Filip Noterdaeme, we have a big problem, our hotel reservation fell through and we have no place to stay. Filip Noterdaeme smiled at him and said, I would be honored to host your company at the belgian embassy. And so for the next ten days, to the great annoyance of the elevator men, the dance troupe resided at the belgian embassy with Filip Noterdaeme. There was a great deal of merriment and going up and down the elevators and Filip Noterdaeme finally began to feel at home in New York for the first time.

He began exploring the city and quickly learned that life in New York happens on the street. One thing that struck him immediately was the homeless one saw everywhere. He had seen the clochards of Paris and gypsies in Brussels, also punks in London but nothing like the homeless of New York. He also did not know what to make of the air conditioners that were hanging out of every other window. He had never seen air conditioners before and found something appalling about the way they disrupted a building's façade. It was not until years later that Filip Noterdaeme bought his first air conditioner. He was by then already living in a rent-stabilized two bedroom at 172 Clinton Street. His apartment was on the top floor and it was unbearably hot in June, July, August and September. He carried his new little air conditioner up to his bedroom and tried to balance it on the windowsill with a brick and all of a sudden the brick slipped and fell. It fell and shattered through a skylight on the second floor below, landing on Paul the landlord's dining room floor.

Naturally Filip Noterdaeme had to apologize and pay for a new skylight. This was his first interaction with Paul the landlord who has since then never ceased to be suspicious of Filip Noterdaeme. Once, several years later, it was Yom Kippur, I was rearranging books on the shelves by the bedroom window and three George Steiner books fell out. They too landed on the second floor terrace but luckily none of them shattered the skylight.

Filip Noterdaeme lived in the belgian embassy by himself for four months. Finally his parents arrived. His mother instantly busied herself with redecorating and furnishing the embassy with the help of an interior decorator but the two never getting along any too well soon put a strain on everybody's nerves. His father, very melancholy and elusive and clear sighted and intellectual was working at the United Nations every day and began avoiding coming home in the evening à tout prix, at all cost. Filip Noterdaeme likewise avoiding à tout prix having to spend time at the embassy joined a residency art program on the Lower East Side in a former public school building on Suffolk Street.

Practically every morning Filip Noterdaeme went to the Lower East Side, worked on his art and then later wandered up First Avenue and usually walking all the way to 1 Beekman Place. He then formed the habit which has never left him of watching New Yorkers, now with one eye, in those days with two. On Sundays he usually had lunch with his father at the Smith & Wollensky steakhouse. Ambassador Noterdaeme never finished his steak and Filip Noterdaeme always asked for a doggie bag.

It was at the residency art program that Filip Noterdaeme met Geoffrey Rees from Boston. They quickly became rather fond of each other. In no time they were knowing each other and knowing each other very well. It was only a little later that the belgian embassy was finally ready to receive and represent and Filip Noterdaeme decided to move out of 1 Beekman Place and in with Geoffrey Rees who was renting a little railroad apartment on 337 Grand Street in Williamsburg. From the embassy Filip Noterdaeme took along only two things, an old Electrolux vacuum cleaner and a vintage Kitchenaid stand mixer. These were his contributions to his first gay household. Of course Raj the driver was there to help Filip Noterdaeme with the move and he was very confused about it all. Why, he said, would you want to move from there to there. And it is true, nobody then thought of moving there.

Williamsburg in those days was populated by poor immigrants and drug addicts. There were old polish delis and shabby bodegas and liquor stores and pawnshops with bulletproof cashier windows. Crime was rampant and sometimes one could see a chalk outline of someone who got shot on the pavement. Everybody's front door was always padlocked and windows had metal bars. The streets were dirty and smelly and at night one frequently passed prostitutes, pimps, drug dealers, crack addicts and tranny hookers.

Geoffrey Rees was a man of full habit, accustomed to a literary life and the delights of the table. He was very fond of origami. He was terribly complicated and never pretended otherwise. He was in short very melancholy and elusive and clear sighted and intellectual. Like many reformed jews he religiously believed in psychotherapy but continued to hold on to old jewish customs like affixing a mezuzah to one's doorpost. Filip Noterdaeme delighted in hearing Geoffrey Rees telling tales of ashkenazi jews and sephardic jews and the correct placement of the mezuzah.

In those days Filip Noterdaeme was very eager to become a real New Yorker and do all the New York things. He and Geoffrey spent a lot of time in the East Village, eating out in cheap ukrainian and caribbean restaurants, going to the double features at a little cinema on Saint Mark's place and sharing pastries at Veniero's. One night they got frightfully drunk and Filip Noterdaeme laughing uncontrollably fell into a garbage can as they were walking down the street.

Filip Noterdaeme also began regularly seeing a therapist on the Upper West Side. One day while talking about his mother he made an interesting Freudian slip and instead of my mother said, my money.

Filip Noterdaeme, having never learned to sing but wanting to also once signed up for a beginners' singing class at the Herbert Berghof Studios. He remembers one female student attempting with much feeling to sing a Bette Midler song that was quite popular at the time, The Wind Beneath my Wings. The teacher said, one must know in one's mind who one is singing these kinds of songs to, now won't you tell us whom you've been thinking of. At this the student blushed and said, my dog. This was the end of Filip Noterdaeme's interest in singing classes. He became vitally interested in theatre and attended a workshop with old Herberg Berghof himself. Since then Filip Noterdaeme has always been perfectly able to understand the enthusiasm that props arouse among actors. He says a good prop is such a useful tool for an actor that one must always have one, in that way the action will come more naturally.

As I said this was the first time Filip Noterdaeme was living with a partner. He was terribly inexperienced and so was Geoffrey. They had two pets, a grey cat named Fluffy and a little dachshund named Rosie, and having them was like having two children who never learn and never grow up. Fluffy and Rosie had to be groomed and fed and taken to the vet. No homosexual or old lady is so poor or so careless or so avaricious but that they can and do constantly take their pets to the vet.

Little by little Filip Noterdaeme and Geoffrey learned to share household tasks and cook dinner for each other. One summer day Filip Noterdaeme cooked an extraordinarily bad dinner. It was a ratatouille provençale after a Julia Child recipe and a big to-do. The recipe gave instructions to cut two eggplants lengthwise into slices one eighth of an inch thick and three inches long and one inch wide. Filip Noterdaeme found these american measurements to be very confusing and annoying. He spent a long afternoon in the kitchen trying to follow the recipe with a ruler and knife. Then it was evening and Geoffrey came home and sat down. Filip Noterdaeme appeared at the kitchen door very exhausted, very unnerved and very sweaty. I have, he said to Geoffrey, been cooking all day and the eggplant is still hard. Geoffrey went into the kitchen to look and it was true it was still hard.

Life at 337 Grand Street was very amusing. Geoffrey Rees played Filip Noterdaeme his favorite records, usually the Carpenters, and baked pot brownies when friends came over for a party. There was also a lot of experimenting with sex.

Sex, Filip Noterdaeme says, was on everybody's

mind in those days, of course everybody wanted it but everybody was also afraid of it. Peter Hujar had just died of AIDS and Keith Haring had just announced that he had it. Everybody knew someone who knew somebody who was very ill or dying and there was a lot of anger and grief and a sense of helplessness among gay men. Filip Noterdaeme says one had to think twice before one did it, and then again while one did it, and that it was very strange to think about it while doing it. Of course most of the thinking happened after doing it when it was too late to make it undone. The next thing one had to do was get an AIDS test and wait for a whole week for the results. Sex became safer sex but it wasn't the same nor was it ever really safe. Abstinence of course was safest but not altogether satisfying or realistic or fair, all of which is to say that everybody was always on the edge.

This brings me to the story of Filip Noterdaeme's first threesome. He has had three threesomes in his life and of the three the first one was the most memorable but for all the wrong reasons. It happened one late night at 337 Grand Street. He and Geoffrey had invited a boy they both liked to come home with them. Being not two but three for the first time in bed was very exciting until all of a sudden the excitement had to be put on hold because it turned out that there was no lubricant in the house and it was unimaginable to safely continue the fun and games without any lubricant. Filip Noterdaeme volunteered to go get some and off he went to a nearby bodega, the only store on the block that stayed open late. At the bodega there was much spanish confusion about what exactly Filip Noterdaeme was looking for. Finally he picked a tube of something that looked and sounded just right to him and he excitedly ran back home to Geoffrey and the boy. No no no they said when he showed them, this is not lubricant. Well, Filip Noterdaeme said very confused, what is it, then. They explained to him that what he had bought was in fact a muscle relaxant, in other words there was nothing gay about Bengay, and then all three roared with laughter and so Filip Noterdaeme's first threesome never really happened.

The second of Filip Noterdaeme's three threesomes happened a few years later with Richard Quadracci and his quiet blond lover John. It was a long night and everything and nothing happened because Richard Quadracci had in him a necessity for sadomasochistic sex practices. In other words he needed a physical as well as psychological justification for the exalted obsession in him. This he could not find, being the lost son of one of the country's richest families, in either business or leisure, money having destroyed for him both business and leisure as a passion. I did not meet Richard Quadracci until a few years ago when he invited Filip Noterdaeme and I to join him and a small group of friends at his new duplex on Park Avenue South for dinner. It was a very curious evening. To be sure there was a dungeon, which Richard's friends much appreciated from previous parties, and it must be said that Richard had always been and always was very promiscuous. It was on the lower floor adjoining the master bedroom but that was alright because the living room and dining room were on the upper floor. It gave more privacy to a dungeon to have it on the lower floor. Dinner was served by a thin pale slave-boy wearing nothing but a black leather choker. We all sat down to eat spiral ham and macaroni and cheese and the slave boy knelt on the marble floor next to his master and gingerly ate from a metal dog bowl, his hands tied behind his back. It was very funny to watch how he tried to defend his spiral ham slice hands-free from Duke, Richard Quadracci's little dachshund. Terry Brown Jr. having arrived as always impeccably dressed in a three-piece suit and colorful bowtie sat at table and shyly lightly patted the slave-boy on the head like a good dog, he did not quite know what else to do in the moment. After dinner everybody went to Bar d'O where I sang Dalida's Bambino song.

The third and last threesome Filip Noterdaeme has had to this day happened during the time he was seeing Gordon Ross, a british artist and son of a dentist. This particular threesome involved a young medical student and it was the only time Filip Noterdaeme ever let himself be tied up and gagged.

But to get back to Filip Noterdaeme's spinach days in Williamsburg.

Among his new american friends was Sidney Long, an animal rescuer who was very fond of eastern mysticism. Filip Noterdaeme remembers one afternoon that he spent at Sidney Long's storefront apartment on Grand Street. She was giving him an I Ching reading on her kitchen table but he says he could not concentrate on the reading because Sidney Long's very large cat was sitting upright on the bed behind Sidney and staring intently at him while slowly awkwardly masturbating with a pillow.

Sidney Long and Filip Noterdaeme saw a great deal of each other for a while and then Sidney moved to Newport, Rhode Island. Filip Noterdaeme shares the same birthday as James Merrill and every year Sidney Long sends him a lovely birthday card to remind him of it.

Then there was Rachel Harrison. Filip Noterdaeme delighted in her work which at the time she made largely out of her used tampons and which were then shown in the only existing art gallery in Williamsburg, now an expensive wine store. In later years she became quite successful with art made of canned peas and olives instead of tampons. Recently Rachel Harrison and Filip Noterdaeme met again for the first time in many years, she happened to pass by Filip Noterdaeme's Homeless Museum booth under the High Line and recognized him. She sat down and the two reminisced. Regarding the art world and success she said, be careful what you're wishing for. But I am once again running ahead of those early Williamsburg days.

Filip Noterdaeme registered at the School of Visual Arts to get a Bachelor's degree of fine arts. One of his fellow students was Robert Lazzarini. The two young men became friends. Robert Lazzarini lived in Hoboken and had a grey bunny named Dürer. He liked all things italian and was quite handsome in the doomed way of young italian american men who have a strong liking of spaghetti with meatballs and blond women. He and Filip Noterdaeme always had a very amusing time together as they never took each other or anything at the school seriously. It was at that time that Filip Noterdaeme created his first museum, the Museum of Belgian Contemporary Art. However all this I will tell about later. Today Robert Lazzarini is best known for his anamorphic sculptures. I remember well the first time I saw them. It was at the Pierogi gallery. When we got there we were indeed early as nearly as possible the first to be there. There was a strangely deformed skull and a strangely deformed hammer and more deformed things. To be sure everybody liked and talked about the skull but I much preferred the hammer, I found it so much more alarming.

One day at the School of Visual Arts, it was during a Julia Heyward class on performance art, Filip Noterdaeme and a fellow student, a petite young woman from Japan created a spontaneous performance. They decided to undress and exchange clothes in front of everybody. It was then that the petite japanese and everybody else realized that her panties had little bloodstains on them. Naturally she was mortified. The bloody tiny panties were very tight on Filip Noterdaeme and his briefs were large on the petite japanese but it was the bloodstains on the panties that made the performance memorable.

The School of Visual Arts in those days had its own gay social club. It was a new thing and called SVGay. Filip Noterdaeme was curious and went to a meeting. Everybody at the meeting was out and proud and happy to be one of a group where everybody was agreeing with everybody. Filip Noterdaeme who has a horror of what he calls pack mentality was bored, frankly openly bored and refused to attend any more SVGay meetings.

One of the advantages of the School of Visual Arts was that it being an established New York institution it was able to every now and then get artists of some renown to make an appearance and conduct studio critiques. Filip Noterdaeme remembers one of the visiting artists being Peter Halley. He says the exchange between Peter Halley and the students was perfectly kind and polite but that it did not have a lasting impact on him. Halley is a square artist he says, excellent if you are a square, but if you are not, not.

This story reminds me of how Filip Noterdaeme and I were once served cake by Peter Halley's daughter Isabel at a big to-do about art and cake. Isabel was one of three downtown artist daughters cutting and serving pieces of a big silver cake made of letters spelling the word Cake and I remember her saying to no one in particular, I am not really good at this. She and her two friends were at the time already known for calling themselves The Delirious Downtown Divas, and no one quite seemed to know or care if they any of the three were particularly good at anything, it was just enough for them to be there and everywhere, together everywhere.

Filip Noterdaeme graduated from the School of Visual Arts in 1990. The commencement speech was given by Susan Sontag and he remembers that she was more resentful than particularly engaging or engaged and urged the students to first and foremost begin their postgraduate lives by boycotting television. Filip Noterdaeme's favorite TV show at the time was the Garry Shandling Show, he says it made him chuckle. Sometimes when a program was too dull he would turn the TV set on its head and it always made watching more exciting, no matter what was on. Filip Noterdaeme and I stopped watching television for good in 2004, coincidentally interestingly the same year that Susan Sontag died of cancer.

After his graduation Filip Noterdaeme began working as an extra at the Metropolitan Opera. He became at turns an egyptian soldier, a Pagliacci clown, a spanish page, a chinese servant, a parisian bohemian, and once, in Salome, a naked corpse. Filip Noterdaeme loved the artifice and drama and glamour of the opera world. He often says he would have been perfectly happy to do nothing else for the rest of his life if it hadn't been for Aida. This opera he did not care for all that much but it happened to be the one that the Metropolitan was putting up more often than any other. In Aida Filip Noterdaeme was always cast as a spear carrier and it was hard work. There was the never-ending Triumphal March that went around and around and called for hundreds of extras in loincloths and several horses who to the great regret of the stage manager always relieved themselves center stage. Filip Noterdaeme often likens the Triumphal March of his years at the Met to the Gay Pride Marches of the same period when to the great regret of Cardinal O'Connor hundreds of horse-hung go-go boys in g-strings would always do an indecent dance routine in front of Saint Patrick's Cathedral.

One spring Filip Noterdaeme and Geoffrey traveled to New England to attend a Seder at the home of Geoffrey's father and stepmother and his two half brothers, Adam and Jeremy. Filip Noterdaeme does not remember Jeremy very well but he fondly remembers pretty Adam who was 12 years younger than Geoffrey.

Filip Noterdaeme had never been to New England or to a Seder and, not knowing the jewish custom, made a blunder by sitting down on the chair reserved for Elijah. Later Geoffrey showed him around the area and they drove to Cape Cod where Filip Noterdaeme ate his first New England clam chowder. He thought it was similar yet different, very different to belgian Waterzooi. One day, in Chatham, they took a walk on the beach and all of a sudden Filip Noterdaeme shrieked because he had stepped on something strange. He had never seen anything as horrid before and Geoffrey Rees explained to him that it was a horseshoe crab.

The two began visiting New England quite frequently. There were family birthdays and more jewish holidays and then there was the occasion when young pretty Adam was to come of age and read from the Torah. The whole Rees family went to the local synagogue for the Bar Mitzvah service and Filip Noterdaeme had to wear a yarmulke. Filip Noterdaeme says that Adam did not really come of age that day, he came of age six years later, at 172 Clinton Street, in his bed. But I am rushing ahead of the years leading up to then.

Geoffrey's mother was a literary agent and owned a very large old country house in Rensselaerville. There was a barn on the property that was filled with old things and Filip Noterdaeme and Geoffrey used to delight in exploring it. One day Filip Noterdaeme found a very beautiful antique oil painting of a female nude that reminded him of La Belle Rosine by Antoine Wiertz. He showed it to Geoffrey's mother and she said, it's yours. The painting is now part of the $0 Collection at the Homeless Museum.

One day Geoffrey's mother phoned the two boys and said, guess who moved in next door. Who is it, they said. It's Richard Prince, she said. Filip Noterdaeme was very excited to hear this and a few weeks later the three paid Richard Prince a neighborly visit. Filip Noterdaeme says Richard Prince looked liked a serial killer to him and that there was something stealthy in the way he showed them his collection of pulp fiction volumes and Claude Cahun photographs.

Not very long after Filip Noterdaeme's graduation at the School of Visual Arts, he and Geoffrey moved out of their little railroad apartment at 337 Grand Street and into a spacious loft on 412 Bedford Avenue. Once again

Geoffrey attached a mezuzah to their doorpost and little by little the two young men furnished the loft with things they found on the street as was common among young artists in those days. They found a very nice armchair upholstered in yellow fabric, an antique little side table, and a golden sun-framed mirror.

Filip Noterdaeme joined the two-year Master of Fine Arts graduate program at Hunter College and Geoffrey began writing his roman à clef, Sex with Strangers.

One day Filip Noterdaeme came home very excited from walking Rosie the dachshund and, bringing out a business card from his pocket said, David McDermott and Peter McGough have hired me as an assistant painter.

Filip Noterdaeme says that at the time there was no one who came closer to living in a state of permanent creation than McDermott and McGough. The couple was famous for stubbornly refusing to be living a twentieth century kind of life and shunning all things modern. Of course this was not possible without the occasional compromise but, as David McDermott liked to point out to anyone who cared to listen, modern inventions played as minor a role in their lives as old-fashioned inventions in everybody else's. The duo walked about impeccably dressed in vintage three-piece suits, appreciated good penmanship and drove a hand-cranked Ford Model T. Filip Noterdaeme knew a great act when he saw one and enjoyed it and knew that this was great art and beautiful.

The McDermott McGough atelier occupied an entire three-story former bank building on the corner of Broadway and Bedford Avenue in Williamsburg. Everybody always called it simply the Bank.

Working at the Bank was an experience. The grand

hall on the ground floor curiously had all the old bank's wooden tellers still intact. This is where McDermott and McGough's high-strung british secretary usually sat typing letters on a vintage Remington and answering calls on an old rotary phone. The second floor housed the painting studio and the third floor housed an old-fashioned photo studio. In those days McDermott and McGough employed many assistants to produce their artwork and so there was always much activity on all three floors.

Filip Noterdaeme's first assignment was to work on a large painting showing a prehistoric jungle done in the manner of Thomas Cole. His job was to paint fern, palm trees and dinosaurs, which he did for two months, until the painting was complete. McDermott and Mc-Gough were very pleased with Filip Noterdaeme's work and every Friday Peter McGough went down to the vault in the basement of the Bank and came back with cash, of which there seemed to be wads and wads, and paid Filip Noterdaeme for his work. The duo took to calling Filip Noterdaeme Heer Noterdaeme our flemish painter. There were a great many people coming in and out at the Bank and McDermott and McGough introduced Filip Noterdaeme to René Ricard, Donald Baechler and everybody else. Filip Noterdaeme was awfully pleased when one day they introduced him to Quentin Crisp who had been living in a state of permanent creation long before McDermott and McGough or anybody else. As a matter of fact Quentin Crisp had been living long before anybody else.

Another project that Filip Noterdaeme remembers assisting McDermott and McGough with was a series of odalisque photo portraits of gay porn star Jeff Stryker. It was only a little later that the duo named him Aesthetic

Director. As David McDermott used to explain to Filip Noterdaeme, we must furnish a quality of merchandise that will effectively disprove every argument of every kind raised against us. Filip Noterdaeme's new task was to remove all late twentieth century plastic stuffs from the Bank and replace them with nineteenth century equivalents. He was also to prevent anybody from entering the building with plastic bags, plastic food containers and such. The Bank staff, not all too pleased, soon nicknamed him the Plastic Police. David McDermott was very fond of Filip Noterdaeme and used to take him along for company whenever he went out for errands. Filip Noterdaeme always went in hopes of getting a free lunch but it turned out David McDermott took him along mostly to get him into his bed. One day Filip Noterdaeme got his free lunch at Angelica Kitchen, a popular vegetarian restaurant in the East Village. During the meal, David McDermott lectured him about potatoes. One should never eat potatoes, he said, because one always becomes what one eats and one might end up looking like a potato. Filip Noterdaeme was obliged there to express what he called the belgian viewpoint and explained everything about real belgian fries being fried twice. In any case David McDermott was all grains and vegetables at Angelica Kitchen but later when he showed Filip Noterdaeme his bed he was suddenly all meat and potatoes. Filip Noterdaeme only thought of saving himself but he after all was still much obliged and so it could be said it had not been a free lunch after all.

He worked for the duo for almost a year and at the end of his employment David McDermott gave him a lovely handwritten recommendation letter that was back-dated as was the duo's habit with everything they signed.

The date he chose was the fifth instance of March 1905, sixty years and two days before Filip Noterdaeme was born.

A few years ago, the Internal Revenue Service gave McDermott and McGough a very hard time and David McDermott decided to renounce his american citizenship and move to Dublin in Ireland, the land of meat and potatoes. Peter McGough remained in the United States. The two still collaborate but there is no longer any evidence of permanent creation in their work.

Another artist duo that made an impression on Filip Noterdaeme at that time was the Rob Pruitt Jack Early duo. They were enamored with pop art and lived in a loft on Atlantic Avenue in Brooklyn that they had filled with pieces of modern furniture. Everybody liked them and their work until Red, Black, Green, Red, White and Blue, their controversial show about african american identity. It was shown at Leo Castelli. Nobody liked two white men presenting images of black people and the ordeal lead to an ugly fallout between the two and one did not hear of either of them for a long time. Rob Pruitt has since then been reinstated as an artist of some importance. The story goes that he endeared himself with the art world again at a group show where he presented a very long line of cocaine that was free for the snorting. As to Jack Early, there have also been attempts at a comeback but it is too early to tell if he will succeed.

The first year at Hunter College Filip Noterdaeme liked well enough. The practice of painting did not interest him any longer, he much preferred conceiving paintings and having them painted by somebody else, the way McDermott and McGough had asked him to do. He hired an assistant painter, a young french actor by the name of Dominique Carrara. Under Filip Noterdaeme's directions, Dominique Carrara painted a series of what Filip Noterdaeme called Unmagrittes, Magrittes without the surrealism. They were very funny if one knew the real Magrittes but if one did not, not. In other words, Filip Noterdaeme engaged in confusing everybody about his intentions and getting mixed up in a lot of stories. He was never bored with what he was doing and once caused for much confusion in Central Park after a La Traviata matinee at the Met where Franco Zeffirelli had cast him as a circus clown. He was still wearing his Pagliacci makeup and proceeded to unroll large sheets of cellophane on Sheep's Meadow and kneeling down began tracing with a black marker in great detail what was underneath. Whenever somebody asked him what it was he was doing there he replied to their great astonishment and in all seriousness, I am drawing the first map of the world in the scale of one to one.

He used to upset his professor Doug Ohlson by saying that all he was interested in was learning how to make a masterpiece. Then another thing that used to irritate Professor Ohlson and the faculty was that he took to walking about Hunter College dressed like a hunter, wearing leather boots, an austrian loden cape and a felt hat. He also put on a fake beard he had bought at Bob Kelly's, the professional wig maker on Broadway, and often stuck a pipe in the corner of his mouth, never once lighting it. This masquerade was intended to make him resemble Gustave Courbet in his self-portrait Man with a Pipe. He had by then already begun introducing himself to everyone as Marcellus Wasbending-Ttum, Homoplagiarist. Sometimes he brought Rosie the dachshund along to the school, introducing her to everybody as his hunting dog and loudly in front of everyone encouraging her to go find a masterpiece.

Filip Noterdaeme delighted in being Marcellus Wasbending-Ttum. There were very few who were able to make out the many references he had used to construct the name and persona of Marcellus but this did not matter to him. He had expensive business cards made at Crane's on Madison Avenue and handed them out to teachers and fellow students alike as if meeting them for the first time. He still has the original copperplate from Crane's. The fake beard from Bob Kelly's became a Filip Noterdaeme staple. He first wore it at Hunter College and then started wearing it again years later when he adopted a new persona, the Director of the Homeless Museum.

And so at Hunter he had a very amusing time. He remembers once exhibiting paintings of urinals in the men's room and how his teachers stood and looked and understood less than ever and were fairly fussed. It was at about this time that he wrote his treatise, On the Superiority of Amateurism over Mediocrity. As I said everybody was confused, even Oliver Herring a fellow student he had become friendly with. It was at about that time that Professor Ohlson once remarked with astonishment, I do not know if this young man is a genius or a con artist.

Filip Noterdaeme and Geoffrey Rees were always hard up in those days but there was a lucky period when their landlord was put in jail for some reason and there was no one around to collect the rent. This came to an abrupt end several months later when the landlord suddenly reappeared and there was nothing to do but to make a quick escape with Fluffy the cat and Rosie the dachshund. They moved to a railroad apartment in Spanish Harlem where they were completely miserable.

Filip Noterdaeme began working as an intern for the outreach program of the Metropolitan Museum of Art. The museum provided him with a slide projector and slides and sent him out to talk about the Metropolitan Museum, its history and its art collection, to people who knew nothing about either and were not all that interested in one or the other to begin with. Nobody at the Metropolitan knew of Filip Noterdaeme's father being the ambassador to Belgium at the United Nations and so it was very amusing for him to be repeatedly told during training sessions that he was now an ambassador for the Metropolitan.

Geoffrey was falling upon bad days. He was having a hard time getting ahead with his writing and earned very little money at his sister-in-law's little sandwich shop on Lexington Avenue, in short his life was bitterness and disillusion and there is nothing more bitter than jewish disillusion. He had also developed severe claustrophobia and categorically refused to take the subway or ride an elevator. It was a restless and disturbed time. Then Fluffy the cat got really ill and had to be put to sleep. It was as Filip Noterdaeme says a true catastrophe. Not much later the two moved once again, this time to Chelsea which was at the time beginning to become very popular with gay men.

Their new address was 342 West 21st Street. The building was called The New Chelsea and their apartment was a small two-bedroom with plenty of light. Geoffrey still claustrophobic and disillusioned insisted they should have separate bedrooms. Filip Noterdaeme undoubtedly no longer having any influence for the good in Geoffrey's life agreed and as may be imagined this was the beginning of the end of their relationship.

Twice a week, usually very early in the morning, the Metropolitan Museum sent a black limousine to the New Chelsea to pick up Filip Noterdaeme and drive him to schools, community centers, rehabilitation facilities, nursing homes, hospitals and churches, sometimes as far away as the Bronx or Staten Island. Filip Noterdaeme showed slides and learned how to talk about art to the very young, the poor, the uneducated, the disenfranchised, the drug addicted, the derelicts, the elderly, the blind, and the dying. Everybody always listened. No one in the world could tell stories about art like Filip Noterdaeme. He says it was very easy to talk about Buddha and nirvana to a group of recovering drug addicts and that egyptian mummies were always a big hit with the young ones but not so much with the dying.

After nine months of working as an ambassador for the Metropolitan Museum Filip Noterdaeme was asked to join the in-house educational staff and hitherto give tours directly at the museum. This Filip Noterdaeme liked much better. Over the years he got to know the collection of the Metropolitan very well and soon felt very much at home in the museum no matter if he found himself in the Gubbio Studiolo or the Petrie Court. This was his first experience of working inside a museum and he delighted in the flow of it all, the grand staircase, the tall flower arrangements, the beautiful courts, the children. And then there was the quantity of objects and beautiful art. It gave Filip Noterdaeme a feeling that there had been so many visitors at the museum who had looked at these things before he came and that there would be so many more visitors who would come to look at these things after he'd be gone. He was interested in art types, he knew there was cold art, hot art and temperate art. There was no doubt that Ingres was cold, but what was Pollock, visitors asked, he said hot, and at this they were usually very pleased. He liked the administration offices less. The continuous tired petty bickering, the never ceasing sound of administrators complaining about administration bothered him. Filip Noterdaeme found interacting with the public so much more simply exciting and interesting. As an educator, he was far from being able to compete with those stupendous volunteering american lady docents, scattered all over american museums, who, prompted by the ulterior motive of self-perfection, managed to infuse innocent wide-eyed museum visitors with a magical knowledge of the arts in an atmosphere of vignettes, sandwiches and decaffeinated coffee.

Once, just before giving a tour to a group of deaf teenagers and their sign language interpreter, Filip Noterdaeme was followed into the men's room by a young man in a soft summer suit with a silk kerchief in his breast pocket. He might have been a scandinavian or a scotsman. In any case in the men's room one thing quickly led to another and the two locked themselves into one of the stalls for a very pleasant wordless encounter of the first kind. Filip Noterdaeme arrived a little late for his scheduled tour with the deaf teenagers and he says that they all had such seeing eyes and then what they didn't see they could feel that it made him wonder if they could not also sense what he had excitedly been doing moments ago in the men's room.

He was the only male tour guide among an all female staff of educators. They were all married and there was always at least one among them being pregnant. Filip Noterdaeme says the education department had hired him only because he was never going to ask to go on maternity leave and could thus always be counted upon to fill in for somebody who did. There were nine pregnancies in nine years and then there were no more pregnancies, not one more. This was in 1999, the year Filip Noterdaeme and I met. It was also the year that the Metropolitan Museum did not renew his contract and that he began working as a freelance gallery lecturer at the Guggenheim Museum. He always says the difference between the Metropolitan Museum and the Guggenheim Museum is that at the Met one walks in straight lines whereas at the Guggenheim one walks in circles, and that he always preferred walking in circles. But now I must talk about the day in 1991 when Filip Noterdaeme's studies at Hunter College came to an abrupt end.

It had something to do with the Pussy Painting that Filip Noterdaeme had conceived in great detail and asked Dominique Carrara to paint for him following his instructions. Filip Noterdaeme had then presented the painting as a Marcellus Wasbending-Ttum self-portrait. Sanford Wurmfeld the chairman of the art department at Hunter College put his foot down, he was not going to have his standards compromised by Filip Noterdaeme. This was a serious school, a school for serious artists and neither he nor his faculty would tolerate such plagiarism. Not everybody agreed, and Filip Noterdaeme was summoned to defend himself in front of a disciplinary committee. He had the support of many teachers and fellow students but Sanford Wurmfeld was a bullish man whom nobody dared to openly contradict. And so Filip Noterdaeme ended up being expelled from the school.

Filip Noterdaeme now never likes to go to Hunter College, he does not like to think about it much less talk about it. Even to me he is hesitant about talking about it, there were things at that time that cut deeply into his flemish pride and he went through a phase of disappointment and disillusion.

Whenever somebody asked him what he was going to do, he used to say that he could foresee a thousand possibilities, knowing well that in fact they were all complete impossibilities. In the meanwhile Geoffrey Rees's state had gone from bad to worse and he was reduced to taking antidepressants. He moved out of 342 West 21st Street and into a basement apartment in the East Village, taking Rosie the dachshund with him. There he finally finished writing Sex with Strangers, and with his mother's help got it published by Farrar, Straus and Giroux but for all that it did not do very well.

Filip Noterdaeme now all by himself alone at 342 West 21st Street felt his way a little and then found refuge at the Gallatin School of Individualized Studies at New York University. He studied the writings of Gertrude Stein and Paul Celan and Louis Wolfson and coined a new term, autotranslation, that became the theme of his thesis. He has tried multiple times to explain autotranslation to me and I have never quite understood it but his teachers in comparative literature all did and they liked it well enough to begin using it among themselves. It was during that time that he began writing a book unlike any book ever written. It was called Je t'aime and was a full rewrite of Jean-Jacques Rousseau's Confessions where every sentence had been replaced with countless, thousands of repetitions of the phrase je t'aime while perfectly respectfully maintaining the punctuation and conjunctions of Rousseau's original.

The manuscript was, as may be imagined, a long one. There was also a very extensive annex with annotations and a preface by Geoffrey Rees describing Je t'aime as the saddest story ever told. Filip Noterdaeme sent the manuscript and annex to several french publishers and writers. Denis Roche from Editions du Seuil wrote to Filip Noterdaeme that Je t'aime was not really a book and yet had one big advantage over other large volumes, namely that it didn't take much time to read it. Filip Noterdaeme also sent a copy to Edmund White who was living in Paris at the time and who praised the book's purity and called it a great experience in contemporary literature. Alain Robbe-Grillet at first found the annex very interesting and entertaining but when he closely looked at the actual manuscript of Je t'aime he said to Filip Noterdaeme, but this means that you are in fact completely and totally out of your mind.

It was at about this time that Filip Noterdaeme's father was knighted in Belgium for his services to the kingdom. He was asked to choose a motto for his title and he chose Persevera et Noli Timere. He returned to New York a baron. It was only a little later that he retired from diplomacy and became a professor at New York University. The Noterdaemes moved out of the embassy and took up residence in an apartment on Washington Square but Baroness Noterdaeme continued to insouciantly chase her ambition to become a true lady artist.

Two semesters went by and then all of a sudden Baron Noterdaeme got very ill. There was nothing to do but go to Saint Vincent's Hospital and there he was immediately diagnosed with terminal cancer. He didn't want to die in New York and decided to return to Belgium and so one very sad day Filip Noterdaeme accompanied his father to the airport. Of course Raj the driver was driving. Filip Noterdaeme escorted his father through customs and all the way into the cabin of the waiting airplane. Everybody from Sabena Airlines waited until the last minute and then the head stewardess approached Filip Noterdaeme and said in sotto voce, we are now ready for take-off and must ask you to please vacate the aircraft. It was a difficult moment. Filip Noterdaeme bid his father farewell and his father made the sign of the cross on his son's forehead and Filip Noterdaeme left the cabin and watched the plane take off. He then took the A train back to the city. As he has often said to me, through the whole first twenty-nine years of my life I had always been the ambassador's son and the day my father left New York I suddenly became just another young man trying to find his way. Nothing to the outward eye had changed but he had changed and he knew it.

Ambassador Noterdaeme died in Belgium on belgian National Day, July 21 and Filip Noterdaeme, having only just received his re-entry visa traveled to Belgium to attend the funeral. A year later he graduated from New York University and was elected Master of Arts Degree Representative of his school and given an award at the one hundredth and sixtyfourth commencement exercises in Washington Square Park. Altogether there were eight thousand fellow students in purple robes and hats and all he remembers of the ceremony is that it was raining very hard and that Steven Spielberg the honorary speaker told the drenched students to take the future by storm. Baroness Noterdaeme who had continued residing on Washington Square after her husband's passing watched the ceremony from her balcony. She had by then found a way to amuse herself with herself again and everybody called her Baroness Ida. In short she was fast becoming more uninhibitedly herself than ever. She delighted in taking art classes by day and going to gallery openings and cocktail bars at night. There she more often than not lost her purse and got mixed up in all kinds of stories. When she moved back to Belgium a few years later she left behind countless cardboard boxes filled with her wayward belongings that Filip Noterdaeme was in charge of bringing to the post office one by one and mailing to her new residence in Brussels. He often wishes that he had been spared the embarrassment of listing the strange contents of each box for customs.

Ever since Filip Noterdaeme and Geoffrey Rees had separated he had been trying to find a new companion. There was beautiful melancholic Luis Moreno who later became quite successful and wealthy, but that was not until long after he and Filip Noterdaeme had broken up. It was Luis Moreno who later told Filip Noterdaeme that I was a keeper. There was also sturdy Jim Bachman who was heavily into showtunes and Bette Middler and later a brief affair with slender Jay Franke a young baptist ballet dancer from Texas. After Jay Franke Filip Noterdaeme was for a while seeing a health-obsessed vegetarian who dyed his hair blond and later a real blond fashionista from Norway who worked for Old Navy and was what gay men call a screamer.

In those days living in gay Chelsea always meant a great deal of cruising and dating but never more than just that, cruising and dating. Everybody was always cruising somebody and everybody was ready at any time and it began to be a nuisance. Filip Noterdaeme concluded it might be better for him to go live in another neighborhood.

He moved into a shared two-bedroom on the top floor of a townhouse at 172 Clinton Street in Brooklyn Heights. He took along all his books, the Je t'aime manuscript, and only one of his paintings, the Pussy Painting. He says that he donated the Unmagrittes, the urinal paintings, and all his other art works to a charity for homeless people living with AIDS. I now wish he had not.

The year was 1996. His roommate at 172 Clinton Street was a promiscuous gay sexologist who was very interested in Filip Noterdaeme's stories about gay Chelsea and then promptly decided to move there. Filip Noterdaeme took a new roommate, Paul Lombardi, a young and charismatic television reporter with a winning smile. Paul Lombardi was only really on when the cameras were on him and he was miserable when they were not. At the time, they were not on him most of the time. Things gradually changed for Paul Lombardi when he became the protégé of a NY1 news anchor and moved out of 172 Clinton Street and in with the anchor.

Once again Filip Noterdaeme had to look for a roommate and one day a young student from Brooklyn Poly called and asked could he stop by and see the room. It was a rainy day and the young man arrived drenched and huffing and puffing from walking up the four flights.

This was Nick Wilkinson. He moved in the next day.

Filip Noterdaeme was still working at the Metropolitan Museum at the time but he was now more interested in literature than art. He signed up for a course on Nathaneal West at the New School and was delighted to find his own sense for the grotesque reflected in the writings of the american novelist.

Nothing much happened in the following year until Filip Noterdaeme was introduced to Gordon Ross at the Cock, which was then the only gay bar in New York that still had a backroom. They met and went quite mad about each other.

Gordon was from England and living in the United States without a visa, leading a true bohemian life on the Lower East Side and sharing a small two-bedroom apartment with a long-haired wigmaker who had been friends with Tom Sachs when Tom Sachs was still just Tom and who later made the famous wig that John Cameron Mitchell wore and sang about in Hedwig and the Angry Inch.

Gordon Ross was working as a window dresser and obsessed with Andy Warhol, in fact he liked to remind everybody that Andy in his early beginnings too had been a window dresser. He was also very proud of having once been shot at like Andy and very happy with the clean small scar the bullet had left behind in his leg. He had a taste for kinky sex and it was he who introduced Filip Noterdaeme to bondage and role-play. All in all Filip Noterdaeme adapted fairly well to Gordon's particular tastes although he soon found the role-playing and make-believe kidnapping scenes a bit tiresome to act out.

One evening the two young men dressed up in Gordon's army gear and combat boots and went to a bondage club in the West Village. They wandered about the club and came upon a scene with a lesbian whipping the bottom of another lesbian who had mousetraps clasped to her tits. At first this upset Filip Noterdaeme and Gordon would tell him, now look, now don't, until he was finally able to look all the time. Later that night he and Gordon had that threesome with the young medicine student during which Filip Noterdaeme let himself be tied up and gagged.

Like Filip Noterdaeme Gordon had once been introduced to Quentin Crisp, and the two sometimes treated Mister Crisp, who was wont to tell everybody in his best Vivien Leigh imitation that he had always depended on the kindness of strangers, to lunch, tea and sympathy.

Filip Noterdaeme always delighted in Quentin Crisp's company. Listening to him was a pleasure and Mister Crisp seemed to accept with candid satisfaction that this should be so. With Quentin Crisp, says Filip Noterdaeme, you were in England in a kind of way that if you only went to England you could not possibly be. Quentin Crisp entertained the two young men with well-rehearsed stories from his life and Filip Noterdaeme could never truly enjoy his scones with Devonshire cream and strawberry jam because the stories were so perfectly enchanting that nothing else could possibly have mattered at the moment. As Jack Smith once said and as Penny Arcade likes to say in her best Jack Smith imitation, sometimes spending just one hour with a genius is enough.

At one time Filip Noterdaeme and Quentin Crisp had lunch all by themselves at Mister Crisp's favorite diner, the Cooper Square restaurant on Second Avenue. Filip Noterdaeme had brought a copy of his Je t'aime book as a gift for Quentin Crisp who had thanked him and said, books, my dear, are for writing, not for reading. After lunch Filip Noterdaeme walked Quentin Crisp home to his notoriously dusty boarding room on East 3rd Street. There the two sat for a while and talked about Thomas Hardy and Miss Greta Garbo. Then Quentin Crisp decided to take a little nap and Filip Noterdaeme sitting close by watched over him. He always says the fifteen minutes he spent watching Quentin Crisp sleep taught him everything about performance art there is to know.

In those days Filip Noterdaeme and Gordon also spent a lot of time with Terry Brown Jr. who frequently treated the young couple to a night on the town. It always started with dinner and then they went on to see a show, maybe Eartha Kitt at the Carlyle and of course usually ending up at the louche Gaiety in Times Square. There the male strippers had commenced doing dance routines in character costumes and then returning to the stage completely naked in a state of arousal, and this state of arousal now so prevalent on the internet but presented exclusively live onstage at the Gaiety at the time was the delight of Terry Brown Jr. and his generation. Not very long ago somebody was talking about how the current burlesque revival owed everything to certain female performers. I laughed. I am quite certain, I said, these girls pay more for their costumes than the male strippers of the Gaiety did then for their outfits but the burlesque revival was in fact long ago started by the male strippers of the Gaiety, long before Times Square was reinvented by Disney and every girl one met was or wanted to be a burlesque performer.

But to Filip Noterdaeme there was nothing in the world more entertaining than Bar d'O on Tuesday nights.

Terry Brown Jr. used to call the Gaiety the Ballet and Filip Noterdaeme used to call Bar d'O the Church.

It was during that time that Filip Noterdaeme began writing a satire of self-help books called US Free. It talked of cosmetics in the style of printed copy, the kind advertisers use in sales catalogues, and was written from the perspective of toads. US Free was never completed but every now and then Filip Noterdaeme delights in reading parts of his unfinished one-hundred-page manuscript. It makes him chuckle.

Gordon was getting restless about his illegal immigration status. He made up his mind to leave the United States clandestinely via Canada and then travel to London to get his immigration papers in order and then promptly return. They spent their last evening together at Joe's Pub where Joey Arias was giving a big solo concert. It was Valentine's Day and they were both depressed because they did not know when and if they were going to see each other again. The next day Gordon Ross boarded a train at Penn Station to travel to Canada as planned. When he crossed the border something happened, at any rate he was caught by US immigration officers and told in no uncertain terms that he was hitherto barred from reentering the United States for 10 years. Filip Noterdaeme was quite beside himself with grief. He stayed at home for several days feeling desolate and listening to a recording of countertenor David Daniels singing Händel arias. Then one Tuesday night he put on the tight white T-shirt with the word Dreamer printed on it that Gordon had given him as a gift and went to his church, Bar d'O. He arrived at the club and there were already many people in the room. He sat down on the red vinyl banquette and just in front of him sitting on an ottoman was a handsome young man with dark hair. He was dressed all in black and every now and then got up to industriously greet and air kiss Joey Arias and Sherry Vine and Raven O, the divas of Bar d'O. The show began and then all of a sudden Joey Arias introduced the young man to the crowd and the young man got up and sang a Frank Sinatra song, The Best Is Yet to Come. That young man was I. After the show Filip Noterdaeme introduced himself and it was as he often later said what the french call a coup de foudre, love at first sight.

IV

Filip Noterdaeme Before He Came to New York

Once more I have come to New York and now I am living at 172 Clinton Street in Brooklyn Heights. Filip Noterdaeme was still working on his book US Free and he had just commenced lecturing at the Guggenheim Museum. He did not create the Homeless Museum until years later and when he did I helped him create it.

Filip Noterdaeme was born in Brussels, Belgium. As I have become an ardent New Yorker and as he has spent many more years in New York than I, I have often begged him to be a New Yorker but he always remained firmly a Bruxellois. He left Brussels when he was one year old and later lived there again for several years and now it looks like Belgium may split in two separate countries and what would happen then to the belgian capital nobody really knows. He used however to delight in being born in Brussels, Belgium when during tours, in connection with work at the Metropolitan Museum of Art, he used to show Magritte's paintings and people always immediately assumed that Magritte was from France. He used to say if he really were a New Yorker as I wanted him to be he would never have had the pleasure of seeing various New York City school teachers get confused about the whereabouts of Belgium. Once, a high school teacher firmly informed him that flemish, Filip Noterdaeme's mother tongue, was in fact a dead language.

When I first knew Filip Noterdaeme in New York I was surprised that he didn't have an accent. But you don't sound like a foreigner, I as well as many others said. No, he replied, you see I feel with my ears and it does not make a difference to me what language I hear, I don't hear a language I hear tones of rhythms and voice, but with my eyes I see words and sentences only with great difficulty and so no matter which language I speak I never have an accent and no matter which language I write I have great difficulty. One of his most notorious aphorisms is Homelessness begins at home.

He was born in Brussels, Belgium, of a very respectable diplomatic family. He always says that he is very grateful not to have been born of a business family, he has a horror of what he calls business people. It has always been rather ridiculous that he who is good friends with everybody and can know them and they can know him, has always been admired of the few. But he always says, some day they, anybody, will find out that he is of interest to them, he and his Homeless Museum. And he always consoles himself that there are some writers who are interested. They always say, he says, that my museum is interesting but they cannot comprehend it and continue to only write about those museums they say they comprehend. The hope that one day a writer will comprehend the Homeless Museum and write about it has at some of his most bitter moments been a consolation. My museum does get under their skin, only they do not know that it does, he has often said.

He was born in Brussels, Belgium, in a house, a twin house. His flemish family lived in one and a family of walloons lived in the other. The Noterdaemes had lived in the twin house for about three years when Filip Noterdaeme was born. A year before his birth, the two families who had never gotten along any too well were no longer on speaking terms. Very evidently the long national conflict between the dutch-speaking flemish and the french-speaking walloons had become very personal.

Filip Noterdaeme's mother was a buoyant energetic buxom woman with a mind all her own. She was a well-known announcer on national belgian radio and the flemish loved the sound of her voice. The only thing was that she lacked a sense of numbers and dates. This sometimes became a bit of a problem. There is a legendary story of her once announcing Beethoven's Nine Hundredth Symphony on the air. His father was a belgian diplomat. They stayed in Brussels until Filip Noterdaeme was about one year old. All he remembers of this is that his mother once took him along to the broadcast studios and that he was allowed to sit on her lap as she made her announcements and that that pleased and terrified him.

Filip Noterdaeme had two older siblings, a sister and a brother. After he was born his mother declared that she was not willing to have another child. However she did get pregnant again. In the meanwhile Filip Noterdaeme's father became very successful and was sent to work at the belgian embassy in London. His mother had to give up her radio career and they moved to London. There she very reluctantly gave birth to a third son. Filip Noterdaeme and his young brother were then raised very much like twins, that is to say in those days Filip Noterdaeme was always a little bit behind in his development and his young brother always a little bit ahead in his and so the two brothers were more or less on the same level for quite some time. Later Filip Noterdaeme began to be ahead of everyone in some ways and his younger brother a little bit behind in other ways and they grew apart.

They stayed in London until Filip Noterdaeme was about four years old. All he remembers of this is that he and his siblings used to play in Kensington Gardens and that often Her Majesty Queen Elizabeth used to stroll through the gardens and sometimes a band played the british national hymn which he liked. Also that his favorite english nanny called him my little prince. He believed for many years that Prince was his real name and he never could come to accept the name as belonging to anybody else.

They lived in London for three years. Then the father was called back to Belgium on business for the belgian Ministry of Foreign Affairs and they moved back to Brussels. Here Filip Noterdaeme has more lively memories. He remembers a little art school where he and his younger brother played with clay. He also remembers an amusement park with a marvelous mechanical donkey that dispensed golden chocolate coins from its behind when one fed it with litter and that was always exciting. He also remembers the family's black cat jumping in front of a car right by their house on the avenue de la Forêt and scaring the driver and he and his siblings burying the cat in the garden. He also remembers that the family that lived across from them was extravagantly wealthy. They had two pet leopards and a Jaguar sports car. He says he remembers seeing the father drive the Jaguar with the two leopards sitting in the back. Just the other day Filip Noterdaeme was reminiscing about the Jaguar and the two leopards with his older brother who said, yes it is true this was the Pierre Salik family of the famous belgian blue jeans but they did not have leopards they had tigers and Monsieur Salik drove not a Jaguar but a Lotus.

Filip Noterdaeme also remembers the fresh waffles for breakfast and he also remembers that they had moules frites for dinner and as he was very fond of frites and not too fond of mussels he used to always eat all of his younger brother's frites. It was not until years later that Filip Noterdaeme developed a taste for mussels like every belgian.

Those early years in Brussels made a very great impression upon Filip Noterdaeme. When in 2002 he and I went to Brussels together for the first time, as soon as we arrived at the Grande Place Filip Noterdaeme said, it is strange, Brussels is so familiar but so different. And then reflectively, I see what it is, there is nobody here but europeans (there were no chinese tourists or businessmen there yet), you can see the salesgirls of the chocolatiers in their white lace aprons, you can fully see the Grande Place because for once there are no scaffoldings, it is just like my memory of Brussels when I was six years old. The air smells like it used (sugar waffles had come back in style), the smell of belgian beer and belgian public gardens that I remember so well.

The Noterdaeme family remained in Brussels for four years and then moved again, this time to Geneva. Filip Noterdaeme's elder brother charmingly describes their last days in Brussels when he and his mother went shopping and bought everything that pleased her fancy, her first fur coat, wonderful hats, a small print by James Ensor, a pointillist seascape by George Lemmen, an antique convex mirror, and finally ending up with a whole set of crystal glassware from the famous belgian manufacturer Val Saint Lambert.

And so once more the family said goodbye to Belgium. They flew to Geneva in first class on Sabena Airlines, the belgian national airline that was lovingly referred to by the belgian diplomatic corps as Such A Bloody Experience Never Again.

The only thing Filip Noterdaeme remembers from the airplane trip to Geneva was the three-course menu they were served on board. There was buttered spinach and a belgian veal dish called oiseaux sans tête, headless birds. And also that on every glass, every plate, every piece of cutlery was an image of a bird in flight. This was L'Oiseau de Ciel, the Sky Bird, by Magritte, who once said that Sabena had paid him just enough to paint the logo so that he could put du beurre sur mes épinards, butter on his spinach. Years later, L'Oiseau de Ciel became butter on the spinach of the Sabena employees when the company filed for bankruptcy and auctioned off the original painting in an aircraft hangar at Brussels International Airport.

The only other thing Filip Noterdaeme remembers from the airplane trip is that he and his little brother were wearing beautiful sailor outfits with matching hats each with little blue ribbons and upon arrival in Geneva his little brother stepping out of the aircraft had his hat blown off by the wind. The stewardess ran down the gangway and onto the tarmac, caught the hat to the awe and astonishment of Filip Noterdaeme's mother.

When the family settled down in Geneva they had to get used to new surroundings yet again. Everybody tried swiss chocolate but agreed that it was inferior to belgian chocolate and so his father continued to bring home Côte d'Or chocolate from his frequent trips to Brussels. This story reminds me of a rather amusing incident that happened in the kitchen at 172 Clinton Street several years ago. I was making truffles and had in front of me a large tray of molten belgian chocolate when Filip Noterdaeme walked in and we had a quarrel. I do not remember what it was about in any case Filip Noterdaeme who has a quick temper suddenly rapidly grabbed the tray wanting to slam it back down on the counter but the momentum being quite strong the warm chocolate lifted off the tray and ended up on the ceiling, on the walls, on the floor and on us, in short everywhere. I cannot say which one of us was more perplexed at that point but Filip Noterdaeme quickly recovered, ran his finger through the chocolate on the floor and tasted it and said, this is real belgian chocolate and can you still use it.

I remember only one other instance where Filip Noterdaeme's temper got the best of him. We were skiing in the italian alps with his family and one day at the breakfast table he got so agitated about a comment his mother made that he started throwing breakfast rolls at her. No one of his family was all that surprised but I was. He later told me that when he was a little boy he often chased his siblings around the dining table with a butter knife.

But to get back to Geneva. The family had moved into the belgian embassy, a very grand nineteenth century villa with a large iron gate and a gravel driveway. It is said that the royal belgian family had briefly stayed there while in exile after World War II. The belgian coat of arms was everywhere and adorned even the fine china and silverware. There were also solid brass signs above every door spelling Cuisine, Salon, Toilettes, Privé etcetera so visitors would always know where to go and where not to go. Behind the embassy was a big garden and Filip Noterdaeme remembers climbing into the cherry trees and eating cherries until his face, hands and clothes were stained purple. He also remembers being afraid that his father might get shot because there had been an assassination threat. The family acquired a rather aggressive watchdog, a belgian shepard named Laura, and for a time the swiss police positioned two guards outside the house but Laura kept attacking them and it became a problem. All this and much more, all the physical life of these days, Filip Noterdaeme has incorporated into the Homeless Museum.

Life at the belgian embassy was extremely formal, with live-in servants and stiff dinners with silver trays and finger bowls. Filip Noterdaeme's mother had an electric bell installed under the dining table to summon the maids from the kitchen. She loved using it and she used it a lot. The maids for some reason were always practicing catholics from Portugal. There was Maria and there was Clara and Zita and all of them always had dark circles under their eyes.

The front and back of the house were very distinct and it was there and at that time that Filip Noterdaeme became interested in what went on behind the scenes and the tension between the external and the internal. He always says living in an embassy felt like being constantly on display like in a museum and one of the things that used to worry him about museums is the difficulty visitors feel, that after all museums are essentially not inhabitable. Well anyway it is that of which he is always talking and he resolved his struggle with it when he created the Homeless Museum in our home at 172 Clinton Street.

Whenever Filip Noterdaeme and his siblings wanted to escape from the formality of embassy life they went up to the attic and visited the portuguese maids in their quarters. Filip Noterdaeme fondly recalls the warm cozy atmosphere in their little rooms, so different from the cold formal atmosphere downstairs. The attic also had an atelier, reserved for Filip Noterdaeme's mother who liked to dabble in painting. Filip Noterdaeme liked spending afternoons in the atelier because it was quiet and because he liked the smell of the oil paint and turpentine. It was also there that he was allowed to keep his little hamster, Picasso. Poor little Picasso died one day from breathing in too many turpentine fumes. Filip Noterdaeme having desperately tried to resuscitate Picasso with warm milk was heartbroken about it.

Another way to escape the embassy was to go across the street to the Intercontinental. The hotel had an outdoor swimming pool and Filip Noterdaeme and his siblings spent a great many afternoons there, lounging and ordering american club sandwiches and milkshakes on tab. It was very convenient and the hotel staff became used to them constantly being there. When it was time for supper at the embassy their mother always called them back to the house by stepping out into the embassy garden and blowing into a french horn. It made a very strange sound that no one but the children recognized.

The important thing to tell about now is Filip Noterdaeme's education.

His father having enrolled him and his three siblings in the very international Institut Florimont so they might have the benefit of a multilingual education insisted that the children should continue to prattle in flemish at home. As Filip Noterdaeme says, ears to him were more important than eyes and it happened then as always that he found himself surrounded by many languages. His parents spoke flemish and his siblings spoke french. In the Geneva household, there were the portuguese maids who of course spoke portuguese, a temperamental cook who cursed in italian, a gardener and his wife who spoke a swiss dialect and Monsieur Charbonnier the chauffeur who never spoke a word. There were also many foreign dignitaries coming and going at the embassy and they usually conversed in broken english, much to the regret of the american and british officials. At Florimont, english was taught by a spaniard with a lisp. Filip Noterdaeme found the potpourri of languages and the maçedoine of accents around him very amusing. His liking of double entendres and word puns commenced at this time. His love for visual puns came later.

Learning how to write was a different matter. Filip Noterdaeme was having a very hard time of it and after a little while his teachers concluded that he was dyslexic. His parents arranged for a private tutor to come and work with him every day. Little by little he caught up with everybody else. Nevertheless to this day he continues to have great difficulty writing.

One day Filip Noterdaeme's french teacher asked the children to write a description of the street where they lived. The embassy was at 26 chemin du Petit Saconnex and Filip Noterdaeme wrote a piece in which the chemin was telling its story, of the arrival of the first automobile and of how it had replaced the horse carriage and how this had made everything soft quiet and slow suddenly become hard loud and fast. The chemin also complained that it was still called a chemin, a path, when it had become a rue, a street. This innocent charming little story Filip Noterdaeme's french teacher for some reason considered a disgrace. He does not remember that he himself did.

As I said the family's chauffeur was Monsieur Charbonnier who never said a word. He always wore a black uniform and driver's cap like every respectable chauffeur in those days. He was very tall and very thin, with a long face, long nose and a fabulous amount of front teeth. In short he looked very much like a horse and Filip Noterdaeme and his younger brother often made jokes behind poor Monsieur Charbonnier's back about being driven in a black sedan by a horse.

Monsieur Charbonnier drove Filip Noterdaeme and his siblings to school every day and also twice a week he drove him all by himself to his sessions with the family therapist, Madame Nicoto. She was a petite phlegmatic woman who was forever sharpening her Caren d'Ache pencils and picking lint off her Cacharel cashmere cardigan, which is to say that she was meticulous in a very swiss way. Filip Noterdaeme spent a great deal of time in her practice looking at the floor and this is where he got interested in persian carpets.

Well.

In the midst of all that there was his father representing Belgium at the United Nations and always wearing a suit and tie. Filip Noterdaeme does not remember his father ever wearing anything else but a suit and tie and even when he was not, says Filip Noterdaeme, he gave off the impression that he was.

At the United Nations Ambassador Noterdaeme in those days was always advocating for a détente. He was negotiating disarmament and it wasn't easy, especially with the russians. Years later when he presided over the Security Council of the United Nations in New York, he tried the same with the iraqis and it was even harder. Then there was Bosnia and Rwanda. In any case there was always disaster looming or already happening somewhere in the world and he and the other ambassadors debated the magnitude of it all in long emergency meetings during the day and then some more over equally long dinners followed by whiskey and cigars at one of the embassies. Filip Noterdaeme's father saw a great deal of the french ambassador Stéphane Hessel at this time. Ambassador Hessel used to recount to Ambassador Noterdaeme the conversations that he afterwards used in his autobiography, Danse avec le siècle, Dance with the Century, and they talked endlessly about the character of de Gaule, Charles.

One day disaster struck at home. Filip Noterdaeme's sister threw herself out of a window. It happened at night and she survived with a broken back and several broken limbs. Filip Noterdaeme remembers visiting her in the swiss hospital where she had to stay for many months, her entire body in a cast. This incident was Filip Noterdaeme's first lesson in human suffering and misery. Years, many years later, he learned from the writings of Vladimir Nabokov and Quentin Crisp that the best way to get people to notice suffering was to show glimpses of it in small intervals with long stretches of time in between.

And then there was the time when the king of the belgians and his wife her majesty Queen Fabiola came to

Geneva.

Filip Noterdaeme was very interested and his mother was evidently very excited. As he always says about royalty, kings and queens are never regal but everybody around them is always trying to be, which is always very amusing.

In any case there was great excitement at 26 chemin du Petit Saconnex in the days leading up to the royal visit. Then the day finally arrived and everybody at the belgian embassy was at attention. Then someone from protocol called and said, His Majesty the King and Her Majesty the Queen are delayed and will you please excuse the royal couple, they will come tomorrow for sure. The next day at the same hour everybody was at attention again and once again the phone rang and this time it was the chief of protocol and he asked to speak to Ambassador Noterdaeme. He said, Your Excellency the Royals have been delayed again and should arrive tomorrow, apologies. This happened several days in a row and every time everything that pleased his and her majesty's fancy, a luncheon of smoked sable and other things, went bad and new orders had to be placed. So much waiting and wasting, Filip Noterdaeme says, created a sentiment of dread rather than eager anticipation. At any moment's notice the king and the queen could appear and one had to be ready and even the chairs had to be ready and of course the maids' white aprons had to be bleached and starched and bleached and starched again every day. He remembers hearing the three portuguese maids with the dark circles under their eyes saying, oh meu deus and, oh meu coração. Otherwise, he says, they really none of them had much else to say.

Finally the king and queen turned up and nobody was really at attention at this time, from exhaustion. Everyone was presented and everybody sat down. Everybody sat down and everybody began to eat.

The belgian royal couple had no children which everyone knew was a source of much sadness in the marriage. Queen Fabiola was of spanish aristocracy and reminded one most naturally of paintings by Goya. She had a certain mad quality that perhaps had to do with her elaborate hairdo and was curiously in accord with her long birth name Fabiola Fernanda Maria de las Victorias Antonia Adelaida de Mora y Aragón. Of course the belgians could never remember such a long name so when she became queen she was simply always Fabiola. She always traveled with a spinsterish spanish governess and both her and the governess gave off the impression of carrying mothballs in their matching purses. The king was entirely a different type. He was quiet, serious and self-effacing, he had the square shoulders and the unseeing fixed eyes of a belgian monarch. He was very gentle.

The conversation around the table was not very lively, nobody had all that much to say besides that it was an honor and a pleasure to meet. The queen complained a little about the stormy weather and also that traveling in the air had had its elements of unpleasantness. Just at the end of the luncheon the king asked Filip Noterdaeme's mother if she had any of the comic supplements of the swiss dailies. Madame Noterdaeme said, why certainly with pleasure Your Majesty and she dispatched Filip Noterdaeme to fetch copies for the king. Filip Noterdaeme came back with several comic supplements and the king was very pleased indeed. Then everybody stood up. Everybody stood up and the king and queen said, à bientôt, we will meet soon, and they went back to Belgium.

The family spent every summer in Italy. They always stayed at the Royal Sporting Hotel in Portovenere, a small fisherman's town on the ligurian coast. From there they made excursions to Florence and Pisa and many other towns to visit churches and museums where they looked at italian masters. Later in his life Filip Noterdaeme spent much time looking at flemish masters and he now says he prefers the flemish masters over the italians. The flemish are so much more simply complicated and interesting, he says.

At wintertime, the family took to the alps to Crans-Montana, a swiss resort for the rich where Filip Noterdaeme remembers once seeing his teenage pop idol Gilbert Becaud sitting alone in a restaurant and eating Raclette, one plate after another, an unforgettable sight for all concerned. Then one day when he was out skiing Filip Noterdaeme shared a lift with a senegalese. The two had a casual conversation about the kind of things skiers talk about, little pleasantries about the weather and the snow. Years later Filip Noterdaeme had another conversation with a senegalese, this time much less casual. It happened at the Homeless Museum booth on Union Square. The senegalese was working as a street sweeper and the two talked at great length about Léopold Sédar Senghor and his political theories of enracinement and ouverture.

The Noterdaemes lived in Switzerland for five years and then returned to Belgium.

Filip Noterdaeme and his younger brother having lived practically as twins first in London and then in Geneva were sent together to a jesuit boarding school in Wallonia.

About boarding school Filip Noterdaeme says, I

have never loved a regulated life with fixed hours or a clockwork existence where thoughts and dreams must end at the sound of a bell. He has often described to me how strange it was to suddenly find himself under the forever low grey skies of Wallonia when he had gotten used to the majestic clear blue skies of Switzerland and Italy. Nevertheless Filip Noterdaeme has never ceased to be thankful to his parents for sending him to boarding school. Imagine, he has said to me, if my parents had stayed in Geneva and me and my younger brother had not been sent off to boarding school, imagine, he says, how horrible. I would have been unreasonably spoiled instead of miserable. I would never have become an artist and created the Homeless Museum.

It was in those years that he and his younger brother although sharing the same classes began to grow apart little by little. His brother being generally happy and Filip Noterdaeme generally miserable, the two were having less and less in common and as a result the next few years were lonesome ones for Filip Noterdaeme and were passed in an agony of adolescence.

In their last 2 years of boarding school, Filip Noterdaeme and his brother attended an elective art history class taught by a jesuit priest by the funny name of Père de Fou, Father of Mad. Beside Filip Noterdaeme and his younger brother there was only one other student attending the class, a very peculiar boy named Marc de Decker.

Père de Fou delighted Filip Noterdaeme. His personality and his teaching and his way of amusing himself with himself and his 3 sole students all pleased him. Filip Noterdaeme always says that it was Père de Fou's class that made boarding school tolerable and that everything changed after that. Once when they were looking at Matisse's famous portrait of Madame Matisse with the green stripe and Marc de Decker objected, but Père, this green stripe does not belong there, de Fou said, yes it does, you should keep your mind open.

And so Filip Noterdaeme having been exposed to Matisse's painting with the green stripe and also Picasso's portrait of Fernande in a Black Mantilla and having become more humanized and less adolescent and less lonesome began to think about becoming an artist.

As I said Filip Noterdaeme's mother dabbled in painting and sometimes she and Filip Noterdaeme traveled in her little silver Fiat to visit museums and art fairs in neighboring France and Germany. They once went to Kassel to see the Documenta 7. There Joseph Beuys had commenced planting his 7,000 oak trees. Joseph Beuys was everywhere at the time. He was in Kassel, in Düsseldorf, in Paris, and also in Ghent. Filip Noterdaeme says that he liked Beuys well enough but that even then he preferred boys over Beuys. In this way Filip Noterdaeme has not changed. When his parents found out about his persuasion they were not amused. They had already lived through this sort of thing with his older brother and would have preferred to not have it repeated with another son. This was of course the time when AIDS was constantly being discussed in the news and sex among homosexuals was regarded as deadly. Filip Noterdaeme's mother made it clear to everybody in the family that she felt like a helpless bystander watching her two older sons risk their lives and once told Filip Noterdaeme of a dream in which she saw him standing in the middle of a deserted highway with a car racing towards him.

Filip Noterdaeme's older brother being an experienced homosexual was at the time living in a bachelor pad in Paris and he sometimes invited Filip Noterdaeme to come and stay over for the weekend. Filip Noterdaeme was very fond of these parisian escapades. He remembers buying his first men's cologne at the Galeries Lafayette. It was Caron's Pour un Homme and he has never taken to any other cologne since then. My favorite men's cologne is the original Man by Bogner and as it was taken off the market long ago I am now reduced to bid on it at auctions. Filip Noterdaeme also remembers buying a beige jumpsuit in the new Les Halles. It had a full-length frontal zipper that made his older brother raise an eyebrow.

Regarding sex, his older brother once remarked, nobody teaches anybody anything, at first everybody is inexperienced and then later everybody is experienced, and nobody has taught anybody anything. He then gave Filip Noterdaeme his first pack of condoms. Filip Noterdaeme has only twice in his life contracted a social disease. The first time remained a mystery for quite some time and the second was during a visit to Venice where he had no choice but to seek a pharmacy and he says it was most embarrassing to explain in broken italian that he urgently needed a remedy against phthirus pubis, pubic lice.

After graduating from boarding school Filip Noterdaeme had to choose if he should study art or philosophy and to Père de Fou's great regret he chose philosophy, mostly to honor a family tradition and to please his father. This was a mistake. Philosophy demands a satisfactory grounding in logic, a subject for which Filip Noterdaeme showed little inclination. At the Catholic University of Namur in Wallonia where Filip Noterdaeme began his studies the jesuits adored Thomas Aquinas and despised Nietzsche, in other words they were more interested in theology than philosophy. Also there was a good deal of intrigue and struggle among the students, those who had been recruited to join the Society of Jesus and those who had not.

Filip Noterdaeme does not remember much of his philosophy studies in Namur but he remembers getting his driver's license and once going parachute jumping. It was also the first time in his life that he had to cook his own meals. He worked out a series of experiments in cooking under the directions of a belgian recipe book and by the end of the year he knew how to cook a perfect rabbit stew with prunes and belgian beer.

After one year it was fairly well known among all his teachers that he was bored, frankly openly bored. And so he wisely left Namur and enrolled at a flemish art academy in Brussels where painting was still being taught in the Van Eyck tradition.

He was very productive in his first year at the academy and had three solo exhibitions, two in Brussels and one in Namur. His paintings were not in the Van Eyck tradition, they were in the tradition of Rubens and Ensor and Magritte, all in one. He now says they were all rather awful but sold very well. Then something strange happened. Filip Noterdaeme came down with a painful eye infection that blurred his vision and had everyone very concerned. No eye doctor seemed to be able to properly diagnose what it was until Filip Noterdaeme was sent to the country's most eminent ophthalmologist, a certain Dr. de Broek, a doctor of such reputation that people traveled from as far as Iran and Pakistan to be seen by him.

Dr. de Broek was a very gentle and cultivated man who was in the habit of receiving all his patients in the living room of his house. He was a passionate collector of persian carpets and his living room was so overstuffed with them that it had more a semblance of a bedouin tent than that of a doctor's practice. Filip Noterdaeme already knew something about persian carpets since the days of his therapy sessions with Madame Nicoto in Geneva, and during his eye examination he and Dr. de Broek discussed weaving motifs of the islamic period. From Dr. de Broek's tactful explanations Filip Noterdaeme understood that he most certainly had contracted his eye infection during his late night escapades in gay Paree. Filip Noterdaeme, finally healed of his temporary blindness by Dr. de Broek, has since then contended that only those doctors and therapists who have a liking for persian carpets are worth consulting.

It was at this time in Brussels that Filip Noterdaeme began to develop a taste for the grotesque. He made it a habit of frequenting a pub called La Mort Subite, the sudden death. His favorite art museum in Brussels was the unfashionable Musée Wiertz with its collection of macabre paintings. Years later in America he learned that unlike belgians, americans do not have a sense for the grotesque in art. Americans, he has often said, like their art to be serious and earnest. He says that the grotesque is too present in every other aspect of life in America to also be present in art. In America the grotesque can be found in the movies, in advertising and in television, in food and of course in politics, but never, as a rule, in art, says he. However there are exceptions. There is the american Jack Smith and there is the american Karen

Finley and of course the very grotesque american Paul McCarthy whose exhibit I remember seeing at the New Museum back when the New Museum was still located on Broadway and still an important place for new art. One was well advised to hold one's handkerchief to one's nose throughout the visit because Paul McCarthy was very fond of including spoiled food items in his installations. I also remember a grotesque video in which he had dangling sausages as fingers.

It was during those years in Brussels that Filip Noterdaeme's attention was attracted by the works of a belgian artist who had promoted a narrative of himself as a destitute poet who having decided to rather make money than write more poems had announced to everybody that from now on he would only make art objects and sell them at a profit in a gallery space. That sincerely insincere artist poet was the late Marcel Broodthaers, and there was something about his work that never failed to move Filip Noterdaeme deeply. A few years ago during one of our european summers, Filip Noterdaeme and I traveled to the SMAK museum in Ghent to see Pense Bête, Broodthaers's sad farewell to poetry and introduction into the contemporary art world. We looked at it in silence for a while and sure enough, Filip Noterdaeme was moved, deeply moved. Filip Noterdaeme always knows a Broodthaers when he sees it, knows it at once and enjoys it and knows that it is great art and beautiful.

Marcel Broodthaers had once famously created a museum in his own home in Brussels and called it the Musée d'Art Moderne, Departement des Aigles. It was not until a good many years later, at the School of Visual Arts in New York, that Filip Noterdaeme also created a museum of his own. It was completely influenced by Marcel Broodthaers and called the Museum of Belgian Contemporary Art, Department of Parrots and Chickens. And so the first time as one might say that a new american generation discovered the works of Marcel Broodthaers was when Filip Noterdaeme showed his. There was among other objects a bowler hat that Filip Noterdaeme had covered with mussel shells. It had something to do with an auction at Sotheby's in London that Filip Noterdaeme had once attended and where to his great astonishment and surprise one of the auctioned objects had been Magritte's personal bowler hat. Filip Noterdaeme knew of a famous photograph of Magritte making a gesture of handing Broodthaers his bowler hat and as he watched people around him at Sotheby's bidding for the hat he became very agitated and upset about not being able to place a bid.

Broodthaers's daughter Marie-Puck was at the time running a tiny little storefront art gallery on the rue Ravenstein called Galerie des Beaux Arts, just across the street from the Palais des Beaux Arts.

Marie-Puck Broodthaers was about the same age as Filip Noterdaeme and great fun to be around. He became a regular at her gallery, which is to say he went quite often to look at her offerings. It was also there that he was first introduced to Maria Gilissen, Marie Puck's mother and widow of Marcel Broodthaers.

There was a famous story of Marcel Broodthaers once entering the Palais des Beaux Arts with a camel from the Antwerp Zoo. The year was 1974, the same year that Joseph Beuys spent three days with a coyote at the René Block gallery in New York and that nine year old Filip

Noterdaeme had helplessly watched Picasso the hamster die of asphyxiation in his mother's painting studio in Geneva. Evidently 1974 was a big year for animals in the arts. Regarding Broodthaers and Beuys Filip Noterdaeme always says, Broodthaers was a poet artist and Beuys was a hero artist and naturally everybody always prefers a hero to a poet. Filip Noterdaeme prefers a poet to a hero and says, it is rather a pity that Broodthaers never visited the United States. Just imagine, he says, he might have led an elephant from the Bronx Zoo into MoMA's gift shop.

From his flemish academy period in Brussels Filip Noterdaeme also fondly remembers a trip to Ghent where he saw Jan Hoet's exhibit Chambres d'Amis, Guest Rooms. There were fifty original art works shown in fifty art collectors' homes. That day in Ghent Filip Noterdaeme visiting one interesting guest room after another made an important discovery comparing the hospitality among the hosts, that friendly hosts were usually showing bad art and not friendly hosts, good art. Chambres d'Amis, Filip Noterdaeme says, made clear how difficult it was to integrate contemporary art in a home without it becoming just décor. Years later Filip Noterdaeme created a museum for a day in several private homes in Kansas City. It was a disseminated version of his Homeless Museum in New York. He called the event HOMU Cribs after a popular show on MTV that tours the homes of the rich and famous. But more of that later.

Another interesting show that Filip Noterdaeme likes to remember from those years is a show at the university of Louvain dedicated to french writer Michel Butor. It was called Ici Butor n'est pas simplement Butor, here Butor isn't simply Butor, and Filip Noterdaeme along with thirty other artists had been invited to meet Butor and create works inspired by his writings. Filip Noterdaeme had a different idea. After introductions had been made he said to Butor, why don't you be the artist and I the model, then neither of us will be simply who we are. Butor very much liked this idea and drew Filip Noterdaeme while everybody looked on with slightly envious expressions. The drawing and photographs of Filip Noterdaeme modeling for Butor are now part of the Archives of the Homeless Museum.

Among the artists that Filip Noterdaeme liked and met during that same period was Carl Andre. This is how they met.

One Sunday in Brussels a gallerist friend of Filip Noterdaeme said to him, would you please pick up Carl Andre at the Gare du Nord for me. Filip Noterdaeme said he would be happy to, and so he went to the train station and waited for the famous american minimalist to arrive. His friend had described Carl Andre as a short man with a beard who always wore blue jeans and warned him that he could be difficult. As a matter of fact Carl Andre was dressed in bib overalls and was not bearded but cleanshaven, and he was delightful. The two drove around town in Filip Noterdaeme's red Citroën 2CV looking for a construction site where they could steal bricks that Carl André needed for his installation. They loaded as many bricks as would fit into the trunk of the car and then headed to the gallery where Carl Andre created one of his floor pieces by simply arranging the bricks on the floor. A few days later Carl Andre returned to America and Filip Noterdaeme created a work of his own by laying out a roll of brick wallpaper on the floor of a construction site.

Filip Noterdaeme also remembers a visit to a contemporary art festival in Münster, Germany. There he saw Robert Filliou's Permanent Creation Tool Shed with its two neon signs, Imagination and Innocence. He also saw The Way Things Really Go, a video by the swiss duo David Weiss and Peter Fischli in which one could see many objects fly, crash and explode with swiss precision, which is to say that nothing really happened but always on time.

Then one day Filip Noterdaeme traveled to Antwerp for the opening of a Keith Haring show. There were a great many people in the gallery when he arrived and the way Keith Haring made his way through the crowd like a star basketball player impressed him immensely. Keith Haring was quickly lost in an excited and voluble crowd, to be sure everybody seemed to be interested, but Filip Noterdaeme did not know why they were so especially interested. After a considerable interval he understood why. Keith Haring was making quick little graffiti drawings on paper and giving them away. It was good publicity. Naturally everybody wanted to have one. When it was Filip Noterdaeme's turn Keith Haring asked for his name and when he heard him say, Filip Noterdaeme, he briefly paused and then drew a Christ on a cross and handed it to him. It was a marvel. The little Keith Haring Christ must still be somewhere among Filip Noterdaeme's old belongings in Belgium.

Filip Noterdaeme like I said in those days often went to visit Marie-Puck's gallery. He always went in the hope of seeing something interesting and usually he did. He remembers seeing works by James Lee Byars and Andre Cadere and he liked them both very much because they were always complicated and simple at the same time. This of course is the perfect combination in all things. Filip Noterdaeme by himself is only complicated and I by myself am only simple but as a pair we are simply complicated.

One afternoon at Marie Puck's gallery Filip Noterdaeme was looking through an array of attractive drawings by Jacques Charlier and there was one that was not attractive. Filip Noterdaeme liked it quite a bit, it was the one that likened belgian artists to slaves in the former belgian colony of Congo. Filip Noterdaeme said to Marie-Puck that he wanted to buy it and Marie-Puck looked up the price in her catalogue. He says it was 10,000 belgian francs. He was in those days working as a clerk in the shop of the Theatre Royal de la Monnaie and the little money he earned there did of course not suffice to pay for the Charlier drawing and so he secretly pawned his mother's reel to reel Revox A77 recorder to come up with the money. It was just about enough and he bought it.

Then came Filip Noterdaeme's 22nd birthday and it was at about this time that his father was nominated to represent Belgium at the United Nations in New York. Filip Noterdaeme decided to move to New York with them. As I said however his father and mother being incapacitated and held back in Belgium for a time Filip Noterdaeme went ahead all by himself and on October 31, 1987 landed at John F. Kennedy airport. Raj the indian driver of the belgian mission was there to pick him up and drive him to the empty embassy duplex at One Beekman Place. At the embassy there was an Entenmann's pound cake in the refrigerator and nothing else, and so Filip Noterdaeme's life in the new world began with a slice of cold cake.

V
1999 – 2005

And so life at 172 Clinton Street began and Filip Noter-daeme created the Homeless Museum and both of us now live in it, and I can begin to tell what happened when I was of it.

When I first came to 172 Clinton Street Nick Wilkinson was occupying the master bedroom. When I moved in Nick agreed to move into the smaller bedroom and Filip Noterdaeme and I moved into the master bedroom.

It was a nice apartment with lots of sunshine and furnished with hand-me-downs in the Brooklyn bohemian style. I in particular did not care for the orange carpet and brown closet doors in the master bedroom. Filip Noterdaeme admitted not having made any changes in the apartment's décor since he had moved in, nor did he care all that much about interior decoration. He said he knew about art and music and books and had confidence in them and he did not know about other things. To be sure there were a great many books and records everywhere, packed into small chests and little bookcases and also stacked on the floor. I said, surely there is a better solution for this, living with that many books and records requires large bookshelves.

I did not own many things when I moved to 172 Clinton Street but there was of course the useless Wurlitzer piano. I called a moving company to transport everything from there to there. Above all, I said to the agent, you must be prepared for a piano and many stairs. Yes, yes, he said, a piano and stairs. And only sent two movers. I was furious. They managed to carry the Wurlitzer down the one flight at 971 Amsterdam Avenue but there was of course no way that they could carry it up the four flights of stairs at 172 Clinton Street. There was nothing to do but bring the Wurlitzer to a storage facility with an elevator. Later I arranged for real piano movers and when they came there were three of them but it was the youngest, a spaniard with a very strong back, who did most of the work, carrying the Wurlitzer up the stairs on his shoulders. It was very impressive.

After the Wurlitzer had been finally delivered I announced to Filip Noterdaeme and Nick Wilkinson that I was now going to redecorate the apartment. Oh, they said. Yes, I said, it is a marvel but it could use some improvement and a fresh coat of paint.

I began by painting the apartment Richard Meier white. Next came the kitchen, which I completely renovated in the industrial Soho loft style. Then came the master bedroom. I ripped out the orange carpet and installed grey wall-to-wall carpeting, I thought the room was much more elegant that way. Paul the landlord when he saw the rolled-up orange carpet pieces by the garbage cans on the street got terribly upset and told Filip Noterdaeme in a very agitated manner, you should have notified me before making any changes. There once, he said, had been a chinese couple living in the apartment and they had lost a diamond engagement ring worth a fortune in the cracks of the floorboards in the master bedroom. He said the loss had been so devastating to the couple that they had had to move back to China, and ever since then he had had hopes of one day finding the ring and get rich but now that we had installed a new carpet in the bedroom it was going to be impossible to search for it. It was a very unlikely story. Later we found out that the couple had not been chinese, it had been from Japan. Of course Paul the landlord, being the owner of several townhouses in Brooklyn Heights was already rich but evidently this did not prevent him from dreaming of finding a lost diamond engagement ring in our bedroom.

The next thing I did was install a long row of bookshelves in the master bedroom and buy modernist dining room furniture. Then I looked at Filip Noterdaeme's friends' paintings and said to him, I have perfect taste and I do not care for any of these paintings. Very shortly the paintings disappeared and I replaced them with simple monochromes in simple frames. They were plainly not art, they were decoration. Years later, Filip Noterdaeme painted several monochromes, and those monochromes were art. They are now on display in the Archives and Meteorology Department at 172 Clinton Street.

As to the Pussy Painting, we agreed to give it a prominent place in the living room. When Filip Noterdaeme told me that Khalil-Bey the turkish diplomat who had commissioned the original Origin of the World from Courbet had hidden it behind another painting and only shown it to select friends I decided to hang the Pussy Painting behind a little set of red velvet curtains.

This completed the first redecoration of 172 Clinton Street. The second redecoration happened 4 years later when Nick Wilkinson moved out. The third and most important redecoration happened when Filip Noterdaeme decided to turn the entire apartment into the Homeless Museum. But that was not until 2005.

The new life at 172 Clinton Street began. I had been very good at keeping house when I had been living by myself and now I became very good at keeping house living with Filip Noterdaeme and Nick Wilkinson. I cooked and cleaned but I refused to vacuum. Filip Noterdaeme was still using the old Electrolux vacuum cleaner he had once taken from the belgian embassy but it was ineffective and made a great deal of noise. I pleaded with him until he gave in and bought a powerful quiet german Miele vacuum cleaner on sale. It was of a very unfortunate yellow color that made one think of the yellow cabs of New York and so I continued to refuse to vacuum, this time for aesthetic reasons. To this day it is Filip Noterdaeme who does all the vacuuming at 172 Clinton Street.

As I said Nick Wilkinson was now occupying the small bedroom. Sometimes he came home late at night with a date. We rarely got to see Nick's dates because we were usually already in bed by that time. Usually we did not get to see them in the morning either because Nick always sent them away in the middle of the night. My roommates cannot see you, he would say to them, they don't allow me to bring anybody home. It was a convenient excuse to get rid of a date after sex and the three of us often laughed about it. Sometimes when Nick was a little more interested he allowed a date to stay for breakfast and on those occasions we did meet his dates. For reasons best known to Nick they were always the same type, always italian americans from Long Island and this once caused me to make a terrible faux pas when I mistook one for another and said, how nice to see you again.

It was at about that time that Jonathan Sheffer called. He was a friend of Eric Ellenbogen and had heard all about my food. Jonathan already had a personal chef, Bill, but, ever curious, asked me come to his townhouse on West 10th Street and cook a tasting dinner for him and his companion, Christopher Barley, a medical doctor who liked the company of young men and never seemed to be working all that much. I prepared and served a dinner and Jonathan immediately lost his heart to my cooking. Bill's cooking was alright but, he insisted, after tasting my dinner he wanted nothing but my cooking. The next day he fired poor Bill and hired me.

There were many stories about Jonathan Sheffer. He was the heir of a paperbag dynasty and had always loved and always lived under the protection of money. He was a short man with very dark eyes and a tense jaw. He was not a little spoiled. More than anything he craved success and admiration. He had studied composition and conducting and had used his family's money to fund his own orchestra, Eos. At first he had had some amount of success but then it became clear that many thought, generally correctly, that his success had everything to do with his family's money. This used to anger Jonathan a great deal. He became obsessed with fundraising and to everybody's astonishment began asking everybody for donations for Eos, usually over dinners I prepared and served. Years later one of Jonathan Sheffer's acquaintances told me that it had become so apparent that Jonathan only wanted his money that he had begun secretly calling him Mr. Pay-Per-View.

For the next two years I spent most of my days in Jonathan and Christopher's kitchen, cooking lunches and dinners for two, for eight, for twenty and once a year a big supper for two hundred guests. It was my pride wanting to cook something different every time. This was made somewhat more difficult by Christopher who only liked very few things and had a long list of what he called food allergies. If I eat a mushroom, he used to declare with immense satisfaction, I will die. Jonathan never took this very seriously but I felt I better had. Christopher also would not eat zucchini, eggplant, cilantro, seafood and many other things and I soon found composing an interesting menu for him a very tedious affair, every time. I also remember an instance where I had preserved lemons the moroccan way, in rock salt. They had been macerating for a week and were ready to use but as I was about to put them into a rabbit ragout Christopher came rushing into the kitchen and said, Daniel under no circumstances can I allow you to cook with these lemons, we could all die of botulism.

Many people have asked me if I ever witnessed scandalous things going on in the notoriously wicked Sheffer Barley household but as I was usually too busy to pay any attention to activities outside of the kitchen I never truly witnessed anything extraordinary except for the time when their freak friend who was known for running a political non-profit strictly to fund his drug addiction left their townhouse in total disarray after house-sitting it for a week. I found upon my return the kitchen in a most dreadful state and when I questioned him about the strange lump in the garbage disposal in the kitchen sink, he yelled, this is my very own sock that I selflessly used to clean the kitchen.

Here I must tell the story of the dachshund.

One afternoon Christopher Barley came into the kitchen and said, Daniel leave everything and come with me to the pet store around the corner, I can't make up my mind. What is it, I said. Tomorrow is Jonathan's birthday, he said, and I want to buy him a dachshund but I cannot decide which puppy I like best. We went and there were two dachshund puppies for sale. I have always considered myself more of a cat person and did not know anything about dachshunds, only that Filip Noterdaeme had once owned a dachshund with a former boyfriend. So there I was standing around in the pet store with Christopher who did not know anything about dachshunds either and the clerk showed us the two puppies. One was a coy drowsy brown-haired female and the other a funny lively black and tan male. Definitely the black and tan, I said, but Christopher could still not make up his mind. The next morning he presented both puppies to Jonathan and asked him to choose. Now it was Jonathan who could not make up his mind. Finally he said, let's keep them both and why not. He named the female Lucy and when he could not come up with a name for the male I suggested Moby, after the whale, not the pop singer. It stuck.

How well I remember those days with little Lucy and Moby in the kitchen in Jonathan's house, Lucy always quiet and sleeping, Moby acting up and keeping me busy with all kinds of mischief. It became rather an ordeal to wash my hands every time after touching him before returning to the stove. In short, Moby and I went quite mad about each other. Jonathan, who never spent much time with either Lucy or Moby, preferring to be left alone in his study on the fourth floor, became awfully jealous and one day said, why don't you just take Moby with you, and this was the beginning of a series of unforeseeable events.

I took little Moby to live with us at 172 Clinton Street and we were very pleased. We liked him immensely and walked him morning, noon and evening and liked him more and more. Then one day Paul the landlord saw us with Moby and he got terribly upset. Don't you know, he said, that you are not allowed to keep a dog at 172 Clinton Street. Not possible, we said, you are living in the same building and you have a waterdog. No, he said, I can do as I please in my building but you cannot, what you can do is continue living here without a dog or keep the dog and move somewhere else.

What to do. I was in a terrible state. I told Jonathan Sheffer about the problem with Paul the landlord and after much back and forth he said, well, bring Moby back here then, but it was only two days later that he changed his mind again. It's no use, he said, I just can't deal with it. Poor Moby became a vagabond and was handed from one place to another until he ended up in Kentucky with David, a lovely elder bachelor who dabbled in pottery. David later told us that people in Kentucky often commented on Moby's blasé attitude to which he always replied, of course he is blasé, he was raised by fags in New York City. David also told us that Moby would not do his business on the grass, alas, only on the pavement like he had been taught in New York. Years later, the story of Moby the dachshund became a number in my cabaret repertoire. It was a reinterpretation of Jaques Brel's Ne Me Quitte Pas as a dog's lament. I always sang it wearing a dog mask I had fashioned after Moby's image and people never knew if they should laugh or cry. Usually they did both.

Filip Noterdaeme was waiting for the Metropolitan Museum to renew his contract. For the last 5 years, he had been in charge of a very popular children's program called A First Look that he had lovingly developed since it had been handed over to him. Something was happening at the museum and he was told that the education department had received additional funding and was being reorganized. Many promises were made, things would get much bigger and better for everyone, and then nothing happened.

Filip Noterdaeme felt very upset about this for a while. In the following months he sometimes ran into familiar faces, parents and children, on the Upper East Side and they always said, what happened and why aren't you at the Metropolitan any more, the children keep asking for you, but there was nothing to be done.

Without his position at the Metropolitan, Filip Noterdaeme's earning capacity, always limited, had dwindled. He was freelancing as a gallery lecturer at the Guggenheim Museum and had become an adjunct professor of art history at New York University. Neither paid a living wage but as he used to say, it's alright, at least I am now entitled to use the big pool at the university gym and have the distinct pleasure of swimming past thin sub-sub librarians and the gargantuan Herman Melville scholar Harold Bloom. And it is true, Harold Bloom also liked to use the university swimming pool and Filip Noterdaeme says his body in the water oddly reminded one of a big white whale. And so Filip Noterdaeme swam and taught at New York University, his alma mater, and it was sink or swim for him.

It was during this period that he had a strange dream.

He dreamt of his family owning a shiny black limousine that was covered in porridge. He woke up and immediately understood the meaning of it all. It is very simple, he said, we the Noterdaemes have always been poor rich, dirt poor and filthy rich.

It was only a little later that Filip Noterdaeme happened to walk by the Loyola High School on the Upper East Side. He stopped and, on a whim, simply walked into the offices and said, hello my name is Filip Noterdaeme and I am looking for a position as an art teacher. The irish secretary looked up and said, are you french. He said, no. We are, said the secretary, in fact looking for a french teacher. Filip Noterdaeme had never taught french or any other language but he said, I can do that, too. One thing led to another and the very conservative school board took a liking to his perfectly french sounding distinguished christian name and hired him. He stayed for three years.

Filip Noterdaeme in all his life has never been as miserable as he was during those years he taught french at Loyola. He found something dismal and infinitely depressing in having to be there every day and being surrounded by closeted homosexual priests and dispirited teachers who smelled of hazelnut coffee and tuna sandwiches. Then there was Sister Nora, the cantankerous cancerous nun who was in charge of the school and naturally made everybody's life hell. How well I remember Filip Noterdaeme cursing every early morning as I knotted his silk tie for him before he ran off to catch the subway to go to the Upper East Side.

It was Halloween and Joey Arias, having gotten an offer he could not refuse to perform at a private event with Raven O and Sherry Vine arranged for Jimmy James and Flotilla de Barge and me to perform at Bar d'O in their stead. Of course I was going to have to perform in drag.

I had in my youth often delighted in dressing up in a long cape and singing along to a Roberta Peters recording of the Queen of the Night aria from the Magic Flute and once had caused quite a sensation in high school when I had lip-synched to a Liza Minnelli recording of Cabaret and so I said to Joey Arias, yes, for Halloween, with Flotilla.

We were very fond of Flotilla de Barge. The first time I ever saw her she was sitting at the counter at Florent's restaurant in the Meatpacking District, and I remember feeling convinced that she had to be a Jessye Norman impersonator. Just about a year ago, Filip Noterdaeme and I saw Jessye Norman in front of the Gerald W. Lynch Theater, after Peter Brook's redux version of the Magic Flute, and there it was she who looked like a Flotilla de-Barge impersonator.

In any case that Halloween night at Bar d'O Flotilla de Barge and I thoroughly enjoyed each other. It was during that evening that she took to calling me her little apple strudel. We had a success. Jimmy James sang with one and many voices, I did my best to look and sound like Liza Minnelli and Flotilla sang that she was gonna sit on the dock of the bay watching the time flow away. Then we all sang the Bar d'O theme song, the Sister song from The Color Purple. Everybody came away with a clear feeling that Bar d'O was cabaret incarnate.

It was at about that time that Judy's, a little Chelsea cabaret and the only downtown cabaret with a purple

111

ruffled silk curtain, invited me to do a show. Filip Noterdaeme said, do the whole show in drag. I was hesitant. Let me direct you, he said, that way neither of us will know what we are doing and this is the only way to create something new.

The first thing I had to do was create a drag look for myself. Not knowing how to go about it I went to talk to the effeminate sales boys at the Patricia Fields boutique. They were interested in types, they knew that there were elegant queens and mad queens and dramatic queens but neither of them could make up their mind as to what kind of queen I should be. Finally they shook their heads and said, it's a pity, such a pretty boy and now he wants to do drag just like everybody else. I bought all kinds of things and began a series of experiments in makeup and looks but it was not until later, when Devon Cass made up my face and took the pictures for the show flier that it became clear that I was a dramatic queen. For the show's title Filip Noterdaeme stole a line from a popular shampoo ad, Because I'm Worth It.

Filip Noterdaeme and I began rehearsing together. I found it fairly easy to stand and walk in high heels but hated wearing a wig. He gave me all kinds of instructions. He wanted me to eat chocolate truffles while singing a song about loneliness and clutch a little leather handbag while singing about generosity. I thought he was making fun of me and I protested, he says now I protest about my autobiography. Finally I did it all and was terribly pleased with the effect.

The show ran for several nights. David Lamarche played the piano and I sang strange songs while eating truffles and clutching my handbag. One night there was a problem with my wig. I had forgotten to pin it onto my head and it began to slide further and further back during the third song so I had to quickly disappear behind the purple ruffled silk curtain to fix it. When the show was over people usually clamored for more and I usually returned to the stage as myself, without the wig or dress, wearing pajamas, to sing Charles Aznavour's La Bohème for an encore. One night Baroness Ida, Filip Noterdaeme's mother, was in the audience. She seemed to be feeling quite entertained and said to me after the show, ah it was so nice to come and hear you sing La Bohème but why only one song and who was that strange lady singing before you.

Joey Arias, Sherry Vine, Raven O and Flotilla de Barge came to see if I was a contender for the drag world. We all agreed without saying it that I was not and that I should get back to performing as myself, simply myself. That settled the matter and I was not a little relieved to throw away the wig and let drag be drag. However I held on to the high heel shoes. It was not until years later that I made an exception for Filip Noterdaeme when he asked me to become Madame Butterfly for the Homeless Museum.

Nothing much happened during the next year. Jonathan Sheffer decided he should learn german like his idol Leonard Bernstein and arranged for a teacher to come and have lunch with him at his townhouse once a week so he could learn and practice german conversation with her. The teacher was a stylish young woman from Austria. Naturally I always served german or austrian food for the lunch lessons. A few months later Jonathan had become very knowledgeable about schnitzel and knödel but still not any more fluent in german conversation and he gave up on the whole idea and there were no more german lunches, not one.

Quentin Crisp who for years had been saying that he hoped to someday soon die in his sleep got what he wanted during a visit to England and the british were very pleased that he should pass away in his native country. His ashes were shipped back to New York and there was a memorial celebration at Cooper Union. It happened to be on Filip Noterdaeme's birthday. Everybody who was anybody was there. I clearly remember Penny Arcade standing away from the lectern and addressing the audience directly. Her golden stilettos were nicely reflected on the shiny parquet of the stage and made her look as if she was floating on gold. She spoke wisely and candidly of Mister Crisp and everyone came away with a clear feeling of their intimacy.

That summer Filip Noterdaeme and I decided to take our first trip abroad together. The place we went to was an island in the french Atlantic that I knew very well from the summers of my childhood. My parents still owned a beautifully modern house there and invited us for a visit. So we went.

I always say that summer in western France has the ideal climate. There is the ocean breeze and moderate heat and the cool Atlantic. In those days it was always at noon that I liked to lie on the beach. Filip Noterdaeme, who has and had no fondness for midday sunshine often accompanied me. Later in the evening he sat on the terrace and wept. As it turned out he was having hay fever, and this made it impossible for him to enjoy himself. He became very somber and unhappy and pleaded with me, let us go somewhere else. Well, I was heartbroken. Don't worry, Filip Noterdaeme said, next year we will go to Italy where there is culture.

This brings us pretty well to the time I had my first cabaret residency in New York, at the Starlight Lounge in the East Village. It had been a home to Raven O who used to perform there with Ben Allison on bass and now Jon Johnson one of the club's owners asked me to perform every Wednesday night. It was the first time I was going to get paid a certain amount instead of a percentage from ticket sales.

The Starlight Lounge did not own a piano. The solution for this problem was to find a good accordionist. I called Walter Kühr.

Every accordionist in New York City knew Walter Kühr. He was the owner of Main Squeeze, the city's only accordion store, on the Lower East Side. He was less known for being the bandleader of a very amusing all-female accordion orchestra, the Main Squeeze Orchestra. Walter was a melancholic german expatriate, with white hair and the financial worries of every Lower East Side shop owner. He drove an old-fashioned motorcycle that always needed fixing, a little bit like Dave Berger's old Mercedes years later.

Walter Kühr knew every german and french song I wanted to sing. We usually rehearsed inside the Main Squeeze shop. There weren't all that many people coming into the store and I don't remember ever seeing anyone buy anything.

Finally we opened at the Starlight Lounge and we had a success. Week after week more and more people came to hear us play. I always say you cannot tell how good a performer you really are until you perform every week. It does something to you that performing once a month can never do. A good many years later Nick Wilkinson said he had never appreciated the quality of my performing until he started coming to see my show every week.

One person who came every week was Shuki Cohen. He was very wonderful. He was very attractive and very interesting. He had a head like one of the late assyrian philosophers. He had a brother whom one heard about but never saw. Shuki was a clinical psychologist and worked in a university and therefore he was reasonably well dressed. He always sat all evening next to Filip Noterdaeme and listened while I sang one song after another. The great excitement was that he recognized every song I sang and that was the beginning of our intimacy. There was also the question under what circumstance was he under the absolute obligation of ordering a drink. It was notorious that Shuki was parted with the greatest difficulty from even the smallest amount of money.

Shuki was extraordinarily brilliant and no matter what subject was started, if he knew anything about it or not, he quickly saw the whole meaning of the thing and elaborated it by his wit and fancy carrying it further than anybody knowing anything about it could have done, and oddly enough generally correctly.

One other regular at my shows at the Starlight Lounge was Temo Callahan. He was a real dandy from the south who had made his fortune in art books. I remember how he once, when there was a problem with the microphone, called out to me, darling just sing like Edith Piaf on the street. One time he came with his friend Kathy Zuckerman. She was rather a madonna like creature, with fair skin and charming hair. She sat and listened and took a great liking to my german cabaret singing. It was only a few weeks later that she arranged for me to sing at a very special event at the Museum of Radio and Television. It was the premiere of a new documentary about Marlene Dietrich. My memory of it is very vivid. There was Marlene Dietrich's daughter Maria Riva and the two Dietrich grandsons and a great grandson who was tall with long blond hair like Dietrich's. I performed in black top hat and tails that Kathy Zuckerman had rented for me and Maria Riva looked up and listened carefully as I sang Johnny Wenn Du Geburtstag Hast. After the show we were introduced and Maria Riva said flattering things of how I had brought her mother's spirit into the room. She also told me to stretch the o in Johnny even longer and that she had plans to write a biography about Walter Benjamin. I believe she said Walter Benjamin but it might also have been Benjamin Franklin, I do not remember.

After six months my residency at the Starlight Lounge came to an end. Jon Johnson said to me, I am afraid the other owners want to now try something else. They did and Wednesday nights at the Starlight Lounge became a bore. A few months later, to everyone's surprise, the Starlight Lounge closed. I imagine the space is still vacant.

It was at about that time that a german television producer contacted me and told me she was working on a film documentary about Walter Kühr and his accordion store, could he and I possibly do one more concert together for the cameras. I proposed doing it at the Gershwin Hotel Lounge where Neke Carson was in charge of programming.

Neke Carson had a long history of being involved

with bohemian nightlife in New York. For some reason he had ended up as a programming director at the Gershwin Hotel where one could often find him in the lobby tickling the keys of the baby grand.

Our show at the Gershwin was well attended. Joey Arias came and John Cameron Mitchell came and Terry Brown Jr. came. The german cameras were rolling and the producer was pleased. After the concert I was interviewed for the documentary and said nice pleasant things about Walter Kühr.

Poor Walter. He fell on hard times a little later and decided to move back to Germany. In what was supposed to be his last week in New York, a few months after our concert, he was house-sitting a friend's penthouse in a high-rise building in the Wall Street area and one morning stepped out onto the terrace with a cup of coffee in his hand. One moment he was enjoying the view of the financial district and the next moment he saw a plane hit the World Trade Center, a few blocks away. He says it instantly made him throw up, right there on the terrace. When I saw him a few days later he was as a matter of fact still green in the face. But I am running ahead of that terrible September day in 2001.

It was once again summer and Jonathan Sheffer asked me to cook a dinner for a fundraiser for the Clintons he was going to host in his East Hampton house. Bill Clinton was no longer in office at the time but there were rumors about Hillary running for governor.

It was a big to-do with hired wait staff and valet parking and over 40 guests. I had been shopping and cooking for days and was confident about the five-course dinner. What I had not expected were the many secret service agents that kept walking into the kitchen two by two, looking for something to eat. I fed everyone as is my habit and Jonathan's irish housekeeper, a cheerful woman with a heart condition and rosatia, was greatly pleased to have so many handsome secret service men sit and eat in the kitchen.

After dinner, there was the customary photo-op with the staff. It was a strange moment. Bill Clinton was more than a little tipsy but like all successful politicians he had perfected the technique of holding a beaming dimpled smile for the cameras. I distinctly saw him lock the corners of his mouth into position. I was asked to stand next to Hillary Clinton who posed with a barely audible sigh and did not look at me once. She appeared to have not had a moment for herself in a very long time.

Terry Brown Jr. whom we all loved very much died. He had been very ill for a long time but had continued to go out and come to my shows and sit and applaud and sigh in all the right moments. To the day of his death, which Filip Noterdaeme insists must have been self-inflicted, Terry never lost his pride and pleasure in being a bon vivant. Filip Noterdaeme was unconquerably sad when he died. When he heard that Terry's conservative family from Milwaukee was going to come to New York to take care of things he hurried to Terry's apartment. How he got in I do not know but it was of the utmost importance to remove all signs of gayness before the family's arrival and so he took along an entire suitcase filled with Terry's immense gay porn collection. Later, a few months later, a memorial service was held and everybody came. We were standing outside the church on Park Avenue and Filip Noterdaeme said to me, look at all those people, there are so many and they are so familiar and I do not know who any of them are. Oh, I replied, they are all the people you used to see with Terry at the cabarets, and you saw their faces every season, year after year, and that is the reason they are all so familiar.

That summer was a comparatively quiet one. Nick Wilkinson had found employment in an office high up in the World Trade Center where his aunt worked and he liked it well enough. Filip Noterdaeme was still teaching at Loyola. I always remember him saying disgustedly apropos of some teachers who said they liked being at the school, they would, he said angrily, they like oppression.

I was bored, frankly openly bored with having to cook every day at Jonathan Sheffer's house. I felt my way a little and finally gave him my notice and my thanks for two pleasant years. Jonathan, accustomed to firing employees but not accustomed to employees leaving on their own terms, was not a little shocked. You must understand, I said, this is not about you, it is about me wanting a change in my life. Of course Jonathan could never imagine anything not being about him. And so I left the Sheffer Barley household never to return.

It was at about that time that I accepted an offer to write restaurant reviews for a small magazine. Filip Noterdaeme often accompanied me to the restaurants I was being sent to. Some restaurants were very good, some were mediocre and some were spectacularly bad. The most amusing review I wrote during that time was about a seafood restaurant called Metro Fish. Very evidently the chef did not know fish from steak and I wrote, seafood for meat lovers. I handed in my review and the magazine editor after reading it hesitated for a moment. Ah yes, he finally said illuminated, you wish to describe a little greek american diner from Long Island.

The most interesting discovery we made from eating at all these restaurants was that we always preferred the food when it was prepared by a woman chef. There was Gabrielle Hamilton at Prune and Rebecca Charles at Pearl Oyster Bar and Vanessa Duan at Vanessa's Dumpling House and later Missy Robbins at A Voce and of course Alice Waters at Chez Panisse in California. All of them had the tired eyes and wan smiles that are so indicative of a first rate chef. There was about them a certain disciplined quality that perhaps had to do with their uncompromising standards and was curiously in accord with their gruff manners. However there was one exception I must mention. That was Jean-Georges Vongerichten. It was during his tasting menu that I discovered my fondness for dry alsatian white wines.

It was at about that time that Cary Davis contacted me. I remembered Cary Davis from the summers I had cooked in Eric Ellenbogen's house in the Hamptons where he had always been the first one in line at the buffet, always inquiring about the protein. He said he was about to move into a townhouse on West 10th Street, just across from Jonathan Sheffer's home and three townhouses down from Andrew Solomon's. It seems everybody was living on West 10th Street in those days. In any case he was interested in hiring me to cook for him and his new partner John McGinn in their new house once a week or so. I had always been fond of Cary Davis and said, yes absolutely. We made an employment contract and it was and is the best employment contract I have ever made in my life.

It was late July and we went to Italy as planned. We went straight to Venice and Filip Noterdaeme immediately lost his heart to Venice, I must stay in Venice forever he insisted. I was very upset, Venice was alright but, I insisted, I needed a cooler place by the ocean, preferably an island in the french Atlantic. Filip Noterdaeme felt he needed nothing but Venice. We were both very violent about it. We did however stay there for a week and Filip Noterdaeme showed me the Scuola San Rocco where one was given a mirror to hold like a tray to conveniently see the painted Tintoretto ceiling. We also visited Peggy Guggenheim's museum where we watched attractive young italian waiters set up tables for a benefactor's dinner. We looked very carefully at a plaque in the garden that commemorated Peggy Guggenheim's beloved babies, her fourteen dogs. Filip Noterdaeme wrote down the names and the years they were born and the years they had died. Oddly it seemed none of them had lived long lives. One Madame Butterfly lived 4 years, from 1954 to 1958. A dog named Pegeen like Peggy's daughter had had an even shorter life, from 1951 to 1953. We couldn't help wondering if Peggy had truly understood the complicated systems of dog keeping and child rearing.

Then we moved on and traveled to Milan and Florence and wherever we went it was the same. It was one hot italian day after another and frescoes and lemon gelato and hotel rooms and no place to wash our clothes. In short I was miserable. I insisted that our next summer vacation would have to include a house with a garden and a pool and a washing machine.

We were back in New York and then 9/11 happened.

Filip Noterdaeme had already left for work with his silk tie tied in a hurry as usual and Nick Wilkinson was about to leave when someone called him and said, there is a fire in the World Trade Center. We turned on the television and looked. Nobody knew yet what had happened. I think, Nick said, this is my office burning and surely my aunt is in there. He was in quite a state. Then the second plane hit the second tower. I can still remember the sound of the explosion from across the river. It was only a little later that everything came tumbling down.

I did my best to comfort Nick and spent the rest of the morning teaching him how to make Vanillekipferl, the viennese moon-shaped almond cookies. It seemed as good as anything to do that morning. One must, I said to him, do something with one's hands when feeling helpless.

Later Nick and I walked to the Brooklyn Promenade and looked at the plume of smoke over Manhattan. There was an eerie silence in the air but we could not help noticing that there were many men out and about cruising each other which did and did not make any sense to us. And so that day indeed felt very much like the old world had come to an end and nobody knew what the new world was going to be like.

It was only a little later that the United States became a war country. Everybody flagged the star spangled banner and life was looking very bleak. Life was looking very bleak but it continued. Filip Noterdaeme taught, I cooked, and Nick grieved.

Cary Davis and John McGinn moved into the renovated townhouse on 10th Street. It had a very beautiful large kitchen. Everything in it was brand new with the exception of an old Fifties stovetop his mother had insisted he put to use. She had explained that since she had just bought herself a new stovetop he should be using her old one that, she said, was in perfect working condition. In any case there was no arguing with Cary Davis's mother and so Cary Davis's brand new kitchen had an old and perfectly impractical stovetop in its center. Cary Davis and I often laughed about it.

In the meanwhile at Loyola School days had gone from sinister to absurd. Cantankerous cancerous Sister Nora had been replaced by an illiterate principal whose foolish incompetence astonished both teachers and students. Filip Noterdaeme recalls a memorial speech that became memorable for all the wrong reasons in which the principal kept referring to 9/11 as 7 Eleven.

To divert his mind Filip Noterdaeme began reading the writings of Thomas Bernard in whose incessant rants he found solace. He also began making drawings again. His chosen subject was an unusual one. It was homelessness.

There had always been many homeless in New York but now that Filip Noterdaeme encountered them every day on the subway to and from work, feeling quite miserable himself, the tragedy of homelessness began to weigh on him. This was the beginning of his most revolutionary work, the Homeless Museum. He developed a compassion for everything that was homeless and filled notebook after notebook with drawings. After a while drawing the homeless was not satisfying enough any more and he began filming them with a little video camera. He made film portraits of practically every homeless he saw on the street or on the subway and filmed them in all manners and styles. African Woman, Mister Slaveman, Ballerina, and Mastering the Asphalt Arts were made during that time. The Butter video in particular I was very fond of. In it, Filip Noterdaeme is seen buying a stick of butter in a grocery store, bringing it home, stamping on it the legend, GIVE TO CHARITY JUST NOT HERE, wrapping it again, walking back to the grocery store and replacing it on the shelf. The legend was borrowed from a New York Transit poster that one saw hanging in every subway car at the time. It was part of a new campaign to rid the subways of the homeless. There was another also often ridiculed MTA poster that read, IF YOU SEE SOME-THING, SAY SOMETHING, that was supposed to entice the public to help identify terrorists. One day Filip Noterdaeme simply stole one of each from a subway car and had them framed.

In what would be his last video about the homeless, a homeless man is sitting on a park bench, vigorously scratching himself. On a second park bench on his right sits Filip Noterdaeme mirroring his every move, making the moment appear like a synchronized dance. He called the little video Mimesis. It has never been shown in public and maybe it never will.

It was at about that time that Filip Noterdaeme went to the Metropolitan Opera to see chilean soprano Veronica Villarroel in Puccini's Madame Butterfly. He was very moved by her portrayal of Cio-Cio-San and came home in a solemn mood. He had understood Puccini undoubtedly and he had a comprehension quite his own of the Madame Butterfly character. It was this experience that prompted him later to nominate Madame Butterfly Director of Development of the Homeless Museum.

In the meanwhile I was beginning a new Wednesday night cabaret residency, this time at Bar d'O where Filip Noterdaeme and I had met. Tony Lauria became my new accompanist. He was an italian american accordionist from Long Island and had that cool attitude that is so attractive in certain musicians. Filip Noterdaeme came to every show and sat with me in the little dressing room. He so thoroughly understood every possible way in which one could be nervous that as he sat beside me telling me all the kinds of ways that one could suffer from stage fright I was quite soothed. The United States was by that time already a war country and I closed every show with Lili Marleen, the song Marlene Dietrich had famously sung in her USO shows in WWII.

Then came the winter of 2002 and everybody was talking about Ronald Lauder opening a museum on Fifth Avenue to show his collection of german and austrian art. It was called the Neue Galerie and there were going to be german cabaret concerts in its café, Café Sabarsky. Limor Tomer was in charge of the programming. She had in past years sometimes booked me for the cabaret nights at the Brooklyn Academy of Music and now she invited me to perform at Café Sabarsky. I did and soon became the official darling of the Café presenting a new show there every season for the next eight years.

I became very fond of performing at the Neue for two reasons, the excellent Linzer torte and the paycheck with the extra digit that made all the difference. Prior to every show, I used to sit with Filip Noterdaeme and whichever pianist was playing for me at the time in one of the executive offices on the fifth floor and wait for two waiters to arrive with our dinner on silver platters covered with silver domes. Filip Noterdaeme always liked domed silver platters and he always said that in his old age he expected to have a handsome young butler in a lace apron serve him dinner on a domed silver platter.

One night Ronald Lauder and his wife Jo Carol came to see my show. Several years had gone by since the day I had served them white truffle risotto and almost destroyed the blue Yves Klein in their home but now they sat at the table of honor and watched me perform in their museum café and they were pleased.

After the show, Ronald Lauder and I talked while Jo Carol looked at me long and hard, which made me wonder if she recognized me from the days of the risotto. I was very impressed with Ronald Lauder's impeccable german. I told him that I had just been invited to perform in Vienna in the spring. Where, he asked, will you be performing. The Casanova Bar, I said. Ah, the Casanova Bar, he said, right next to Café Havelka. You will have a wonderful time.

Spring came and Tony Lauria and I flew to Vienna on Austrian Airlines. I was very impressed with the little red mini dresses and red hats and red high heels that the stewardesses at Austrian Airlines were wearing, it was so much more stylish than the uniforms of german or american stewardesses. It was a night flight and when I told the stewardesses that I was going to give a concert in Vienna the next day they let me have a seat with extra leg room so I could get some sleep.

We arrived but for some reason my luggage did not. There was nothing to do but to perform the first show at the Casanova Bar in the black Brooklyn tracksuit I had worn on the plane. The stylish viennese thought I was making a very sophisticated New York fashion statement.

The next morning I went to Café Havelka like Ronald Lauder had recommended and ordered a cup of coffee. I sat and waited for a very very long time. Frau Havelka small and frail was there greeting every guest and talking to her made waiting for my cup of coffee, well, if not altogether pleasant then at least less unpleasant.

During my stay in Vienna I also went to see a Thomas Bernard play at the Burgtheater. It was called Elizabeth II and oh what a delightful play it was. Gert Voss played a cantankerous old viennese man who kept complaining about everything, especially the viennese and the Burgtheater, and every time he did there was a delectable shiver running through the ardently viennese audience. It was in Vienna and after having seen the Thomas Bernard play that I realized how much Evee Lynn was eine echte Wienerin, a real viennese, through and through.

Then Tony Lauria and I gave our last performance and we flew back to New York where Filip Noterdaeme had in the meanwhile made up his mind to quit working at Loyola High School at the end of the school year and become the director of a new museum of his own making.

This is the story.

At first he considered calling it Madame Tussaud of the Gutter. I was not all that fond of that name and we disagreed violently about it.

The next thing that happened was Abi Maryan calling and saying, my father is going to direct and premiere a new version of a Gertrude Stein opera called Doctor Faustus Lights the Lights, I told him all about you and your cabaret act and he would like you to audition for the Mephisto part. I went and sang Alanis Morissette's You

Oughta Know with which I had always had much success at Bar d'O. Abi Maryan's father and Stanley Walden the composer said, thank you and, you are hired. We rehearsed for four weeks and there were good days and bad days. Then it was opening night and it happened to be Filip Noterdaeme's thirty-seventh birthday. He was very preoccupied, not with Doctor Faustus Lights the Lights but with finding the right name for his museum. At intermission he visited me backstage, whispering, it's so bad it's not good. He then excused himself and left to take a walk in the neighborhood and therefore never saw my big Mephisto scene in Act II. After the show we went to celebrate his birthday at Vong and he excitedly told me that he had had an epiphany during his walk. He had spotted several homeless men and seeing them had made him decide to not call his museum Madame Tussaud of the Gutter after all but the Homeless Museum. I very much liked the new name and so that night we not only celebrated his birthday but also the birth of the Homeless Museum with whose beginnings so many things began whose beginnings still haven't ceased to begin.

Filip Noterdaeme began telling everybody about the Homeless Museum and how he was now not an artist any longer but a museum director and naturally everybody objected. Peter Krashes, Oliver Herring's companion pronounced the project doomed and said that Filip Noterdaeme would never succeed in the art world with a project of that name. He and Oliver Herring had just moved into a townhouse they had bought and renovated with their parents' money and were currently petitioning against the opening of a homeless shelter on their block. It is a remarkable fact that only a few years earlier the couple had been volunteering with Filip Noterdaeme at a homeless shelter.

One of the first things Filip Noterdaeme did as the director of the Homeless Museum was having his portrait taken. He asked his friend, photographer Tom Cinko to take it.

Tom Cinko had that pleasant kindly agitated calm that photographers always must have. His specialty was food photography and years later, when I wrote my cookbook, Discomfort Food, Authentic Recipes from the Homeless Museum, it was he who took all the photographs. But this time it was a portrait he had to do and Filip Noterdaeme decided it had to be a double portrait. After all, as he always contends, it takes two to make a truth and my truth exists between the museum director and the homeless, it always will.

Filip Noterdaeme arrived at the photo studio and first posed in a pink Paul Smith suit to portray the museum director handing out a dollar bill and then he posed again in rags and the fake beard he still owned from his days at Hunter College, which made him look rather like a bum indeed. Later, Tom Cinko made the two portraits look like a single image of Filip Noterdaeme the director handing a dollar bill to Filip Noterdaeme the panhandler and Filip Noterdaeme was very pleased. The double portrait was only shown once and then completely forgotten but never lost.

Little by little, Filip Noterdaeme began having a delightful way of amusing himself with himself again in a way he had not since his days at Hunter College. All his creations for the museum were based upon his years of working for art museums and the many hours he had been watching and thinking about the homeless and it was like a kaleidoscope slowly turning, all falling into place and creating miraculous things.

This brings me to the story of the first open letter Filip Noterdaeme wrote as the museum director. It was addressed to Thomas Krens, the director of the Guggenheim Museum. In the letter, he proposed an extraordinary partnership and asked him to let the Homeless Museum establish headquarters on the rooftop of the Guggenheim building on Fifth Avenue. With the letter he included a little drawing of the Guggenheim with a clothesline on its roof. It was the first of many unanswered open letters. In the following years, Filip Noterdaeme wrote 25 of them. Most of them were written to other museum directors but some were written to artists and businessmen. There was, for example, the letter to Monsieur Arnault, the chairman of Louis Vuitton Moët Hennesy, the french luxury group, in which he proposed that the Moët Champagne house put pictures of homeless people on the back label of their bottles, in the style of the missing children milk carton campaign. He wrote, LVMH should consider building a Dom Perignon shelter for homeless men and a Veuve Cliquot shelter for homeless women. He made two prototype bottles using the picture Tom Cinko had taken of him as a panhandler. They were a big success at the inauguration of the Homeless Museum but that was not until several months later. Naturally Monsieur Arnault never replied to his letter. All of the open letters were eventually printed as a limited edition. But I am running far ahead of those early days when the Homeless Museum was just beginning to come into being.

One day Filip Noterdaeme came home with an automatic toy robot. He had a clear idea in mind and worked on it with hammer and saw until it looked rather battered and disheveled, in other words like a homeless robot. He candidly facetiously named it Robobum and made a short video in which the robot is panhandling on the street and asking passersby, can you spare a dime. Then another day Filip Noterdaeme came home with a plush monkey from FAO Schwarz on Fifth Avenue. It had a name, Jean, and came with a certificate that declared the owner honorary guardian of a live chimpanzee from the Los Angeles Zoo. In short it was all monkey business and Filip Noterdaeme named Jean Programming Director of the Homeless Museum. This was the beginning of a long list of trustees he nominated for his museum board. Soon Jean the Chimp was joined by Madame Tussaud whom Filip Noterdaeme named Creative Director and Beethoven's Second Symphony, Beethoven's least performed symphony, was put in charge of marketing. Robobum became the treasurer and, as I said earlier, Madame Butterfly was nominated Director of Development. Then Filip Noterdaeme called for the museum's first board meeting at 172 Clinton Street. Of course, Filip Noterdaeme said to me, I will film everything with my camera and you will have to play Madame Butterfly. This was news to me and I was less than thrilled. I did not yet own the vintage silken kimono and geisha wig and japanese white facial powder I became known for wearing in later years and had to make do with white bed sheets for a kimono and a black velvet scarf for a wig. I do not remember what I used to whiten my face. Filip Noterdaeme put on his pink Paul Smith suit and his fake beard. The combination of these two things, the elegant suit and the shaggy beard became for a long time the definite defining look of the Museum Director.

We staged and filmed the board meeting in the living room. It began with Filip Noterdaeme asking the board members if the Homeless Museum should establish headquarters or remain homeless. I made tragic faces to a recording of Maria Callas singing Butterfly, renegata e felice, Jean the Chimp was humping a banana, Robobum asked everyone, can you spare a dime, Beethoven's second symphony remained silent, and the candles before a framed portrait of Madame Tussaud were dripping wax onto the table. In the meanwhile Filip Noterdaeme poured himself one whiskey after another to stay awake. We kept filming and restaging things and it went on and on until night turned into day. After a silent vote and a vote count, we ended the board meeting video with Filip Noterdaeme declaring a tie and saying that the meeting had to be adjourned. Then Filip Noterdaeme had to put on a fresh suit and rush to work and I went to bed.

Then there was the making of the gummy bums. They were a failure but later Filip Noterdaeme sculpted two beautiful bums out of marzipan and they became a vital part of the notorious Morgue & Library. And then we flew to Berlin.

It was a charming trip. We had heard all about Berlin, how it was becoming an interesting and open city again. I remember so well my first impression of the city, an impression that indeed has never changed. Berlin was very spread-out, decayed and forcefully modernizing and rebuilding. I was of course already used to the directness and ruthlessness of New Yorkers but found the Berliners even more direct and ruthless. Filip Noterdaeme only remarked on the Berliners' bad hairdos and said, just imagine what a busload of french hairdressers could do here.

We wandered about and visited the Alte Staatsgalerie, sat under the linden trees at Unter den Linden and ate herring salad with sour cream and Guglhupf at KaDeWe. Filip Noterdaeme became accustomed to the Berliner Luft and began wondering if life in Berlin perhaps was not favorable to life in New York. As always in those days Filip Noterdaeme saw homelessness everywhere we went. He saw it in all sizes and shapes, all degrees of wealth and poverty, sometimes very charming, sometimes simply rough, and every now and then very emotional. He was still preoccupied with the thought of establishing headquarters for his Homeless Museum somewhere and one day, while visiting the Neue Nationalgalerie, he began to wonder, if not in New York, why not in Berlin, and if not the circular rooftop of Frank Lloyd Wright's Guggenheim Museum then why not the square rooftop of Mies van der Rohe's Neue Nationalgalerie. We went to the St. Matthäus church nearby and walked up the steps of the church steeple to see the roof of the Neue Nationalgalerie. It was completely flat and seemed quite accommodating. Filip Noterdaeme was delighted. He ran back to the Nationalgalerie to measure its height. It was ten and a half meters. Do you think, he asked me with a radiant smile, we can find a ladder tall enough to get onto the roof.

Joey Arias and Sherry Vine were also in Berlin during that time, performing their show at the Bar Jeder Vernunft Spiegeltent in the old Berlin West. Of course we went. When the two saw me in the audience they invited me onstage to sing a song and I sang Charles Aznavour's La Bohème. This was a mistake. Joey and Sherry's show was frivolously outrageously american and everybody was pleased with it being so and there I was singing an earnest poetic french song and I was singing it in german. There was icy silence and I almost stopped the song short. Later backstage Sherry sweetly said to me, but you sang so beautifully, and Filip Noterdaeme comforted me in his best german, saying, die Berliner sind wirklich ein undankbares Volk, the Berliners are truly one ungracious bunch. That evening I decided that one day I would return to Berlin and change the Berliners' minds about me.

We returned to New York and did the usual things. Then came the summer and Filip Noterdaeme officially resigned from Loyola and we decided to celebrate it with a trip to Provence. We packed and I realized I had no swimsuit to wear and started to look for one all over New York City. It was all about spandex is spandex and cotton is cotton or spandex is complex and cotton forgotten. Finally we boarded the plane to France. We had new carry-on luggage and we were very proud of our carry-on luggage.

That summer in Provence was a beautiful one. We rented a villa near Aix-en-Provence with a pool and a washing machine and I was immensely pleased. We took long walks around the countryside and hitchhiked to Aix to go to the marché where the fruits and vegetables were so much more colorful than in New York and the fish so much more expensive. Here I must tell of the incident with the house gardener.

From the day we arrived in France, wherever we went it was always, Bonjour Madame Bonjour Monsieur. It is true that to the french I look and sound like a Madame, but never to the germans or the americans. The germans see me as a boyish frenchman and the americans as an alien of extraordinary ability. Filip Noterdaeme sees me as his indispensable german hausfrau. In any case we never thought of correcting the french, we simply nodded and smiled and went our way, sticking strictly to polite form and accepting the french way of seeing me. Then one morning, standing in the kitchen in my spandex swimsuit, I opened the shutters and there stood the old gardener watering the plants. Naturally he greeted me right away with Bonjour Madame but then he saw that I could not possibly be a Madame after all and there he did not know what more to say.

The next thing that happened was Filip Noterdaeme's younger brother pulling up in a big car. We ran outside to greet him and out jumped his wife and three children. Everybody was milling around and so Filip Noterdaeme said, let's make a video. He told us exactly what he wanted it to be. Everybody listened quietly. It will be, he said, an adaptation of Hänsel and Gretel with me playing Cézanne as the witch. The two older children were going to play Hänsel and Gretel and his brother and his wife were going to play Pablo and Jacqueline Picasso, the parents.

We filmed in front of the magnificent Mont Saint Victoire and Picasso's chateau in nearby Vauvenargues. Under Filip Noterdaeme's direction the Grimm story became a tale of a greedy Picasso chasing away his children and Cézanne welcoming them in his studio in the woods and teaching them the art of begging. We made the video in record time and then Filip Noterdaeme's brother and family jumped back into the big car and we waved goodbye.

One day during our stay in southern France we drove to the coast. On the way we visited Le Corbusier's Cité

Radieuse where we were charmingly entertained by the handsome tour guide. The concrete building was beautifully radiant with the light of the south. Then we took the autoroute to the coast. There was heavy traffic, and it was one péage after another and gas stations all along. We drove no further than Cassis and there we suddenly realized how nervous the driving had made us. We were just nervous.

We drove around Cassis looking for a parking spot. Cassis is by the Mediterranean and it is hot. Filip Noterdaeme who has never wanted it hot and hotter has not been enthusiastic about driving since that experience. He said he had been just like a belgian waffle in that car, the heat above and the heat below, and trying to park the car in the narrow streets of Cassis. I do not know how often he used to swear and say, forget about it, that is all there is to it, just forget about it. I encouraged and remonstrated until we found a parking spot.

One night towards the end of our stay in Aix we were having dinner on the Cours Mirabeau. There are of course many excellent french restaurants in Aix but Filip Noterdaeme and I have always preferred italian to french food and so we went to an italian restaurant. It was a lovely dinner. The table next to ours was soon occupied by an elderly married couple from England, Mr. and Ms. Peltz. He was a tall burly man with a big red nose and sharp blue eyes under bushy grey eyebrows and she was a petite lady with shiny linden-colored eyes in a flowery dress. They were delightful in many ways. Mr. Peltz ordered a whisky soda even before he sat down and told the italian waitress in great english detail how his drink was to be prepared. Do you think, he asked us after she left, that she can be trusted with my drink order. We assured him that he was in good hands.

It was a lively evening. Mr. Peltz spoke of the british in Provence and said with great satisfaction, we practically own this country. This Filip Noterdaeme found most amusing. After dessert the waitress served everyone a glass of grappa on the house. Mister Peltz took a careful sip and placed the glass back on the table. How do you like it, Filip Noterdaeme asked. Oh it's quite nice said he. You mean to say, said Filip Noterdaeme, that it is terrible. Why yes, Mister Peltz said, it is perfectly dreadful. Before leaving Mr. and Mrs. Peltz made us promise to pay them a visit on our next trip to London. To this day we have not managed to go to London together but one day we will.

I flew back to New York just in time for Labor Day weekend to cook in the Hamptons for Eric Ellenbogen and Cary Davis. Filip Noterdaeme stayed in France a little longer and joined his older brother in Hyères. It was there that he first had spaghetti à l'ail, similar but different to spaghetti aglio olio. Later in New York he prepared spaghetti à l'ail for me. I can still see him standing in the kitchen at 172 Clinton Street that day, sweating whole garlic cloves in olive oil. The garlic was sweating and he was too.

We were back in New York. Filip Noterdaeme was no longer working at Loyola but he found work as an adjunct art history professor at several universities. First there was New York University and soon he was also teaching at the City University of New York, Kean University, Marymount College and later also the New School. And so he was working part time, all the time, and he continued to earn very little. No wonder he was always hard up. He had students of all ages, from 18 to 81. Filip Noterdaeme maintains that they all had one thing in common, wanting to be changed not wanting to be changed. He used to tell them, what we have to study is the feel and the taste of the cream that Vermeer's milkmaid is pouring out of her jug. Of course he had to bring slides for all his courses and my memory of seeing Filip Noterdaeme, desperately late for class, crouching on the floor at 172 Clinton Street looking through a pile of scattered slides is very vivid. It was in those moments that he sometimes would say to me, you have it easy, all you have to do for a fat check is to simply peel an apple whereas I have to astonish everyone with rotting apples by Cézanne.

Filip Noterdaeme also began working as a clerk at Book Court, a small bookstore near 172 Clinton Street. One of his tasks was to sort books in alphabetical order and it brought back all the anxiety of his youth when he had been diagnosed with dyslexia. He never got fluent with the alphabet and always used a handwritten chart that he carried in his pocket. At the bookstore, he also learned how to wrap up books in gift paper and count the cash in the register at the end of his shift. But most of the long hours he spent there he simply sat behind the counter filling one Moleskine notebook after another with thoughts on the homeless and his museum. He wrote that the homeless were more dramatic than Hannah Wilke, more Zen than John Cage, more happenstance than Alan Kaprow, more cunning than Andy Warhol, more vulgar than Jeff Koons, more abstract than Ad Reinhardt, more thrifty than Joseph Cornell, more repetitive than Daniel Buren, more preachy than Barbara Kruger, more obsessive than Louise Bourgeois, more angry than Penny Arcade, more foul than Paul McCarthey, more banal than Julian Schnabel, more rigid than Martha Graham, and more manipulative than Lars von Trier. All this Filip Noterdaeme wrote and then one day he simply wrote, Homeless is more.

It was at about that time that he decided that the Homeless Museum should have an acronym, naturally concluding that the acronym would be HOMU. Everybody called the Modern MoMA and now everybody was going to call the Homeless Museum HOMU. Of course there had to be a website and Nick Wilkinson, always helpful, helpful as a friend and helpful as a computer geek, designed it. And then we ordered one thousand pin-back buttons with the HOMU logo. In short, it was the beginning of the HOMU brand.

A little later that year Filip Noterdaeme took me to see something at Sean Kelly Gallery in Chelsea. It was called The House with the Ocean View. As we came into the gallery there seemed to be a great many people present and on an elevated platform was a dark-haired woman in a pajama curiously standing still and looking into the distance. I did not know what she was doing, it was evidently not ordinary. What is that, I whispered to Filip Noterdaeme. Oh, he said, that is Marina Abramovic, and I'm afraid she has been standing up there for a week already. Everybody around us seemed overcome at Marina in her pajamas but I in my german way said to Filip Noterdaeme, it is all nonsense, there is no house and no ocean, Marina is doing everyday things and she is not looking at us and we are looking at her, and they call this a performance. We began to laugh uncontrollably. Then we recovered and Filip Noterdaeme once more explained about Marina Abramovic. He said what she wanted was to become one of those marvelously tortured adulated martyrs of which the Catholic Church has several examples.

We went to a concert of Jimmy Scott, little Jimmy Scott and it was very beautiful. I had first heard of little Jimmy Scott in 1993, shortly after my arrival in New York, and I remember buying one of his albums. Later Larry Woodard had compared my voice to his and tried to get me to lower my vocal range. You will not, Larry Woodard used to say to me, have a career unless you develop a more masculine lower range, look at little Jimmy Scott who suffered a great deal because of his high voice, no one in the industry would give him a break. In any case we went to hear him sing and it was an experience. Little Jimmy Scott's face looked old in the way of newborn babies and the wide suit he wore clung to his body like to a scarecrow. When he started singing his voice immediately filled the room with sadness. After the show, we went backstage and Jimmy Scott said to me, no matter what happens, keep singing. I promised I would.

Then under my strenuous impulsion we traveled to Spain and spent New Year's Eve in Barcelona. I knew Barcelona well from the time when my parents had lived there in the Nineties and we did have an awfully good time.

We dined very pleasantly at the Pinotxo tapas bar in the Boqueria and thought that the old owner behind the counter indeed looked like an aged pinocchio. We did the usual things and then I showed Filip Noterdaeme my favorite building in Barcelona. It was not a Gaudi building, it was the Barcelona Pavilion by Mies van der Rohe with its beautiful white Barcelona chairs. Then we went to the zoo. In all those years I had been visiting my parents in Barcelona I had never been to the zoo but Filip Noter-daeme insisted that no one could visit Barcelona without seeing Barcelona's living mascot, Floquet de Neu, Snow-flake the albino gorilla. We went and Floquet was there doing everyday things and he was looking at us and we were looking at him. It was a great performance. Natu-rally we had to buy a plush Floquet de Neu at the souve-nir shop and Filip Noterdaeme began thinking of what it would be like if Floquet and the white Barcelona chair were to switch roles for one day. Just imagine, he said, Floquet would do everyday things at the Barcelona Pavil-lion and meanwhile the white Barcelona Chair would be on display in the gorilla cage. Poor Floquet died of skin cancer not very much later without ever having seen the Barcelona Pavilion or the white chair.

We returned to New York. The next thing that hap-pened was Eric Ellenbogen asking me to cook for a board meeting at his mansion in East Hampton. It was a strenu-ous three-day affair. Everybody ate and talked business and then ate some more. Then it was over and everybody left and Eric Ellenbogen said, you are welcome to stay at the house for a few days and invite Filip to join you, in other words make yourself at home. I called Filip Noter-daeme and said, do come. He took the next train to East Hampton, and brought along all HOMU board members in his suitcase.

We stayed for a weekend and had a wonderful time. We enjoyed the ocean view and took steam baths in one of the guest bathrooms. I cooked elaborate meals in the well-appointed kitchen and Filip Noterdaeme raided the wine cellar. Then it was time for a group photo with the HOMU board members and I once again had to improvise a Madame Butterfly costume. This time I used Eric Ellenbogen's Frette sheets for a kimono, black leather napkin rings and chopsticks from his dining set for a geisha wig and white clown make-up from a drugstore in East Hampton to make up my face.

Then came the spring and Nick Wilkinson moved out of 172 Clinton Street and into a little West Village studio. We decided to not take another roommate and turned Nick's former bedroom into a study.

The next thing that happened was Matthias Hollwich with a letter from Omar Akbar, the director of the Bauhaus in Dessau.

I remember very well the impression I had of Matthias Hollwich when I first met him in Munich in 1991. He was an attractive-looking tall blond german, with passionately interested, rather than interesting eyes. He was studying architecture by day and working as a waiter at night in Munich's only late night supper club, the Nachtcafé. He was always behaving like someone with a sunny disposition but there was a deeply sad side to him that came out whenever he was tired and overworked which was most of the time. He had a liking for very austere-looking architecture and the building designs he made for his studies always made one think of prisons.

I had introduced Matthias Hollwich to Filip Noterdaeme at the time he was doing an internship at the offices of Diller and Scofidio in New York and the two had had a long conversation. Filip Noterdaeme told Matthias Hollwich about a new idea. It had something to do with expanding the Guggenheim Museum brand into airport lounges. Matthias Hollwich sat and listened and looked and put Filip Noterdaeme's ideas to paper. He understood a good deal of Filip Noterdaeme's ideas, he used to dream at night that there was something there that he did not understand, but on the whole, he was very content with that which he did understand. In any case Filip Noterdaeme had delighted in seeing his ideas expressed in Matthias Hollwich's architectural drawings. Then Matthias Hollwich had become a docent at the Bauhaus in Dessau and now Omar Akbar had sent him to New York to complete a Bauhaus survey concerning the fate of the Walter Gropius Director's House in Dessau. The house had been built in 1926 and destroyed in 1945 by allied bombers and the question now was should it be rebuilt or not, and the Bauhaus was reaching out to architects and artists around the world to debate the question. Yes, said Filip Noterdaeme, rebuild it, but not until the building's centennial, in 2026, and then destroy it again in 2045 to commemorate the centennial of its bombing. Repeat the same scenario every 100 years, he said. Filip Noterdaeme called this grotesque Gropius House proposal Shock and Awe. It was later included in a Bauhaus publication, and it was the only proposal by an artist that made it into the book. Naturally Filip Noterdaeme was awfully pleased.

Matthias Hollwich and Filip Noterdaeme then having been introduced to each other by me became friends but later they became enemies. Now they are neither friends nor enemies.

They exchanged ideas as was the habit in those days. Filip Noterdaeme helped Matthias Hollwich develop ideas for architectural competitions and Matthias Hollwich gave Filip Noterdaeme design suggestions for his museum ideas. It was only a little later that Filip Noterdaeme approached Matthias Hollwich with an idea that mattered most to him. He wanted to realize a self-imploding museum made out of orange glycerin soap, completely and entirely out of orange glycerin soap. He called it the ISM, the Incredible Shrinking Museum. Matthias Hollwich was very interested and together they built several glycerin soap models of the ISM to show how it would gradually shrink. It is over this museum that a year later their friendship turned into war.

In the meanwhile I became involved with a new variety cabaret show called Rouge. It was there that I first began working with burlesque performers. There was Ami Goodheart, Worldfamous Bob, and Julie Atlas Muz and many more. One night Lutz Deisinger the director of the Bar Jeder Vernunft Spiegeltent in Berlin was in the audience and he said to me, perhaps you should come and perform in Berlin. I told him I was very interested.

I flew to Berlin to meet everybody and discuss the details. Of course, Lutz Deisinger said, you will have to pay for everything. Oh, I said. Yes, he said, and you will have to develop the Berlin show in Berlin with a local director and local musicians because our audiences here in Berlin are not at all like audiences in New York. I said, I know.

I flew back to New York and felt that maybe it was not such a good idea after all to do a show in Berlin. I discussed the matter with Filip Noterdaeme. Just imagine, he said, if it works out you can be a star in Germany and get rich and I can retire. I called Lutz Deisinger and told him I was coming to Berlin. Lutz Deisinger said, very well, come in the fall.

Matthew Barney was having a big retrospective at the Guggenheim Museum and we went to the opening. It was a rather dull exhibit. We went from one ramp to another and quite frankly we had no idea which of the installations were awful and which were not. I say we did not know but yes perhaps we did know. Matthew Barney, Filip Noterdaeme explained, is the vulgarization of Joseph Beuys just as Jeff Koons is the vulgarization of Andy Warhol. Joseph Beuys had conceived and was struggling with the problem that a society should have the makings of a social sculpture and that these makings should be the result of conceiving of human labor and creativity in so tenuous a fashion that it would induce such makings in the people forming it. It was his way of achieving the transformative. It was this idea that conceived commercially influenced Matthew Barney's Cremaster Cycles.

During this period Filip Noterdaeme was very restless. He was intensely a museum director and he was technically an adjunct professor, a gallery lecturer and a bookstore clerk. Everybody being confused about his Homeless Museum many began to refer to it as his Waterloo. Then there were the open letters. It seemed every week he wrote another of his open letters to another museum director, completely expressing the complete actual present of the museum world. He was always hopeful for a reply but he never received one to any of them, not one.

Finally Elizabeth Kley, who was looking for someone to rent one of her two artist studios in Chelsea managed to help Filip Noterdaeme out of his troubles. Elizabeth Kley was a New York artist and acquaintance of Oliver Herring. She looked like a spinster but it was just the look she was working, New York artists are always working a look. Elizabeth Kley made art with clay and had her own kiln in her studio. She was obsessed with Salvador Dali and

146

earned her living as a unionized usher at Carnegie Hall. In any case when she couldn't find anyone to rent the second studio she said to Filip Noterdaeme why don't you show your museum in it for a week or two, it will help spread the word for you and for me.

Filip Noterdaeme thought about it and then did it. This was the inauguration of the Homeless Museum and it was all about the $0 Collection.

The opening was a very jolly affair. Everybody was curious and soon the little studio was full of people. Friends came, and friends of friends. There was Robert Lazzarini and Luis Moreno who had said I was a keeper and pleasant agitated calm Tom Cinko. Peter Krashes and Oliver Herring came. It was the only time we ever saw them at a HOMU event. Everybody read the open letters and watched the videos and had pretzels and beer and talked at great length about one thing or another. I stood next to Tom Cinko who was silent. After a little while I murmured to Tom Cinko that I liked his double portrait of Filip Noterdaeme. Yes, he said, everybody says he does not look like a museum director or a panhandler but that does not make a difference, he will, he said.

Everybody was wondering about the cardboard member-ship desk. Filip Noterdaeme had invented a member-ship policy that had members pay their membership fee not to the Homeless Museum but to a homeless person of their choice. Elizabeth Kley felt that she ought to be the first patron of the Homeless Museum and signed up for $150. Filip Noterdaeme and I often wondered if she ever really gave $150 to a homeless person. There was also a HOMU shop with T-shirts and coffee mugs that all carried the HOMU logo but of course it was an installation like everything else, which is to say that nothing was meant to be for sale, ever. This brings me to the $0 Collection. It was rather impressive. We had gotten yellow page phone books, several dozen of yellow page phone books, from the hallway downstairs and had aligned them along one wall with white boards on them to create a little platform and on these boards Filip Noterdaeme had placed found objects from the street that he carefully arranged in 5 color-coordinated sections. Above each section he had hung an industrial milk crate in matching color that served as a frame for a postcard of a famous artwork. There was brown Paul Cézanne, black Yves Klein, red Michelangelo Caravaggio, blue François Boucher and yellow Wolfgang Laib. I have hopes that one day Filip Noterdaeme might be doing a $0 arrangement under original artworks in a museum, in other words bring his $0 Collection to a million dollar collection.

To everyone's surprise critic Walter Robinson of Artnet came and gave Filip Noterdaeme the first review ever of the Homeless Museum in which he called it an arch Gesamtkunstwerk. We were awfully pleased.

Among the people that came and that we did not know was Gabrielle Giattino. She was a young italian-american woman with a very noble intelligent face. She had for some years been working at the information desk at the Metropolitan Museum but now she was an assistant curator at the Swiss Institute and she had heard about the Homeless Museum. She came and saw and understood.

Filip Noterdaeme, in his work, has always been possessed by an intellectual passion for insincerity in the fabrication of art. He has produced an ambiguity by this concentration, and as a result the destruction of sincerity in art. He knows that earnestness, righteousness, virtue, the result of emotion should never be the inspiration, even political stances should never be the inspiration for art, nor should they be the material of art. Nor should emotion itself be the inspiration for art. Art should consist of an exact reproduction of an insincere reality. It was this conception of insincerity in art that made the close understanding between Filip Noterdaeme and Gabrielle Giattino.

Gabrielle Giattino also conceived insincerity but in her, insincerity had a mystical basis. As a mystic it was necessary for her to be insincere. In Filip Noterdaeme the necessity was intuitive, a pure passion for insincere art. It is because of this that his work has often been compared to that of the dadaists and by a certain american performance artist to the work of Jack Smith.

The most moving thing Gabrielle Giattino has ever written is the eulogy dedicated to her father. She read it at her father's memorial service. At the time she had a charming boyfriend named Becket. Later she fell in love with a woman, Andrea Merkx, and the two moved in together. We politely tried to not act surprised and soon grew very fond of Andrea who had just the right head for the stylish brown Borsalino hat that Gabrielle had inherited from her father.

A few months after the inauguration of the Homeless Museum, Gabrielle Giattino invited Filip Noterdaeme to take part in Quixotic, a group show she was guest curating for the Slingshot Gallery in Soho. He was terribly excited and decided he should present a machine to simulate homelessness the way flight simulators simulate flight and this is how the idea for the first Homeless Simulator came about. Filip Noterdaeme invented it and Matthias Hollwich helped him built it. It was a very large tall translucent plastic box that one could crawl into through a latch. Inside, there was an old blanket, a coyote, and a record player with a vintage educational record from the McCarthy era that Filip Noterdaeme had stolen from Loyola's history department.

It is difficult now to reconstruct the specifics of why Filip Noterdaeme thought of placing a coyote in the Simulator, but he did at the time often express the hope that once inside one should feel at least for a little moment the isolation and the strangeness of homelessness that all artists geniuses and poets know so well, as well. He had at first considered getting a plush coyote from a toy store but Anthony Coleman the pianist for my Café Sabarsky show that season insisted that Filip Noterdaeme should get a real taxidermy coyote, which is to say that Anthony Coleman knew his Joseph Beuys from his Kurt Weill. I must admit we both liked Anthony's suggestion and Filip Noterdaeme placed a special order for a stuffed coyote with a taxidermist from the Adirondacks. It was only a little later that a big crate was delivered to 172 Clinton Street. It arrived on a Saturday morning and I was as usual during the summer months out in East Hampton, cooking. Filip Noterdaeme called me and he was very agitated. Guess who is here and looking at me, he said. Who is it, I said. The coyote arrived, he said, and she is so beautiful, I just know that the Homeless Museum will flourish with her. He instantly named her Florence and promised to one day take her to Venice. Florence has not been to Venice to this day but Filip Noterdaeme once took her to Copenhagen.

Quixotic opened at the Slingshot Gallery with Florence sitting inside the Homeless Simulator and making everybody a little uncomfortable just as Filip Noterdaeme had hoped. Everybody who entered the Simulator came out a little disturbed and a little sweaty, in short not a little transformed by homeless simulation. Filip Noterdaeme was very pleased and named Florence Director of Public Relations of the Homeless Museum.

Since I needed to earn money to pay for my Berlin shows in the fall we did not travel that summer. I cooked every weekend for Eric Ellenbogen and Cary Davis and their two companions, Chris Mooney and John McGinn. Eric Ellenbogen needing to earn money to pay for the renovation of his new townhouse on Gramercy Park had rented out his East Hampton mansion and rented an old little pink house for the summer. It was close to the beach but much to the regret of Cary Davis did not have a pool or the same level of comfort as Eric's modern mansion. Like most americans Cary Davis always preferred a pool to a beach, he found it so much more agreeable.

It was a very humid, very hot summer. One night I had a dream of seeing myself in the mirror with spiky bleached hair like Laurie Anderson's. I decided that I should do my Berlin shows with spiky bleached hair. I went to a hair salon and it was an ordeal to get my dark hair as light as it had been in my dream. I cannot say that anybody cared for it but I wanted at least to have my bleached portrait taken for the posters in Berlin before dying my hair back to dark brown. I asked Steven Speliotis to take it.

I had once before worked with Steven Speliotis when I had for a short time thought of trying to become a fashion model. He had an accomplished way with lighting and made me look like a pretty girl looking like a beautiful boy, not just to the french but to everybody. I had high hopes that this would be of interest for Calvin Klein or Steven Klein or perhaps Ellen von Unwerth but I never found work as a fashion model and soon gave up on the whole idea.

In any case, Filip Noterdaeme and I went to Steven Speliotis's studio and it took only very little time to take my portrait because I knew exactly what I wanted and Steven Speliotis knew exactly how to get it done just right. Later when we looked at the prints we liked the one with my eyes closed and we liked the one with my eyes open but we particularly liked the double portrait Steven Speliotis had taken of me and Filip Noterdaeme at the end of the session as a spontaneous little favor.

The next thing that happened, quite unexpectedly and inconveniently, was the famous Northeast Blackout of 2003. Filip Noterdaeme was having a night out in Williamsburg with Gabrielle Giattino and Becket and I was staying at the old little pink house in East Hampton preparing a birthday dinner for Cary Davis.

I can still hear John McGinn's gentle voice echoing through the house, relating the latest news he kept listening to on a little battery-operated radio, and then everybody discussing at great length the technical details of the power surge in Ontario and how everybody must help themselves. John McGinn immediately bought a dozen cans of tuna at the columbian bodega, which made Eric Ellenbogen desperately unhappy. It was on that occasion that I served the vitello tonnato that had a smoky flavor because I had to cook the veal on the barbecue. In the city, Filip Noterdaeme utterly exhausted from the heat said to Becket, where is Ontario. Don't you know, Becket said. No, he said, nor do I care, but where is it.

Then came the end of the summer and I flew to Berlin. There were posters with my portrait hanging wherever I looked. It was not the beautifully elegant picture Steven Speliotis had taken of me. Lutz Deisinger had refused to use it and instead had used an older photograph of mine that made me look like an italian hooligan. He also insisted that I hire Peter Hahn as my director.

Peter Hahn was well known for having made Tim Fischer a Berlin cabaret star in the Nineties. I of course had been hearing a great deal about Tim Fischer from my mother in Munich who often liked to point out that I could have had Tim Fischer's career had I stayed in Germany and not moved to New York.

Peter Hahn at first did not want to direct my show, he feared that everybody would say that he was just trying to repeat what he had done with Tim Fischer. He was always concerned about the politics of tingle tangle, show business, which perhaps had something to do with him having lived in West Berlin during the cold war. He was convinced that the Berliners would not want to hear me sing any songs that Tim Fischer had already sung. He also did not want me to hire any musicians that had ever worked with Tim Fischer and instructed me to hire a cabaret pianist from former East Berlin as my musical director and a violinist and a cellist, both from Japan. I got along rather well with the japanese. With the East Berlin pianist, less. We rehearsed tirelessly and always had lunch in a little restaurant behind the theater. Of course I always had to pay for everything. Regarding the food that was served I

153

remember once whispering to the japanese, this must all seem so primitive to you. They shyly lowered their eyes and said, yes.

With the help of Peter Hahn I put together a very mixed program of Robert Schumann Lieder, Barbara chansons, Roy Orbison hits and Abbey Lincoln ballads. It was a very unconventional mix and we facetiously gave the show a very conventional title, Liederabend, song recital. We rehearsed for three weeks and then the show opened. I performed in the black Brooklyn tracksuit I had worn on opening night in Vienna after my suitcase had not arrived on time and this time it was a statement. The Berliners, who are not stylish like the viennese were not amused. In those years of the american Iraq invasion the Berliners took great pride in their contempt for anything american and were very mistrustful of german expatriates who lived in the States. One critic wrote of how surprising it was to see something heartfelt coming from America. At last my nerves could not bear it any longer and I blurted out, why does he say that, why does he not say that he does not know America.

The show ran for three weeks, the longest three weeks of my life. However it had some success with expatriate americans, lesbians and straight young couples, but not so much with the press and the gays. One night Deutschlandradio came and recorded the show for a live broadcast. That night was a pleasant one. Later I turned the recording of the broadcast into a CD, Isengart Live in Berlin. On the cover, I put my bleached hair portrait, the one that Steven Speliotis had taken and that Lutz Deisinger had refused to use for the Berlin posters.

The gloom and the loneliness I felt in Berlin brought

back all the melancholy of my adolescence in Germany. Filip Noterdaeme came to visit but he could only stay for a few days. He was full of understanding and tender encouragement. Berliners, he said, are like the chinese, they are uncouth and cruel. They are not brutal they are cruel. They have no close contact with style such as most Europeans have. Their history is not the history of victory, of glory, it is the history of resistance and defiance. They are not welcoming, Filip Noterdaeme said. And it is quite true. The Berliners whatever else they may be are not welcoming. They are very blunt, they are very direct and sooner or later they always demand that you do things their way. New Yorkers are welcoming, they are frank and they are generous. Perhaps with renewed contact with New Yorkers the Berliners will learn these things.

One night after the show a beautiful young woman appeared in my dressing room. This was Meow Meow. She thoroughly understood everything about Liederabend, understood its irony and its mix of styles. It was the beginning of our intimacy. It was not until a little later, in New York, that I saw her perform for the first time and shared a stage with her.

It is very difficult now that everybody is accustomed to everything to give some idea of the kind of uneasiness one felt when seeing Meow Meow perform for the first time, she broke so many boundaries of the cabaret world. It is true that she usually performed in cabarets but she was not really a cabaret entertainer, she was a deconstructivist performance artist disguised as a cabaret diva. It was this additional level and her australian outrageousness that made all the difference and set her apart from everybody else. There have since her emergence on the scene been many attempts to copy what only Meow Meow can do. It was Lance Horne who coined a delightful term to describe such actions and so, whenever we see a performer attempting such shameless imitations we call it, she or he is doing a Meow.

I always delighted working with Meow Meow. In the following years she often came to New York and we performed together in Rouge the burlesque show and once gave a special late night performance at Joe's Pub where we sang a Dalida Alan Delon duet that was all about empty words.

Meow Meow was chronically hard up from having to pay for her airline tickets to go from here to there, always traveling, never truly at home anywhere but on stage, any stage. I called Limor Tomer and said, you must book Meow Meow at Café Sabarsky, which she did. Meow Meow's show at Café Sabarsky was a great success until the night she called for a pizza delivery during her show, telling the audience that no one had cared to bring any food to her dressing room. Kurt Gutenbrunner the Café Sabarsky chef who did not understand deconstruction, not in food and not in cabaret, got very upset and forbade Limor to book Meow Meow again. But all this was years later.

I was back home in New York. I felt bad for a while, having worked all summer to earn money and then promptly lost it all to Liederabend, and then I went on with my life.

This brings me to the winter of 2004, when under very strange circumstances the Homeless Museum held its third board meeting on the french island of St. Barts in the Caribbean.

I had heard all about St. Barts from Cary Davis and

Eric Ellenbogen. Every wealthy gay man in New York was awfully fond of St. Barts in those days and lived but to get there. It was on Thanksgiving that they all liked to travel there with frozen turkeys and canned cranberries in their Gucci bags. Cary Davis wanted me to go to St. Barts so badly he gave me and Filip Noterdaeme two round trip tickets for Christmas. You will love it, he said. We went, hesitatingly.

In St. Barts everybody was lounging and shopping, shopping and lounging, there really was nothing else one could possibly do. I remember seeing a few palm trees but mostly luxury boutiques and luxury hotels and luxury restaurants where young french waiters who were forever tired by day and partying at night served inevitable cheese omelettes with wilted lettuce that had been flown in from Paris. We felt very much out of place.

We had a few adventures. We stayed at a little studio with a very damp mattress, as a matter of fact everything was damp in St. Barts because it was rainy season. Filip Noterdaeme refused to sleep on the damp mattress and grudgingly made do with a hard wooden bench for a bed during our entire stay.

We rented a little jeep and constantly got lost on the steep winding dirt roads. More than once we got caught in a tropical downpour. One day we came across two little old ladies from Jamaica who were selling tiny red hot peppers and pineapple rum. They looked to us like they had been drinking rum all their lives. In any case we bought some of the tiny red hot peppers and I roasted and skinned and diced them for a pasta dish. Then without thinking I went to the bathroom and touched what I should not have touched. Well. I have never been in such pain, not before and not since. I frantically paced around the room, moaning, cursing, crying and laughing at the same time. Filip Noterdaeme laughed and laughed. And then the next day the same thing happened to him.

Then there was the time when we saw a wild peacock curiously picking at Filip Noterdaeme's copy of Goethe's The Sorrows of Young Werther he had left on the terrace.

Before we left the island, Filip Noterdaeme, having once again brought along all the HOMU board members in his suitcase insisted we take a group photo on the beach. He was very adamant about it. I had to improvise a geisha look for the third time and ended up using white toothpaste to whiten my face, a very bad idea indeed.

So there we were on a white beach next to a hotel for millionaires trying to take our second HOMU board member group photo. The wind kept blowing away the sheets of Beethoven's 2nd Symphony, Filip Noterdaeme's fake beard was itching his face, my face was burning from the toothpaste, the framed portrait of Madame Tussaud kept falling over in the sand, Jean the Chimp was almost washed away by a tropical wave and there was a problem with the camera's self-timer. The following day we returned to New York, not a little overwrought.

The next thing that happened was the HO Cracks controversy.

For some time Filip Noterdaeme had been noticing the cracks on the façade of the Guggenheim building on Fifth Avenue. He sent Director Thomas Krens another open letter, innocently mischievously proposing to highlight the cracks with orange paint. He called the project HO Cracks. It was only a little later that a secretary from the Guggenheim offices became incensed about an illustration of HO cracks on the HOMU website and Filip Noterdaeme became the one Guggenheim employee she wished away. The relationship between her and Filip Noterdaeme became just that. Filip Noterdaeme refused to remove HO Cracks from his website and the secretary thought he should not be allowed to give any more tours at the Guggenheim. I cannot say that anybody else did. It was not until several months later that Thomas Krens launched his own proposal to restore the Guggenheim façade. The restoration took several years to complete and cost 27 million dollars. The patented paint that ended up being used for the façade was not orange, it was a sort of light beige called Elastocolor Rasante code 7F353520 color 3535. Around that time Filip Noterdaeme found some leftovers of it in a dumpster outside the museum building and used them to paint what became known as the Guggenheim Monochromes. They are now hanging at 172 Clinton Street and are perhaps my favorite paintings of the Collection of the Homeless Museum. However the Guggenheim just launched a commercial line of Guggenheim-inspired wall paints for $130 a can and so now everybody can paint their entire home in Guggenheim gallery colors.

The Signature Series was created next, one canvas at a time. Filip Noterdaeme took to the streets, armed with square blank white canvases and a black sharpie pen and asked any homeless men and women he encountered to sign the canvases for him. Many did and this pleased Filip Noterdaeme immensely. Eugene Washington signed and Thomas McDougal who called himself Tee signed, and then there was Speedy, Josephine and one Michael Jackson and many more. Looking at the canvases Filip Noterdaeme used to say to me, I am trying to be as contemporary as I can be. And then sometimes a little worried, is it not too contemporary.

We did not make any traveling plans for the summer. I had once again agreed to cook for Eric Ellenbogen and Cary Davis in the Hamptons and had hopes of teaching myself to play the accordion and perhaps take driving lessons to get my driver's license. Then one Friday evening I had a terrible fall at 172 Clinton Street and this was the beginning of a very funny string of coincidences. First I had to go to the emergency room. There the doctor said, you shattered your right wrist. He put my hand in a temporary cast and said, it must be operated on within three days, find a good surgeon.

The next morning I took a train to the Catskills to see a matinee of Cabaret the musical. I knew the director, Stephen Nachamie, from my dance school years and everybody was talking about how he had cast a black man in the role of the german Emcee. When I arrived, Stephen Nachamie introduced me to the show's producer. She was a lady with short blond hair in a pink shirt. She looked at my cast and said sharply, what happened to your hand. I said what had happened. She then told me that she was a retired hand surgeon and it was through her recommendation that I was able to get my hand operation done by the best hand surgeon in New York, Dr. Salvatore Lenzo. The operation was a success. Two months later he removed the screws he had put in my wrist and sent me to rehab. The rehab therapist was a pretty woman with long curly hair and the stifled yawn of someone who has to spend the whole day in a doctor's office. We always chatted during the tedious hand exercises. When I told her that I lived in the attic apartment of a townhouse in Brooklyn Heights she said, ah those attic apartments in Brooklyn Heights, I used to date someone who also lived in an attic apartment of a townhouse, years ago, his name was Paul. That is curious, I said, that is the name of our landlord and I happen to know that before he bought the townhouse he used to live in the attic apartment we are now renting from him. How very bizarre and what a coincidence that his name should be Paul too, she said. Yes, I said, isn't that curious. And then she asked me about his last name and I said such and such and she said, how very bizarre and what a coincidence, that was my Paul's last name too. And so it turned out that she had been Paul the landlord's girlfriend before he got married and bought the townhouse at 172 Clinton Street. When I told her about Paul now owning several buildings she very much regretted having broken up with him years ago. Just imagine, she said, I would be on easy street and would not have to sit here and show you wrist exercises. But all that happened later in the fall and first I had to get through the long Hamptons summer with screws and a metal fixator sticking out of my right wrist that used to put the butchers at the local meat market in a state. Eric Ellenbogen and Cary Davis had hungrily patiently agreed to hire one or another houseboy for extra help and so it was a strange summer of handicap and handy houseboys, in other words, all meals were prepared by two left hands.

In the meanwhile Filip Noterdaeme as usual had to stay behind in the hot city. How well I remember that phone conversation he and I had one late Saturday evening. We said charming soothing things and then we talked about new plans for the Homeless Museum. Why don't we, Filip Noterdaeme said, simply install it in our home. Just imagine, he said, our entire lives will become part of the museum, everything of it will be on display for everyone to see and we will live a life of permanent creation. We must do it, he said. But nobody will believe it is real, I said. It makes no difference, said Filip Noterdaeme, it is the essence of the thing that they must see and we must turn every room into a museum department, and then, his voice softening he added, I always wanted to live in a museum and what's the good of being the director of my own museum if I cannot live in it. He knew he was right and that it had to be done. But how.

The Museum of Modern Art having been closed for renovation for several years announced its grand reopening by blanketing the city with ads that said, Manhattan is Modern Again. Then word got out that the new admission would be $20. This mattered a great deal to Filip Noterdaeme. Now everybody is accustomed to pay $20 or more to visit a museum but back then it was big news. Filip Noterdaeme designed a flier that said Manhattan is Robbed Again, and for several days went to the new MoMA entrance on 53rd Street and handed out his leaflets to VIPs on their way into the museum for their exclusive preview. One evening, Filip Noterdaeme snuck past the security guards and crashed a big private reception in the new atrium. There was Ellsworth Kelly, Brice Marden, James Rosenquist, Jeff Koons, Rachel Whiteread, and Louise Lawler and even Oliver Herring and Peter Krashes. Everybody was drinking champagne and celebrating the new MoMA. Filip Noterdaeme spoke to Jo Carol Lauder about the problem of the 67% percent increase of the admission price and she told him, if twenty dollars is too much people can always get an annual membership for $75. She insisted it was quite a bargain. Filip Noterdaeme sadly shaking his head walked away, saying under his breath that Jo Carol Lauder was not very good with numbers and the Modern all too good at it. He continued handing out his leaflets to party guests and later had a dispute with a junior associate who violently tore up one of his leaflets in a rage and threw it on the floor. He also talked to Fran Lebowitz about the high admission price and she said, yes, yes, it is scandalous.

In all of New York there seemed to be only one other artist who was as incensed by the Modern's new admission price as Filip Noterdaeme. This was Dan Levenson. He had commenced standing by the Modern's entrance wearing a sandwich board that looked like a giant twenty-dollar bill. The two having become friendly from jointly picketing the VIP guests that kept entering the Museum during these days frequently discussed all matters of art and money. Once on 53rd Street when they saw Glenn Lowry the director of the Modern about to enter the museum they engaged him in a cordial debate. Filip Noterdaeme and Glenn Lowry had difficulty in talking not having a common language but they talked enough to confront each other. Filip Noterdaeme chided Glenn Lowry for failing the Modern's mission to make art accessible to a wide array of people, concluding that he had expanded the museum physically but shrunk it spiritually. Glenn Lowry told Filip Noterdaeme and Dan Levenson in no uncertain terms that he had had no other choice because the Modern did not receive any operating money from the government. Filip Noterdaeme replied, be that as it may, on opening day I am planning to visit your museum with my supporters and we all will pay our $20 admission with penny coins only.

That week The New York Times ran an article on the cost of culture, reporting on Dan Levenson and Filip Noterdaeme's protest and Glenn Lowry's explanation about not receiving any funds from the government. Later the paper ran a correction that clarified that the Modern in fact was receiving operating funds from the government, and Filip Noterdaeme had several special bathroom plaques made that read MUSEUM DIRECTORS MUST WASH HANDS. He mailed one to director Glenn Lowry as a gift. The image of the plaque was later used by Paul Werner in his book, Museum Inc.

Then came the day when the Modern was finally open to the general public and Filip Noterdaeme completed his Penny Campaign as he liked to call it. He went to the Modern with a good dozen of supporters, each of us wearing a HOMU pin-back button and paying the $20 admission with two thousand pennies just as he had announced to Glenn Lowry. The little copper coins weighed twelve and a half pounds per admission, and the cashiers were awfully polite and obliging, holding out little white laundry baskets to collect the many thousands of pennies while trying to act normal. This I thought was rather amusing. Very evidently they had been warned about us and instructed to behave in such nonchalant ways.

Our group then began touring the new museum and after a while it became clear that we were being followed by several security guards and a very stern-looking little man in a gray suit. We continued to calmly inspect the museum and nonchalantly remarked on the noble simplicity and calm grandeur of the escalators, so common in shopping malls, which prompted Filip Noterdaeme to rename MoMA the Mall of Modern Art. Finally the little man in the gray suit could not stand it any longer and pushed us into a corner. His name was Mr. Simoncini, he was the head of Security at MoMA and he said, I have been watching you and don't you dare try to do something sinister or I will have you escorted out by my guards. We thought this was also most amusing and assured him in the nicest way possible that we had no such intentions. I tell the story for what it is worth. It was only a little later that Filip Noterdaeme began thinking of creating a miniature version of the Modern as a Boîte-en-Valise to show MoMA highlights on the streets, free of charge.

It was at about that time that Gabrielle Giattino called us and said to Filip Noterdaeme, the Swiss Institute will have an exhibition booth at the Armory Show early next year and I would like you to come and perform inside our booth as the Homeless Museum Director. Filip Noterdaeme said he would be delighted to. He then mentioned that he had been thinking of installing and presenting the Homeless Museum at 172 Clinton Street. Gabrielle Giattino liked this idea. She immediately called Katlijne de Backer of the Armory Show and told her all about the Homeless Museum. And so this, one of the most important conversations of Filip Noterdaeme's life, led to the Armory Show announcing the first Homeless Museum opening at 172 Clinton Street. We decided that it should take place on a Sunday morning and that we would serve a light brunch. The Armory Show sent out invitations to its VIP patrons and the reservation list began filling up with names, american names and european names and japanese names, names of art collectors and socialites. When there were 30 names we kindly requested that the reservation list be closed. We cannot, I explained, possibly accommodate more than 30 brunch guests at 172 Clinton Street.

We began transforming 172 Clinton Street into a live-in museum. Our friends said, but your apartment doesn't look like a museum. It will, Filip Noterdaeme said.

In the weeks leading up to the Armory Show and our opening I often urged Filip Noterdaeme to create more art works for the Homeless Museum exhibits but he was much more concerned with creating museum departments. Creating art works is easy, he used to say, it's the museum that is hard to create and a museum must have departments. In other words, to Filip Noterdaeme the museum itself was the exhibit and the art was décor.

Having had a love for signage since the days he and his family lived at the belgian embassy in Geneva he decided we should have plaques above every doorway to designate each room as a museum department. The first department he created was the Curatorial Department. We installed it in the bathroom, and it had a slide projector one could use with a remote control while sitting on the toilet. Curating a show became our favorite new expression. We also had our white bath towels monogrammed with the orange HOMU logo and affixed a MUSEUM DIRECTORS MUST WASH HANDS sign above the sink. The finishing touch was the HOMU Pharmacy equipped with special HOMU pills, but more of that later.

It was an exciting exhilarating time. We turned every room, every nook and cranny of the apartment into a museum department and every object into an exhibit. Filip

Noterdaeme had all the impractical ideas and I had the practical solutions. As a rule he didn't like to see work being done. He never knew how anything was going to look until I showed him but once I did he always knew right away everything about it that was right or not.

We began with the Curatorial Department and then there was the Main Hall and Café Broodthaers and the Museum Shop and then the Staff and Security Department and the Archives and Meteorology Department and later the Wurlitzer Atrium, genial exhibits, amusing exhibits and might-be-offensive exhibits, and I listened to Filip Noterdaeme describing his ideas and then set about planning and realizing them.

An awful lot of things had to be ordered and bought and brought home and installed in those weeks that led up to the opening. Filip Noterdaeme does not care for shopping and detests buying clothes or any other practical things but he loved bringing home things he found on the street and use them for the museum, like the red Coleman ice box and the old Madama Butterfly record with Renata Tebaldi in a red kimono on the cover he found one day that together became an installation he called the Development Department.

Another thing Filip Noterdaeme was very preoccupied with in those days was the cultural climate inside and outside of the museum. He always was, he always is, interested in the problem of the external and the internal. It was at about that time that he found a vintage weather map of North America in a little shop on Varick Street. He bought it and made small subtle changes to it to express the cultural climate in America under the influence of different art forms. The finished Cultural Weather

Map had cold art movements like Dada and Minimalism and hot art movements like Abstract Expressionism and Arte Povera and hurricanes named after Marcel Duchamp, Andy Warhol, and Joseph Beuys.

Of course, Filip Noterdaeme said one day, we must have a hygrothermograph to monitor the climate inside the museum. We found a used one for sale on ebay and placed a bid. We won and the seller promised to ship it promptly. And then we ordered a weathervane to monitor the cultural climate outside the museum. Filip Noterdaeme asked for it to be in the shape of a coyote, a howling coyote because of Florence who had by then become not just HOMU's director of public relations but also the mascot of the Homeless Museum. All this, the Cultural Weather Map, the hygrothermograph and the weathervane became part of what Filip Noterdaeme called the Archives and Meteorology Department. It was housed in Nick's former bedroom and to this day the Homeless Museum remains the only museum with its own meteorology department.

When the weathervane arrived there was the question of how to attach it on the slanted roof above the living room so it could be seen through the skylight. We brought the weathervane to Vinnie the sicilian blacksmith on Bergen Street. Would you, said Filip Noterdaeme, be so kind and create a heavy metal base for this. Oh yes, said Vinnie the blacksmith, certainly I can do that. Also, said Filip Noterdaeme, looking at the weathervane, would you please remove the directional rods. I am, he explained, not interested in monitoring the wind, I am interested in monitoring cultural currents. Vinnie did everything just as we told him to and when we went back to his shop a few days later the weathervane was all finished and ready to be safely set up on our roof, looking rather nice with a very heavy shiny black steel base. There you go, said Vinnie and, it will cost you such and such. I am not so easily shocked but when I heard Vinnie say, such and such, I was. But since we had not come to a prior agreement on the price there was really nothing we could do and so we paid him such and such, and I imagine he was grinning for a long time behind our backs as we were walking home carrying the very heavy weathervane back to 172 Clinton Street.

But now I must tell about our trip to Las Vegas.

Bar d'O had been forced to close shortly after its tenth anniversary and Joey Arias and Raven O had moved to Las Vegas to star in Zumanity, an erotica show produced by Cirque du Soleil. We had promised to come and visit one day and so we went. Who first recognized how bad an idea it had been to travel to Las Vegas I do not know. When we landed at the airport we were at first amazed at how everything looked but by the time we arrived at the hotel we were already overwhelmed and soon very soon we were appalled, just appalled. We stayed for three long days.

Our hotel room was on the twenty-seventh floor of the New York New York Hotel and there was a hot tub next to the bed. We looked at it critically and said, how impractical. I remember also that the windows could not be opened. Very evidently the hotel management was afraid of hotel guests jumping out the window after losing all their money to gambling.

We spent our first day in Las Vegas wandering about the strip and watching people gamble. There were more losers than winners. Later we had dinner at the Bellagio's all-you-can-eat buffet and we were seated next to a man who talked incessantly emphatically about craps on his cell phone while wolfing down an astounding amount of steamed king crab legs.

The next day we came upon an Elvis impersonator in a white jump suit singing in a casino lounge. He had the heavy-set body that of course is a characteristic of all Elvis impersonators. He had been impersonating for seven years and he had been faithful to Elvis in the fashion of Las Vegas, that is to say he had sat in an easy chair and ordered room service. I imagine he is still there. Las Vegas had quantities of performers from all over the world, and it was our first experience of the fake but convincing smiles of Las Vegas performers. To be sure there were also lions and tigers, as a matter of fact one of them had mauled Siegfried of Siegfried and Roy just a few weeks before our visit.

Zumanity having replaced animals with humans had a great deal of commercial appeal and was not alarming. Joey Arias made an entrance wearing Thierry Mugler couture and sang and then the circus show began. We sat in the front row and there were acrobats doing strange titillating things on ropes and inside a very large champagne coupe and a contortionist who dislocated his limbs, one after another, and Filip Noterdaeme said, I'm sure I don't know what is the matter with me but I am bored, I want to see more of Joey. Perhaps you would have preferred real animals, I said. Then Raven O made a very feline appearance and Joey Arias teased the audience and everybody screamed and moaned. Then it was all over and we went out for dinner with Joey Arias and Raven O and a group of dancers from the Celine Dion Show. Joey told us that he had been named the Diva of the Strip, and of how he had said in his acceptance speech, I cannot possibly accept this title, it should be given to Celine Dion. She, he had said, is a diva, I am a goddess.

Recently Joey Arias said about those six years of performing 10 shows a week in Las Vegas that one did not live in Las Vegas one only worked in Las Vegas and continued to live in New York and one went through a lot of coming and going between Las Vegas and New York on the red-eye. Lady Rizo once asked him if he had been able to buy a New York apartment from the money he had earned there or if he had possibly put a lot of money aside for retirement. I don't believe in retirement, said he, when you're done, you're done.

In Las Vegas we also made a reservation for a Gladys Knight show at the Flamingo Hotel. I went to the concierge and he presented me with the tickets. He said to me, you must remember, sir, these shows start on time and do not last very long so you must be prepared for disappointment. And so it was. Miss Knight after barely forty minutes left the stage and did not reappear for an encore. Instead, the audience had to sit through a strange video advertisement of her latest single. But I still cried when she sang, Neither One of Us Wants to Be the First to Say Goodbye.

The Guggenheim galleries Rem Koolhaas had designed for the Venetian Hotel were another Las Vegas disappointment. The Kandinskys and the Picassos were hung on very expensive steel walls that were the color of milk chocolate and we did neither like it or see the point of it all.

Perhaps the strangest thing that we saw in Las Vegas was the m&m store. There were m&m handbags and m&m tape dispensers and m&m toasters and m&m hairbrushes. There was also a computer station where one could order m&m's with customized messages printed on them. Filip Noterdaeme said, let's place an order. We ordered five hundred white m&m's imprinted with HOMELESS IS MORE. At first, the computer rejected our order because the word HOMELESS was not allowed but I tricked the system by adding a hyphen between HOME and LESS.

On our last day in Las Vegas I suggested we should walk to the Liberace Museum just outside the city limits. Filip Noterdaeme said he preferred a cab on such a hot Nevada day but I insisted upon walking. And so we found ourselves walking along the highway of the Nevada desert for miles and no Liberace Museum in sight and Filip Noterdaeme was furious. I have since then learned to admit that I not only have no sense of orientation but that I am also quite inept at reading a map. In any case we arrived at the Liberace museum quite unnerved.

And then we were back at 172 Clinton Street.

The imprinted white m&m's arrived. I went to every pharmacy in Brooklyn Heights and beyond to ask for little orange plastic prescription drug vials to create a little HOMU Pharmacy for the Curatorial Department. There was a great deal of friendly rivalry among the pharmacists about who would give me more vials. I designed and printed HOMU Pharmacy labels for each vial and filled them with the white m&m's and lined them all up in the little mirror cabinet above the bathroom sink. This completed the Curatorial Department. A year later, when we ran out of m&m's I found out one could by now order printed m&m's over the internet and at first it seemed like the system accepted the word HOMELESS without a hyphen. Then a few days later I received a phone call from a very nice very american young lady asking if she might speak to Mister Noterdaeme. Yes, I said, here he is, and passed the receiver on to Filip Noterdaeme. She said, I am calling from the m&m headquarters. Yes, he said. You see, she said slightly hesitant, the director of our public relations is under the impression that perhaps your agenda. But I am a museum director, Filip Noterdaeme said indignantly. Yes yes I understand that perfectly now, she said, but perhaps you have not considered our image. I suppose, said he laughing, you were under the impression that I was trying to advertise something sinister. She stuttered, why no, she said, but you might not have considered our image. Oh yes, he said, oh yes. Well it's alright. I will write to your director and you might as well tell him that everything about my museum was created with the intention of it being the way it is and all he has to do is have the white m&m's printed with HOMELESS IS MORE and I will take the responsibility. The young lady thanked him and the conversation was ended. Later we received the new m&m's in the mail and they were exactly the way we had always wanted them with HOMELESS printed without a hyphen. This story became known among our friends as the HOMU Pharmacy Case. But all this happened after the museum had already been open for a good year.

The next thing we did was install a large letter board for the board of trustees. Filip Noterdaeme listed every director and trustee of the Homeless Museum on it. It was at about that time that we heard that Snowflake the albino gorilla from the Barcelona Zoo had died of skin cancer and so Filip Noterdaeme made him a life trustee and added his name on the board. He also listed Philippe de Montebello the director of the Metropolitan Museum of Art and Thomas Krens the director of the Guggenheim Museum as honorary trustees. The board was very heavy and I almost dropped it when I hung it by the entrance.

The hygrothermograph arrived and we set it up and began using it immediately. Filip Noterdaeme put a new paper chart into it every week and after one week we could already tell how uneven the climate inside the Homeless Museum was, so very different to the controlled climate inside the renovated Museum of Modern Art. The charts together with the open letters and Filip Noterdaeme's notebooks were all going to be on display in the Archives and Meteorology Department.

The kitchen was going to serve as our museum café and be named after Marcel Broodthaers. There was never any question about the menu, it had to be a simple serving of a cooked shelled mussel, a peeled hardboiled egg and a glass of chilled milk, in other words a very Broodthaersian menu.

One thing that Filip Noterdaeme and I had an argument about was the Homeless Simulator. The first Homeless Simulator with Florence Coyote and the record player had left a very great impression on everybody at the Slingshot Gallery but now Filip Noterdaeme had other plans. Like I said Florence Coyote had been promoted to mascot and Director of Public Relations and now he wanted her to be in the master bedroom which was going to be the Staff and Security Department. And so he completely reinvented the Homeless Simulator and turned it into a simulator of the american dream which, as everybody knows, is about making dough, the more the better. To realize this he placed the vintage Kitchenaid stand mixer he had once taken from the belgian embassy at 1 Beekman Place inside the Simulator and filled its metal bowl with pennies. All fine and well I said, but I do not under any circumstance want it in the living room, it will take away too much space. You are absolutely right, said Filip Noterdaeme, it will not fit anywhere else and that is why it will have to stand in the living room. We argued about it and then I grudgingly assembled it and set it up. There it stood in the middle of the living room leaving just enough space for the Wurlitzer piano on one side and the dining table on the other. I cursed and sighed but Filip Noterdaeme insisted that we leave it there and eventually, little by little, I got used to it. When we opened the Homeless Museum on March 13, 2005 the Simulator was an instant success with everybody and no one who has ever been inside the new Homeless Simulator at 172 Clinton Street can forget the sound of the pennies churning against the metal bowl.

As Filip Noterdaeme continued to insouciantly create department after department I got more and more nervous about art works. What, I asked him, is the museum going to exhibit. Sure enough, we already had the Signature Series, the Champagne Campaign, and the $0 Collection and a large orange body print of the two of us in a spooning position but to me it seemed not enough to fill a museum. Filip Noterdaeme told me not to worry and then, every now and then, to appease me, he would create a little work of art. He made Captive Audience, the art gallery model with the glue traps for visitors, and Museum Guard, his homage to Mister Simoncini of the Modern. It was also around that time that he found a light box to display the orange glycerin soap model of the ISM.

As to the Pussy Painting, we decided to hide it behind the flap door of a little storage space high up under the ceiling. We called this little arrangement the High Gallery and it was always a moment of suspense when I opened the flap door with a long metal handle to reveal the Pussy Painting to our visitors. It was so much more effective than a little red velvet curtain.

Of course, Filip Noterdaeme said to me one morning, you'll have to greet visitors as Madame Butterfly. Well I nearly dropped my butter knife when I heard him say that. I had not minded posing as Madame Butterfly for the camera during that long never-ending night when we shot the board meeting video and then again one cold winter afternoon on the balcony of Eric Ellenbogen's mansion in East Hampton where I was dressed in nothing but napkin rings and a bed sheet and of course in St. Barts where I had to use toothpaste in lieu of white makeup. But, said I, becoming Madame Butterfly for museum visitors was a different thing entirely. I was very agitated. Filip Noterdaeme insisted that there had to be a Madame Butterfly in his museum and there was no one but me to play her. I sulked for several days and then gave in, there is no way to say no to Filip Noterdaeme. But this time I was not going to take any chances with my look. I bought a real geisha wig, a vintage silk kimono and japanese socks and sandals. I also placed an order for a special geisha make-up kit from Japan.

The important thing to tell about now is the Education Department. We set it up in the fireplace. We were being very modern in the way we did it. We simply thought of Andy Warhol who had famously said, if it moves they'll watch, and installed a video monitor directly in the fireplace that showed a selection of HOMU videos. There were many to choose from. We chose Hänsel and Gretel and Mastering the Asphalt Arts and Charity and a few more. I placed two kindergarten chairs with headphones in front of the fireplace and hung the framed IF YOU SEE SOMETHING SAY SOMETHING poster above the mantelpiece.

Like I said the master bedroom became the Staff and Security Department. It had its own short circuit camera system. The camera we aimed directly at Filip Noterdaeme's desk and the monitor we put on a shelf above the desk. It had a strange effect when Filip Noterdaeme sat at it. He liked to explain to everyone that he had the system installed so he could watch his back while working but what it truly was was a live reproduction of Magritte's Not to be Reproduced painting.

Filip Noterdaeme had already introduced his museum membership policy at the inauguration in Chelsea and now he placed the membership forms in the freezer compartment of our refrigerator. This did not surprise me, it was not the first time he was placing important documents in the freezer. It must have been the very first time I came to 172 Clinton Street when I, as was and is my habit, looked for ice cubes for my sparkling water and found in the freezer a copy of Marcel Proust's A la recherche du temps perdu inside a ziplock bag. I saw it and once again a bell within me rang.

Of course we had to have labels next to every

HOMU art piece and also wall texts and decals on doors and windows. We always got our vinyl decals at a little sign shop in Chinatown, around the corner from a delightfully tiny authentic little dumpling place where we liked to eat potstickers while waiting for the decals to be ready.

The Homeless Museum was almost ready to receive its first visitors, all that was missing was the audio tour which I still had to write and record. But first came the day of the opening of the Armory Show.

As I said Filip Noterdaeme had agreed to perform there as the Homeless Museum Director and now it occurred to him to build a little booth of his own to use inside the booth of the Swiss Institute. I said, let's make it look like Lucy's psychiatric help booth from the Peanuts comic strip series. We went to the Armory and I built a little booth out of plywood and used colorful plastic letters to write, THE HOMELESS MUSEUM and, THE DIRECTOR IS IN on it. We equipped it with two kindergarten chairs, one for the Director and one for a visitor. Gabrielle Giattino when she saw me build the HOMU Booth said, ah yes, Lucy's booth. She now says it is a proof that I am very wicked. Filip Noterdaeme laughed and said, yes I know Gabrielle, the world is a playground for you but there are playgrounds and playgrounds and when you gave me this opportunity and gave it to me so graciously without knowing what I was going to do then I do say that you are very wicked.

The Armory Show opened and Filip Noterdaeme sat at his booth in his Paul Smith suit and wearing the fake beard and thoroughly enjoying talking and listening attentively to one stranger after another and not caring one bit for what they said. The wicked rickety plywood booth stood out among the sleek Armory Show exhibits and many artists and collectors and curators with tired feet sat down on the little kindergarten chair in front of the booth.

Jerry Saltz sat down and showed Filip Noterdaeme a bag of talking popcorn he had collected a little earlier from Nina Katchadourian. That is what she called it, Talking Popcorn. He asked Filip Noterdaeme if he truly felt that performing inside a commercial art fair and not putting anything up for sale would change the art world. Filip Noterdaeme said, you are mistaken I don't do this to change the art world, I do this so the art world won't change me.

Maurizio Cattelan who never wears socks sat down and Filip Noterdaeme showed him his pink socks and Maurizio Cattelan took photographs of him, one after another. And then there was Eric Doeringer, not too popular with the Armory Show because he was a bootleg artist. He was selling his bootlegs outside and it was cold. Filip Noterdaeme offered to bring him a cup of hot coffee and they immediately became friends and have been ever since. They understand each other's work very well and it is rare that two artists ever do.

With everything that was going on I had still not found the time to record the audio tour and so it was not until the eve of our opening at 172 Clinton Street that I finally sat down to do it. When I was finished the sun was rising. I had an hour of sleep and then it was time to get up again and cook and shell 30 mussels and boil and peel 30 eggs for the brunch service. Filip Noterdaeme walked about the apartment looking at everything one last time. He looked at his Homeless Museum and he was very satisfied with it and said, for me it is I, I am the museum and the museum is me, it is the only representation of me which is I, for me. He put on his Paul Smith suit and fake beard and then he decided to quickly vacuum the rooms with the yellow Miele vacuum cleaner before everyone arrived. But before he did, he applied a laminate HOMU logo onto the vacuum cleaner and it made him very happy that now even the vacuum cleaner was a museum piece.

He was still vacuuming when the doorbell rang and we said, who is it. It was Gabrielle Giattino and the little staff from the Swiss Institute. The Homeless Museum is not open yet, we said and, please do come back in fifteen minutes. There were giggles on the intercom and promises to return promptly. Filip Noterdaeme finished vacuuming and I finished peeling the eggs. Then it was time to do my make-up with the special geisha make-up kit from Japan. Applying whiteface with the japanese make-up was at once easier and more difficult. First one had to apply a thin layer of special wax onto the face and neck and then the very fine white powder and finally draw the eyebrows black and paint the lips red. This worked quite well in the beginning until it suddenly did not work all that well. However one must learn the proper technique. Years later it took me only a few minutes to get it just right but until then, it always made me nervous to have to make up my face. Finally I put on my new geisha outfit and we were ready to receive and represent.

Gabrielle Giattino and the little staff from the Swiss Institute returned and I welcomed them all with awkward little Geisha bows. After introductions had been made I gave everybody a headset with the audio tour and everybody wandered about the apartment looking and listening, listening and looking. Everybody seemed pleased and amused, especially Gabrielle and Erin McMonagle, her buoyant irish american assistant. Marc-Olivier Wahler, the swiss director of the Swiss Institute took a particular liking to the Pussy Painting.

And then we sat and waited for the VIP guests of the reservation list to arrive. We waited and waited and finally the Swiss Institute staff needing to be present at the ongoing Armory Show left and Filip Noterdaeme and I continued to wait for the VIPs. I sat at the kitchen counter in front of the long row of small plates with one hard-boiled peeled egg and one shelled cooked mussel on each plate and he paced the floor and began bickering about the smell of the eggs and mussels, he has a reprehensible habit of bickering whenever anything unpleasant happens and always tells me he learned this from real New Yorkers and as I am a loyal New Yorker I can then say nothing. We opened all the windows and it was rather cold sitting there in my thin vintage silk kimono and japanese sandals.

As morning turned into midday a handful of friends whom we had invited to join us for the opening brunch came by and who were they all. Cathleen Chaffee was one of them. We had been hearing a good deal about Cathleen Chaffee. She was a friend of Gabrielle Giattino. She looked at all the exhibits and read all the letters on display in the Archives and she understood everything better than anybody else. She and Filip Noterdaeme enjoyed each other thoroughly. They found out that they both had had and continued to have Broodthaers as their great concep-tual artist. They did not care so much about Beuys, either of them. They had always and still liked Broodthaers. In later years they planned collaborating on a Société des Amis de Broodthaers, a society of the friends of Broodthaers. Filip Noterdaeme still likes to think about this possibility.

Then came Eric Doeringer and a little later a shy young woman with a very sturdy fringe of heavy hair over her forehead, heavy long lashes and a baggy green sweatshirt. She toured the entire museum without saying a single word. When she left, she looked very perplexed but still did not say a word. Who she was we never found out.

We were still hopeful for arrivals of the VIPs when Ed Schmidt the playwright, not the car dealer, came with his son Jack and his daughter Beatrice. We always liked Ed Schmidt. Filip Noterdaeme had gone several times to see his play, The Last Supper, Honest to God Dinner Theater, which Ed had presented in his kitchen in a brownstone in Prospect Park. I had gone with him the second time and Filip Noterdaeme had wickedly refused to tell me what it was all about. The performance began and it was all Ed Schmidt and only Ed Schmidt and he seemed to be quite terrible at trying to act and prepare a meal at the same time and then suddenly there was the miracle of the frozen fish turning into french lamb stew. Ah, there he had me completely fooled.

So now Ed Schmidt had come to our opening. He chatted with Filip Noterdaeme and the children took a ride in the Homeless Simulator. Later Jack sat at the Wurlitzer and played, Hit the Road Jack. And then they left.

Paul Werner came. He looked at everything. Later he wrote in his book, Museum, Inc., that visiting the Homeless Museum was like opening the door to a gust of iced air.

Then it was time for Filip Noterdaeme to rush to

the Armory Show and once more sit at his booth. And so the opening had come and gone and not one of the thirty VIPs who had so eagerly made a reservation for the brunch at the Homeless Museum had shown up. This was a good lesson about art collectors and socialites wanting to be everywhere, not wanting to be anywhere.

When Filip Noterdaeme left that afternoon he took with him one of the audio tour headsets to listen to for the first time. He listened to it on the subway and told me later it had made him laugh so hard that everybody on the subway had been looking at him in a funny way. In any case he left and I stayed behind at 172 Clinton Street and made a big bowl of egg salad with the dozens of leftover peeled hardboiled eggs. Then I closed all the windows and took off the geisha make-up. Then I suddenly realized how tired I was. I was just tired.

When Filip Noterdaeme came home later that evening he was very excited. He had met and talked with someone at the Armory show who was very interested in the ISM, the Incredible Shrinking Museum project. Her name was Stacy Switzer and she was the director of Grand Arts, a nonprofit in Kansas City. Filip Noterdaeme had invited her to come to 172 Clinton Street and take a look at the ISM model. She arrived a little later with her husband Colin and Filip Noterdaeme showed them the glowing model on the light box and it was then that she decided to try to one day have it built in Kansas City. I will tell the whole story of how this almost came to pass and then did not. In any case this first meeting was the beginning of our friendship with Stacy Switzer.

Like I said none of the 30 invited VIPs ever showed up for the brunch. Later we heard that practically every

Armory event held in private studios had had nothing but no-shows that day. However to us this was no consolation. Filip Noterdaeme took the VIP reservation list, declared everyone on it persona non grata at the Homeless Museum and brazenly displayed it in the Archives for everyone to see. A few days later we found a picture of two of the VIPs in the Scene and Herd column from Artforum, art expert Kim Heirston with beautifully straightened hair and carpet tycoon wife Andrea Stark wearing heavy jewelry and a fur coat. We printed out the photograph and displayed it next to the persona non grata list. Every now and then a visitor recognizes Kim or Andrea on the photograph and tells us that they are not all that bad really, as people.

Filip Noterdaeme insisted that we should continue showing the Homeless Museum in our home, and it was in this way that the Sunday openings began. Over the next two years we held quite a few of them. 172 Clinton Street became a haven for the curious the incurious and those in the know and Filip Noterdaeme became a living museum piece, long before Marina Abramovic.

In short in this spring and early summer of two thousand and five the old life was over.

VI

At Home

Our friends did not believe that we would continue to allow strangers into our home at 172 Clinton Street to show them the Homeless Museum. Filip Noterdaeme always tells about Bert the handyman who, doing repairs in our apartment, would regularly every time he came assure us that Paul the landlord was going to force us to close the museum as soon as he found out about it. Once my parents came to visit from Germany and we were having tea. It was the time of the publication of the first write-up about the Homeless Museum in Time Out Magazine and we were all talking about it. Terrified my mother dropped her teacup and cried, and is Paul the landlord now going to try to evict you.

As we knew that Paul the landlord liked to go boating on weekends, taking along his wife, their two children and their black waterdog, we planned accordingly to hold openings only on Sundays. We established a routine. I had to boil and peel a large amount of eggs and cook and shell mussels for the service at Café Broodthaers and put on my Madame Butterfly costume and make-up. Filip Noterdaeme put on his fake beard and a pair of burgundy silk pajamas and disappeared in the Staff and Security Department where he laid down in bed and waited for visitors while reading the papers. There he stayed for the entire duration of the opening. In the meanwhile I simply sat

185

by the kitchen counter and waiting and getting up to open the door and letting visitors in. I usually opened the door to the doorbell and the usual formula was to ask, how did you hear about the museum. The idea was that everybody could come but for form's sake and in New York you have to have a formula, everybody was supposed to be able to mention the name of somebody who had told him about it. It was a mere form, really everybody could come in and as at that time nothing in the museum was of any real value and there was no social privilege attached to knowing anyone there, only those came who really were interested. So as I say anybody could come in, however, there was the formula. I once in opening the door said as I usually did, by whose invitation do you come and I heard an aggrieved voice reply, but by yours, Daniel. He was a young man I had met somewhere and with whom I had had a long conversation and to whom I had given a cordial invitation and then had so promptly forgotten.

Many people came to the openings and who were they all. Artists and groups of museum administrators, it happened that some museum administrator had once been brought to the Homeless Museum and the word had spread from her throughout the little cubicle offices in other museums, any museum where there was a young woman with disappointment about the museum world heard of 172 Clinton Street and then lived but to get there and a great many did get there. They were always there, all degrees of age and intelligence, some very engaging, some very dull, and every now and then a very beautiful middle-aged lesbian. Then there were quantities of young artists, not too popular because they always wanted to look behind the scene and there was no behind the scene, and also they tended to want to steal ideas and Filip Noter-daeme has a horror of people who have no ideas of their own. Then there was a fair sprinkling of New Yorkers, an acquaintance would bring a group, and occasionally a tourist would accidentally get there. And then there were the habitués, among them Georgia Krantz of the Guggenheim Museum, always attentive and charmingly thoughtful, and Eric Doeringer the bootleg artist. Sara Bodinson of MoMA and Colby Chamberlain of PS1 often came. We liked them both.

Sara was one of those admirable MoMA administrators in other words excellent office workers of all tasks, good organizers thoroughly occupied with the welfare of their employers and of themselves, firmly convinced that everything Modern can be made bearable with a stiff drink after work.

Colby was a true New Yorker. Talking about the weather he always said that the degree of comfort he feels could be measured by the number of corduroy layers one had to wear. He and I agree that two layers are optimal.

Nobody who came ever quite knew what to expect at first and there were some who after having seen everything still did not quite know what to think of it. I often wondered whether they thought they were not supposed to know or just did not know.

A visit to the Homeless Museum always began with everyone being weighed on a doctor's scale that was marked with the slogan Pay What You Weigh. We charged one cent per pound. Some visitors the ladies especially were not very fond of our admission policy and there were some who were terribly upset about it and pleaded with me to not say their weight out loud and write it down instead so no one would hear. I remember one short young woman who turned a whiter shade of pale when I told her that her admission would be one dollar and forty-seven cents. This cannot possibly be said she. Well, I said, what did you have for lunch. Her face very rapidly went from white to red and, looking very sheepish she said, I had a burger. I am afraid the burger will have to pay too, I said.

The next thing for me to do was to hand each visitor a HOMU pin-back button and encourage everyone to take the audio tour. The audio tour lasted about 15 minutes and was always a success. Years later Dan Shaw in describing it in The New York Times wrote it was recorded in an academic voice that sounded as if it belonged to a castrato cousin of Philippe de Montebello, the director of the Metropolitan Museum of Art. There were eight headsets and so whenever there were more than eight people touring the museum at a time, which was often, I had to find ways to keep those who were waiting occupied. I usually sent two visitors to the Education Department where they could sit on kindergarten chairs and watch HOMU videos. It was a very effective way to keep them quiet and occupied for a while. If there were more than two people waiting I sent everybody else to the Archives and Meteorology Department to read the Director's open letters and notebooks.

The first two exhibits mentioned in the audio tour were the Pussy Painting and the Homeless Simulator and I always observed everybody's reaction. Sometimes there was nervous laughter, sometimes perplexity. Those who were perplexed usually stayed perplexed throughout their visit and those who laughed continued to laugh.

Everybody had to stop by Café Broodthaers for a serving of the Broodthaers Menu. Usually everybody tried at least something. Some ate everything. In general the mussels were more popular with women and the milk more popular with men. Those who were on a diet, and most americans usually are, did not eat the yolk of the peeled hardboiled egg. While they sat at the café counter I always showed visitors the Membership Department in the freezer, explaining about our cool members and popping the question, would you care to become a member of the Homeless Museum. Many filled out a form and I promised them that we would mail them their membership cards. It was Colby Chamberlain who once arranged for the membership forms of the Homeless Museum to be shown as art objects, at the Rotunda Gallery in Brooklyn Heights. The name of the exhibit was The Dotted Line.

Over the years, the Homeless Museum has acquired a considerable number of members and we like to think that all of them have paid their membership fees directly to a homeless person as instructed on the form. Most signed up for the five dollar membership which we called the friend membership. But there were some who signed up for the 150 dollar membership, the patron circle. Boykin Curry and his wife Celerie Kemble did. We always liked them. They were a couple with many pedigreed New York and Palm Beach connections and first one then two then three delightful children and a little Jack Russel terrier named Anchovy. They loved to eat and they loved my food. They lived in a penthouse on Central Park South that had a very small kitchen and a very green large terrace with a very chic chicken coup on it. Celerie Kemble adored shoes. There were shoes in every closet and in the hallway and under the grand piano and one day I found a lonely pair of Manolo Blahniks in the dishwasher. Filip Noterdaeme delighted in this little story of ingenious cosmopolitan shoe care and asked me to encrust a pair of plexiglas mules with rhinestone letters to spell the word HOME on the right strap and LESS on the left strap. But to get back to our openings at 172 Clinton Street.

The audio tour then led the visitors through all the other exhibits and ending up in the Staff and Security Department. There Filip Noterdaeme sat expecting them, upright in his bed and welcoming them to his office and introducing them to Florence whom we had positioned behind a little microphone stand, and engaging them in lively conversation, always charming always cunning. Every now and then he secretly activated a little sound device under the bed sheets that made Florence appear to be making philosophical observations about generosity and altruism and the ground of our being, wretchedly concluding that we're a flawed species, and all of that in the voices of Lawrence Wiener and Huston Smith.

There was something so strange and attractive about the way Filip Noterdaeme behaved and talked during those long hours in the Staff and Security Department that many visitors became quite enamored and stayed and stayed not wanting to ever leave. It is in bed that he developed his performance technique that later became so notorious when he brought his act to the street. Now it does not matter where he is anymore, he can do it anywhere.

We made it a habit to go out for dinner after everyone had finally left. We usually went to a little fish and chips place nearby and there we ate and gossiped about

the visitors of the day, each of us having been in a different room throughout the opening and thus having had a
different experience. Tell me, oh do tell me, he always
said, how did they react to the audio tour and what did
they say, did they like what they saw and did they laugh.
We sometimes joked that one day we should switch roles.

It was at about that time that I built the Boîte-en-
Valise version of the Modern that Filip Noterdaeme had
first envisioned in the days of the Penny Campaign. It was
an elaborately miniaturized construction and took a long
time to fabricate. It had among many other things a little
Wassily Chair, a Broodthaers egg shell table, a Giacom-
etti, a helicopter, of course, and a tiny little Richard Serra.
The most difficult part was to make everything fold and
fit into a little black cardboard valise. Filip Noterdaeme
called the collection his MoMA HMLSS, as in MoMA
Homeless, and announced that he would display it in
front of the Modern on the first anniversary of its reopening. When the day came, we went to 53rd Street. We took
along the valise and Florence with her little microphone
stand and the sound device. We stood there for many
hours and Florence appeared to be repeatedly asking,
HAS. ANYBODY. SEEN. LOWRY, a funny sound bite
I had taken from Brazil, the Terry Gilliam movie. All in
all MoMA HMLSS was a perfect expression of the inside
of the Modern for those kept on the outside. But first it
traveled with us to Kansas City.

We went upon the invitation of Stacy Switzer of
Grand Arts to meet with Margaret Hall Silva, the Hall-
mark heiress and founder of Grand Arts, and talk to
her about the ISM, The Incredible Shrinking Museum.
When we passed through security at the airport with the

little black cardboard valise all hell broke loose. I remember catching a glimpse of the x-ray monitor with MoMA HMLSS showing on it. It looked very beautiful with transparent layered textures and shapes and ever since then I have been obsessed with getting a print of an X-ray of MoMA HMLSS. In any case the security very sharply asked us about the steel blades and Filip Noterdaeme very patiently explained to them that they were not blades but a miniature Richard Serra. Oh it's only art they said, very relieved and maybe a little disappointed, and finally we were allowed to board the plane with the valise.

It was an odd trip. We flew on Midwest Airlines and the seats on the plane were extra wide which perhaps had something to do with midwesterners being extra wide. This was curiously in accord with the stewardess handing out warm chocolate chip cookies that I remember being awfully sweet.

We arrived in Kansas City. Stacy Switzer always charming, charming as an artistic director and charming as an inexperienced hostess came to meet us. She first drove us to Grand Arts to show us the guest quarters and the workshop and then we drove to her home for a homemade fish taco dinner. We were very nervous about being in Kansas City and Stacy Switzer was very nervous about cooking for us. When we got there her husband Colin who was a dear introduced us to their two adopted mutts, Seal and Mousse. Seal and Mousse were not used to guests and got into quite a happy loud state. And then Stacy Switzer realized that she had forgotten to turn off the oven and that the fish had by then been baking for 3 hours. It came out quite a bit on the dry side but the evening was rather pleasant nevertheless and we all felt much more relaxed after having eaten and laughed about Stacy's dry fish. When she came to New York a year later we took her to dinner at Esca where the chefs had commenced serving crudo, italian style raw fish.

On our second day in Kansas City we had our meeting with Margaret Hall Silva. She had a pit bull named Samson and both her and Samson were very serious and firm and liked to sit. Samson had a little condition of the bowels and everybody politely pretended not to notice until Filip Noterdaeme said, I believe Samson is letting loose one Delilah after another. We all laughed and held our noses and then Filip Noterdaeme presented MoMA HMLSS and Margaret Hall Silva was very interested in its miniatures. Her mother had been an avid collector of miniatures of all kinds and there was in Kansas City a museum full of her dolls and dollhouses and things. Then she and Filip Noterdaeme discussed the ISM and she said, well let's see if we can make this happen but it really does look like you will need an awful lot of orange glycerin soap and I will also need to talk to my lawyer about liabilities. After all, we don't want anyone to slip, fall and sue, she said.

We flew back to New York and once again sat in the extra wide seats of Midwest Airlines and were served the same awfully sweet chocolate chip cookies. We wondered a great deal about the trip and the meeting. Filip Noterdaeme wanted to see the ISM built so badly but he wondered if Kansas City was the right place. He was terribly worried and agitated. I remembered the sock method my neighbor across the backyard at 971 Amsterdam Avenue had used and put an open newspaper, I think it was the Kansas City Star, over Filip Noterdaeme's lap and with my right hand and my left sock did my best to make him relax. The stewardess was going up and down the isle and I was going up and down as well and so there was a lot of coming and going on the plane. When we landed in New York I was only wearing one sock. I can still remember the cold draft on my left ankle when we stepped out of the plane. And now I must tell of how I got paid to sing on the sidewalk on Fifth Avenue.

Scott Gutterman the deputy director of the Neue Galerie called and asked, would you be willing to perform on the street in front of the Neue during the Museum Mile Festival. I said, why certainly with pleasure. The Neue Galerie installed a big sound system for me on the corner of Fifth Avenue and 86th Street and I sang german cabaret songs with David Pearl playing the keyboard for one whole afternoon. Fifth Avenue was full of people walking up and down from one big museum to another and they all stopped by to hear me sing and once they stopped they usually stayed to listen until the end of my set. Filip Noterdaeme walked around selling CDs of my Berlin concert and he was a very good salesperson. I sang one song after another and then a little girl started dancing in front of me and this became a bit of a distraction for me and the audience. And so I took her by the hand and danced a little waltz with her and then swung her around and around in the air. Naturally she got a little scared and quickly ran back to her mother a little dizzy and a little wiser and that was the end of that.

We had been looking for a photographer to come to 172 Clinton and take pictures of the museum and we also wanted a portrait of us disguised as the Director and Madame Butterfly. Harry Heissmann who had in the meanwhile moved to New York and was beginning to find recognition as an interior designer said, call Russel Gera, he is famous for using only natural lighting.

Russel Gera was a tall man, very tall because he was industrious and he had the long thin legs that give the characteristic beauty to all norwegian men. It was rather a pity that full beards later became fashionable again because until then one could plainly see in him the beautifully angled facial features of the average northern european male without it being obscured by facial hair. Men with beards always look like pussies to me. We hired him and to this day no one has photographed the Homeless Museum better than he. It was he who shot the delightfully funny double portrait of Filip Noterdaeme and myself in bed that I staged to be reminiscent of Pierre et Gilles' La Panne, The Breakdown.

It was the end of July and time for our summer vacation. Once again we went to Italy. We spent a few days in Tuscany with Filip Noterdaeme's older brother and his companion. We rented a car and took daytrips to Florence and Lucca and once had a wonderful dinner in a restaurant on a hilltop that was very difficult to find. I wanted to at least see the mediterranean and so after a few days Filip Noterdaeme and I went on to Cinqueterre. We stayed in Corneglia and took daytrips in one or the other direction. After four days we had seen everything to our right and everything to our left and thought, where do we go from here. We heard of a charming hotel near Como and placed a phone call. Yes, they said, we have vacancies. We traveled several hours by train and bus to get there and when we arrived at the hotel, it was vacancies all over. The owner, charming and polite, handed us the keys to our room with balcony on the second floor and we went upstairs. There was nothing wrong with the room or the view but there was also something not quite right. Wrong or right, said Filip Noterdaeme, I am not staying here. We went back downstairs and I charmingly politely returned the keys to the owner and said, regrets but we cannot stay. We took the next bus back to Como. In short, we came, we saw, we left.

We have had since then a few other misadventures with hotels. There was the time we had booked a room in a hotel in eastern Bavaria and when we arrived and went up to inspect the room the owner's dog had just relieved himself right in front of it. Naturally we didn't stay. And then there was the incident where we were compelled to leave a hotel room in the middle of the night. That hotel was the Waldorf Astoria in New York, but I will come to that later.

That evening in Como we spent long hours looking for a good restaurant that was open for business. We found that in this way, Como in August had very much in common with Paris in August. We took the last train to Milan and there we had another most unpleasant hotel experience where we should have left in the middle of the night but did not, we were just tired.

We were back in New York and one day there was suddenly water on the dining room floor. Evidently it had been raining and there was a leak in the roof. I placed a bowl on the floor to collect the dripping water. The bowl quickly filled up with yellowish water and we called Paul the landlord. He never liked it when we called with a problem and once told us there was nothing a roll of duct tape could not fix. Well. We showed him the leak and the bowl of yellowish water and to his great regret duct tape clearly would not do this time. A few days later he climbed onto the roof with a bucket of something black and Filip Noterdaeme said, oh Paul the landlord is applying shoe polish onto the roof and let's see how long it holds. For a while the ceiling did not drip. I say it did not drip for a while but sooner or later it started all over again and this went off and on for several years until, not many months ago, it was leaks everywhere and a part of the ceiling collapsed in the Archives and Meteorology Department. In any case at the time of the yellow water leak Filip Noterdaeme combining the sarcasm of amusement with the indulgence of contempt filled the yellow water into little glass flacons and labeled them Liquid Gold, Anonymous Donation to the Homeless Museum.

In the meanwhile Marina Abramovic spent a whole week doing reenactments at the Guggenheim Museum. She had not yet become the Sarah Palin of the art world and it was several years before her Baked Alaska but she was already calling herself the grandmother of performance art. Filip Noterdaeme went to see what it was all about and there was Marina doing five easy pieces by other artists and two of her own. She reenacted Joseph Beuys talking to a dead rabbit from 1965 and Vito Acconci masturbating from 1972 and one day she reenacted her own Lips of Thomas, a favorite from 1975 where she was flogging herself and bleeding a little here and there and eating honey and finally lying down on a cross made of ice blocks.

The next day when Filip Noterdaeme went back to the Guggenheim to give a VIP tour to Carlo Tunioli and the Bennetton family he saw Marina's bloody ice blocks melting away in the gutter by the staff entrance. He quickly ran to a nearby supermarket on Madison Avenue to buy a freezer bag and put one of the ice blocks into it. He then showed the united colors of Guggenheim to the Bennetton family and then excitedly hurried home with Marina's ice block. At 172 Clinton Street he immediately placed the rescued ice block in the Membership Department, next to the membership forms and the Proust, and for several days thought of nothing but of what to do with it. Then one day he took the ice block out of the freezer placed it in a bowl and watched it melt and then filled the water into glass flacons, the same kind he had already used for Liquid Gold. He named the water Eau d'Abramovic Facial Tonic and I made labels for the bottles and we put them on display next to the Liquid Gold bottles.

I was preparing my fourth show for Café Sabarsky and decided to create a one-man version of Weill and Brecht's Seven Deadly Sins. This had never been done before, as a matter of fact it had been written for a full orchestra with a male quartet, a mezzo-soprano, a ballerina and a corps de ballet. I began looking for a pianist and asked John Cameron Mitchell if perhaps he knew of someone. He told me of Christopher Hamblin, a young precocious pianist from Tennessee.

Christopher Hamblin was still new to New York City. He had a very alert slightly manic presence. I remember how once when we invited him for Thanksgiving he would not touch my pumpkin soup. He was very adamant about it. He often talked about his first night in New York where he had met everybody and done all the New York things he had always wanted to do and how the night had ended with breakfast at a diner sitting next to John

Cameron Mitchell, Justin Bond and Rufus Wainwright. This had created all kinds of expectations in him that of course did not come through and he became very restless.

We rehearsed tirelessly. I wrote a new translation of the libretto and Christopher Hamblin learned to play the rather difficult score. I was Anna I and the family chorus, that is the father, the mother, and the two brothers, and Christopher Hamblin was Anna II. We gave a preview performance at Michael Warner's salon in Chelsea. As expected there were many queer radicals with facial hair and glittery makeup present and everybody was curious. Christopher Hamblin was extremely nervous and I was not. The house of cards that I used as a prop collapsed just in the right moment, at the end of the epilogue, and there was a beautiful collective sigh and then, applause.

The next day we opened at Café Sabarsky. We had a success and Limor Tomer said, why don't you bring your version of The Seven Deadly Sins to the Brooklyn Academy of Music next month, Ute Lemper will be performing it with the Brooklyn Symphony Orchestra and you could go on in the BAMCafé right after her. That way, she said, the audience will first see the old-fashioned regular version and then yours, so different but so familiar. We signed a new contract and it was only a few days later that my phone rang. It was Limor Tomer and she said, the Neue Galerie has received a letter from Schott Music Publishing. What is it, I said. They are threatening to sue if we continue presenting your show, she said. But why would they sue, I said. Because they say, she said, that The Seven Deadly Sins can only be performed by a female singer and a full orchestra. Well. I wrote to Schott and argued with them but they replied, cease and desist, and Limor got very nervous and everything was cancelled, the remaining Sabarsky shows and the Brooklyn show. Christopher Hamblin who had put in so many hours to learn to play the piano score of The Seven Deadly Sins moved back to his family in Tennessee, grew a beard and became the musical director of a church that allowed him to play Dolly Parton songs.

In the meanwhile upstairs at the Neue Galerie offices there was excitement of another kind. Director Renée Price had become quite mad about Milly von Barsky her new pet schnauzer. She commissioned designers to create special Milly von Barsky doggie items for the museum shop. There was the collectible Milly von Barsky doll for four hundred and fifty dollars and a weekender dog apothecary in a hand-stitched pebbled calfskin travel case with green silk moiré for seven hundred and ninety-five dollars and of course the glass-beaded dog collar for two thousand four hundred dollars. Milly became notorious for unraveling rolls of toilet paper in the bathrooms but whenever somebody remonstrated Renée Price roused like a lioness defending her cub.

And now I must tell you about the HOMU Outreach Program. As with the Met's outreach program it was all about sharing culture but Filip Noterdaeme had culture of an entirely different kind on his mind. He had read about wild yeast cultures and instantly decided that the Homeless Museum should have its own sourdough starter or mother, as bakers call it. He said, we must capture and nurture the wild cultures inside the Homeless Museum and share them with the needy. The sourdough mother was thriving in no time and soon I was able to bake a fresh loaf of sourdough bread every week. Now,

Filip Noterdaeme said, we are ready to reach out. We went to Central Park with half a loaf of the HOMU Bread and Filip Noterdaeme fed it to the pigeons. It was an instant success and Filip Noterdaeme said, how remarkable, they are just as receptive to the HOMU Outreach Program as the sick, the dying and the underprivileged used to be when I reached out to them on behalf of the Metropolitan Museum of Art.

It was at about this time that Filip Noterdaeme went to Paula Cooper to see the latest work of my compatriot Hans Haacke. It had been a long time since Haacke had invented institutional critique and by now he had become an institution himself. The show was all about american flags and Filip Noterdaeme said to me, I believe Herr Haacke has lost his bite, his show simply, very simply does not cut the mustard. And then, with a mischievous grin, could you create a Haacke 'n Das ice cream. Well of course I can, I said. I took out my little ice cream maker and created a honey-mustard ice cream with custard, honey, a touch of Dijon mustard and a few roasted mustard seeds for added crunch. Filip Noterdaeme designed a Haacke 'n Das ice cream container and we began offering a little scoop of it for dessert at Café Broodthaers during the Sunday openings. I always delighted in watching everybody's facial expressions as they tasted the Haacke 'n Das, all honey and cream at first and then suddenly all mustard and bite. I remember one astonished-looking young woman shaking her head, saying again and again, that is just so wrong. Nobody ever asked for seconds.

The long eventful year drew to a close. Boykin Curry invited me to come to the Dominican Republic to oversee a big dinner event he was going to host there. He had just bought a 2,200-acre plot of land on the north coast of the island named Playa Grande and wanted to show it off to find investors and realize his dream of building a social utopia for hip millionaires. There were going to be over one hundred of his friends and acquaintances from New York and one reporter from the New Yorker, witty shy Ben McGrath.

And so on Christmas Day Filip Noterdaeme and I boarded a plane to the Dominican Republic and it was filled with cheerfully loud dominicans carrying Christmas gift packages with big bows. Next to us sat a young blond woman with blue eyes and freckles. She introduced herself and said, I believe we have the same destination. Her name was Charlotte Morgan and she was a friend of Boykin Curry's. Naturally this being Christmas Day our flight was delayed a great many minutes and so we sat and waited and chatted and waited some more and then finally the plane took off.

We arrived in Santa Domingo very late at night. Boykin Curry had arranged for a driver to bring us and Charlotte Morgan to the hotel and when we saw the driver Filip Noterdaeme said to me in french, il a l'air d'un Botero, he looks like a Botero. A false Botero, I said. We drove a very long three hours through the night and the road was full of potholes. Charlotte Morgan told us she was a producer on a little television show. What show, we asked. Oh, she said, you probably have not heard of it, it's called Charlie Rose. Ah, the Charlie Rose, we said, with long hands like a basketball player and a double-breasted Ralph Lauren suit like a Wall Street banker and a penchant for beautiful actresses like Catherine Deneuve. And then finally the Botero driver pulled into the parking lot of our hotel and we said thank you and good night and see you mañana.

The next day I went to examine the kitchen at the golf club where I was to cook the large dinner. When I arrived the kitchen staff was busily preparing a large pot of lobster bisque. I introduced myself and everybody was very polite and a little wary. The cooks showed me around the kitchen and there stood a beautifully large new blender. Oh, a Waring, I said, can I use that. Sì sì, they said, their faces full of satisfaction, claro que puedes. Then I went outside to look at the view from the terrace and when I returned there was mayhem in the kitchen, lobster bisque everywhere, on the ceiling, on the floor and on the stack of parchment paper baking sheets I had brought with me to bake my famous biscotti. What happened, I said. Oh, nada, nada they said sheepishly. Very evidently the top of the Waring had blown off while the machine was running. Sure, I said to them in half english half spanish, when you puree a soup for the first time, it is so easy making it that you forget holding down the top and it is bound to make a mess, but those who see it blow up once don't have to worry about it and they can do it safely.

Then the Botero driver arrived to take me to the market where I saw yucca, plantains and papayas and to my great astonishment a real traditional german Schwarzwälder Kirschtorte. I also remember seeing a woman in a flowery dress stirring milk and sugar in a very large caldron set over an open fire and a little old man frying cheese empanadas, one after another. I bought everything that pleased my fancy and the Botero driver took me back to the golf club and I began preparations for the big dinner.

Philip Rubin, nobody quite knew why he had been invited, he was the son of famous former Treasury Secretary Robert Rubin. He had become a chef and married a cook, Lauren, but he was a typical son of a millionaire, brooding and insecure. One evening during our stay at Playa Grande he overheard someone say something that outraged his feelings and after that he hated everything about the whole operation. He said the remark had been very offensive, no one could deny that, and he could not bear it any longer. We showed him every mark of sympathy and he grudgingly agreed to teach the little cooking class Boykin Curry had asked him to do, however no one being all that interested in his class only sympathetic Rebecca Lieberman attended it. He then prepared a bread pudding that was extraordinarily bad. In any case there was no need for another dessert because everybody was deeply satisfied with the four-course menu and three kinds of dessert I had served. A year later we heard that Philip Rubin and his wife had started their own catering company and published a cookbook about apples but I had seen the worm in the apple and was not interested.

Then there was actor Christopher Meloni with his wife and young son Dante. Dante was a very noisy child and I can still hear Christopher Meloni's famous voice continuously calling out his name in reprimand and how every time he did Filip Noterdaeme muttered under his breath, Inferno.

We returned to New York just in time for me to sing a few songs at Florent's restaurant on New Years Eve. Tony Lauria played the accordion and I sang a very popular song by the Propellerheads, History Repeating. When it was about a quarter to midnight the waiters began passing out funny hats and flutes and we made a very quick escape.

It was a new year and the New Yorker published witty Ben McGrath's article about Boykin Curry's Playa Grande utopia and there was much gossip about Boykin Curry's vision of an updated athenian village where, as Ben McGrath had slyly written, op-ed columnists David Brooks or Thomas Friedman might gather to discuss anti-terrorism strategy with Fareed Zakaria or Charlie Rose and then join Moby and Michael Stipe for a concert on the beach. Boykin Curry became a little more wary of talking about Playa Grande to journalists after that.

Filip Noterdaeme in those days liked to entertain himself by coming up with rules for museum visitors and writing them down in his notebooks. There were countless do's and don'ts and they were all very funny. I decided to make a scrolling text video of the transcripts and began showing it on a flat screen monitor in the Main Hall above the cheeky Morgue & Library. We called the video Museum Policies and it made everybody chuckle.

The Sunday openings at 172 Clinton Street continued. Since everybody who came to the Homeless Museum always insisted on coming back with somebody to experience everything once more our live-in museum had by now become an open secret and reporters began inquiring about it. We had already had our first write up in Time Out Magazine in which Liz Webster had written that the Homeless Museum was raising the roof and now Vincent Trivet of the L Magazine wrote about the Homeless Museum in greater detail, explaining that it was something else altogether than what one might expect. Needless to say lesser publications like Brooklyn 24 Seven also wrote about us.

The Brooklyn 24 Seven story is rather funny. Filip Noterdaeme had received a call from someone from the editorial office asking for pictures of the Homeless Museum for an article and he had sent them a copy of Russel Gera's double portrait of the two of us in bed. Naturally we expected that a reporter from Brooklyn 24 Seven would come and interview Filip Noterdaeme sooner or later for the article but no one ever called or came. We had all but forgotten about it when one morning on my way to the bagel shop I saw our double portrait on the front page of the new Brooklyn 24 Seven issue on every news box on every corner. The headline, if I remember rightly, was Serious Nonsense, Inside the Hallowed Halls of the Homeless Museum. We thought this was rather strange as no one from the paper had ever been inside the Homeless Museum. Luckily, Paul the landlord did not seem to take any notice of it.

Petite Samantha Topol, however, when she wrote about the Homeless Museum, interviewed Filip Noterdaeme many times at 172 Clinton Street, in spring, summer and fall. When the article was finally finished she did not know what to do with it and Filip Noterdaeme said, send it to the Believer Magazine. She did and the Believer promptly published it.

I was very pleased when Andrew Potter from Canada came with his partner Elizabeth Wasserman one Sunday. I had read and liked his book Nation of Rebels and was excited to welcome him to the Homeless Museum. Andrew Potter had a deep understanding of how counterculture had created mass consumerism. He loved making fun of Naomi Klein and hated everything that presented itself as authentic. I showed them the HOMU Shop with the inauthentic Director's Cut cigarettes that Filip Noterdaeme had stuffed with clippings of his pubic hair and Elizabeth Wasserman said with an intelligent inner smile, how extraordinary. I liked her instantly and had a feeling that perhaps she was Andrew Potter's secret weapon.

This brings me to the spring of 2006 when Christie's was putting a collection of Donald Judd pieces up for auction. I had always adored Donald Judd's sculptures. I liked their deceiving simplicity and uncompromising exactitude and had greatly enjoyed fabricating a miniature Donald Judd replica out of tiny little green rectangular plastic prisms for MoMA HMLSS. We went to see the exhibit and I liked it quite a lot. When we left, Filip Noterdaeme gingerly pocketed the reference copy of the auction catalogue. In it was a listing of the starting bids and he showed me how some were as high as one and a half million dollars. The auction catalogue also had a reprint of an interesting essay by Donald Judd from 1977 in which he said, my works are simply art and not on the market, not for sale, not subject to the ignorance of the public and not open to perversion. One week later Filip Noterdaeme returned to Christie's with a class of students from New York University to show them the Judds and one student pointed at them and proudly loudly declared that she had a CD rack from IKEA that looked just like that. One year later Filip Noterdaeme created a series of minimalist sculpture that would put an end to all such comparisons. But more of that later.

In the meanwhile I had been doing one Weimar-style cabaret show after another and felt eager to sing a more modern repertoire. I became very interested in the songs of the late pop countertenor Klaus Nomi and began looking for a musician who could rearrange and play Nomi's songs for me. One night at a show at Galapagos in Williamsburg there was among other performers a very handsome young man singing and playing the keyboard and it was completely contemporary. This was Rami Ramirez. He did not know me and he did not know Nomi but he agreed to work with me and find completely contemporary ways to play his songs. The next thing to do was to find someone who could give me lessons in countertenor singing. I called Ira Siff.

Ira Siff had made a name for himself as Madame Galupe-Borszkh the diva of the famous all male opera company La Gran Scena. He had since then become a co-host of the Live from the Met broadcast on National Public Radio. He loved lyrical opera and hated concrete music. His bohemian apartment in the East Village was filled with memorabilia, there were many posters from his days with the La Gran Scena and a framed letter from Renata Tebaldi that was his delight. He listened to me singing all but one scale and simply said, my dear child you are not a countertenor, you are what we call a tenore di grazia.

I worked tirelessly for several weeks, vocalizing with Ira Siff and rehearsing with Rami Ramirez, and then we had our first Klaus Nomi concert, at Galapagos. Rami Ramirez played contemporary arrangements on his keyboard and I sang the Cold Song and Do You Nomi Now etcetera. We had a success and soon repeated the show at other places with bad sound systems and unruly audiences. There were good nights and bad nights. On the bad nights I sounded more like a drowning cat than a countertenor and I was always very nervous before each show not knowing if it would be a Nomi night or a cat night. We also brought the show to the BAMCafé and there it was all Nomi for a long time and then suddenly it was not any more. In any case it was a success alright and when Karen Brooks Hopkins the director of the Brooklyn Academy of Music was being honored at a luncheon in East Hampton in the early summer Rami Ramirez and I were invited to present an excerpt of our Klaus Nomi act. We went and it was there that I first met Jonah Bokaer.

I remember very well the first impression I had of Jonah Bokaer. He was an extraordinarily good-looking young man, twenty-six years old. It was not long after that that everybody was middle-aged. It became the period of being middle-aged. During the next two or three years everybody we met was middle-aged. There were one or two under twenty, for example Juan Olivares but they did not count as Filip Noterdaeme carefully explained to them. If they were young men, they were twenty-six. Soon, very soon, they would be middle-aged.

So Jonah was twenty-six, tall and athletic, looking rather like a young frenchman perhaps because his haircut was french or at least his clothes. He had been a Merce Cunningham disciple and protégé and had that elegant distinguished poise only a Cunningham dancer can have. Jonah knew how to give the nicest flattering compliments and when he worked, which was most of the time, he worked with measured precision. We immediately became friends and have been interested in each other's work ever since.

During all this time Filip Noterdaeme had been in correspondence with Stacy Switzer of Grand Arts about the Incredible Shrinking Museum, a project that would portray the museum world in so tenuous a fashion that it would induce an understanding of its imminent self-implosion. They had been and were still waiting for Matthias Hollwich to gather the necessary information as to how to build it out of glycerin soap, nothing but glycerin soap. Stacy Switzer always patient always anticipating said to Filip Noterdaeme, why don't you in the meanwhile come to Kansas City with Florence and create a special event to introduce the Homeless Museum to Kansas City. We went and brought with us Florence Coyote. There, we created a Homeless Museum for a day using highlights from 172 Clinton Street. It was called HOMU Cribs and completely influenced by Jan Hoet's Chambres d'Amis. The name however was taken from MTV Cribs, the popular television show about the homes of the rich and famous. We had five homes of volunteers to work in, one day to set everything up, one morning for the official HOMU Cribs tour and one afternoon to break everything down. It was endlessly amusing. Over fifty people came to take part in the HOMU Cribs tour and among them were two curious nuns. It was a very hot day. Florence looked very regal in a beautiful large vintage pram that Grand Arts had bought for her and Filip Noterdaeme naturally in his pink Paul Smith suit and wearing his fake beard conducted the tour with her at the helm. They went from home to home, from museum department to museum department and everybody was looking and asking questions. HOMU Cribs concluded with a feeding of HOMU Bread to gold fish in a backyard pond with a recording of the rants of a New York Subway panhandler playing in the background.

The next day we left Kansas City in hopes of one day

returning to see the ISM realized.

It was at that time that Matthias Hollwich who prides himself of being eternally selfless declared that he ought to get shared credit for the concept of the ISM. No, said Filip Noterdaeme, you had nothing to do with the concept, what I had asked you to do is to find a solution on how to build it the way I conceived it. But, said Matthias, I wouldn't know how to do that. Then what, said Filip Noterdaeme, are you doing in my project. Stacy Switzer arranged for a lawyer to settle the dispute but by then the dispute had turned into war and as may well be imagined things quickly turned from bad to worse. Finally there was nothing else to do but fire the architect but by that time Margaret Silva Hall's patience had worn thin and much to Stacy Switzer's regret the project had to be cancelled.

In the meanwhile my parents having sold the beautifully modern house on the little french island had been looking and looking in other places to buy another summerhouse. They had looked in southern Spain and in southern France but wherever they went it had been too hot or too crowded or too expensive. Finally they said, it's no use, we still like the little french island best. They returned to the island and bought a small modern house close to the harbor. I said to Filip Noterdaeme, hay fever or not, we really ought to give it another try as well. We went and stayed at a charming little renovated pied-à-terre summer rental with moroccan furnishings and a german washing machine.

We did have a good time on the island. Filip Noterdaeme completely forgot his early dismal memories of the island and has liked visiting there immensely ever since.

That same summer we also traveled to Munich for a

few days and the most surprising thing there was the Isar river, it was so much cleaner than I remembered it. We also visited the delightfully absurd Valentin Musäum and had a traditional bavarian luncheon of weisswurst pretzels and beer at the museum's tower café. The weisswurst were served floating in a large clay pot filled with steaming hot water and Filip Noterdaeme remarked, how peculiar. I said, no, not for Bavaria. Just a few days later we visited a thermal bath in the bavarian countryside and sure enough we spotted a great many sallow looking elderly men and women afloat in the steaming hot water of the shallow pools.

We were back in New York and the next thing that happened was a call from a reporter from a japanese television station. Her name was Miyuki Nomura and she said she wanted to do a little feature on the Homeless Museum. I was terrified, simply terrified at the thought of being filmed in geisha drag for japanese television. Filip Noterdaeme said, it doesn't matter it's only television. Miyuki Nomura very petite and polite arrived with her camera team. She was very curious about everything and everything about us was curious to her. They stayed for a long time, filming everything and interviewing Filip Noterdaeme on camera. Later Miyuki Nomura sent us a video copy of the feature but it was all in japanese and only years later we finally had a friend who was able to translate it for us. This was Ashley Rawlings, and afterwards Filip Noterdaeme said, I knew it was a wonderful feature in japanese, but it is even, well, I cannot say almost really more wonderful but just as wonderful in english.

It was at about that time that Filip Noterdaeme and I did a presentation about HOMU where we finally switched roles. He had been asked by Marc-Olivier Wahler of the Swiss Institute to talk about HOMU to a group of graduates from the curatorial studies program at Bard College and we decided I should go as the Museum Director in his pink Paul Smith suit and fake beard and he as Madame Butterfly in wig, whiteface and kimono. We had a very amusing time dressing up and made fun of how we much we resembled one another. At the Swiss Institute I did all the talking and Filip Noterdaeme sat quietly demurely next to me. Everybody listened and looked at us with polite, slightly vexed expressions on their faces. At the end of the presentation I revealed that we had taken them for a ride and that he was I and I was he. At that, they lost it, they just lost it and told us they thought we were completely and totally out of our minds.

We heard that Etta James was going to perform at B.B. King's on 42nd Street. It was going to be her first concert since she had had her stomach stapled to lose weight and we were curious to see how the surgery had changed her. We went and there was Casimir and his partner Rachid. They were a very odd couple that had once come to one of my shows at Café Sabarsky. We thought they were interesting. I remember my first impression of Casimir very well. He looked like a sailor from a Nineteenth-century novel, wearing a long dark coat over a wife beater. He had steel blue eyes with more than a touch of madness in them. Rachid was a cheerful R&B singer who idolized Marlene Dietrich and wore his afro platinum blond yet no matter what he did he never looked like Dietrich in Blonde Venus. We all sat down and ordered drinks and fried food.

Then the music started and Etta James appeared,

very thin, very girlish and very coy. She wore tight jeans and a petite red tube top that kept rolling up and exposing her belly button. Who is responsible for dressing this poor woman I said to Filip Noterdaeme, and just then Etta James announced, I want to thank Norma Kamali who is here tonight for creating this outfit for me. Filip Noterdaeme was delighted when Etta sang Sugar on the Floor but he said she had been so much more sweet and low when she was a big mama in a sequined muumuu.

We saw Casimir and Rachid again the next Sunday when they came to our opening at 172 Clinton Street. They came and Casimir was quite overcome by the Homeless Museum and told us of the time he and his twin brother who he said was now in a mental institution had been homeless in Los Angeles. When Casimir signed our guest book he wrote a little mad poem into it, all in large script: TO BE BEREFT, STRIPPED OF EPAULETTES, TO SEE ALL IN THEIR, YOUR NAKEDNESS, TO BEG, TO FEIGN TO CHOOSE AS BEGGARS MUST DO, TO SLEEP IN CHURCH PEWS, TO WASH IN CUSTOMER-ONLY BATHROOMS, TO STINK IN UNWASHED CLOTHES, TO HUNGER AND DRINK WARM WATER THE COLOR OF COCA COLA, TO BE FREE TO BE LOST, TO BE. Casimir also gave us a print of an Egon Schiele drawing of a little girl in a red dress. Filip Noterdaeme liked it well enough but he did not start loving it until he bought a fried egg look-alike made of rubber and glued it onto the Schiele print, now calling it Egg on Schiele. Later Filip Noterdaeme also created a Francis Bacon With Extra Bacon.

I had throughout those years continued to pay regular visits to Evee Lynn in her little studio on 57th Street where she had lived since 1952. The studio had no kitchen because Evee Lynn did not care about preparing food, she preferred calling for take-out delivery. However she delighted in my home-cooked food whenever I brought her some. We talked about everything, about life and America and her history of growing up an orphan in Vienna and Berlin and having then been trained to become a ballerina and survived the war and how she had become an international varieté star in the Fifties and then had had a nervous breakdown and gone through electroshock therapy in the Sixties. One day I brought her a Sony so she could begin recording her remembrances for her memoirs. Evee Lynn teased me and said, naturally you want me to write my memoirs because I had this amazing talent and had to work hard all my life while you always had it easy because you're a lucky child.

Then one day Evee Lynn and I quarreled vehemently and she was very adamant about not wanting to ever see me again. When I die, she said, don't you dare come to my funeral and if you do anyway believe me I will know it. She returned my letters unopened but not before writing on them, forget that I exist. Over a year went by and then one day the phone rang. It was Evee Lynn and she said, alright I need your help, you must bring me to the dentist. And so our friendship was renewed and we have been very close ever since.

The Bilbao case was more difficult. Bilbao had for a long time been a tormented and not particularly sympathetic city. It was very poor and very backwards and naturally desperate and willing. Thomas Krens who wanted to expand the Guggenheim brand was invited by the basques, Frank Gehry was able to come along and help not a little. He was very eager.

It was at this time that Thomas Krens undertook it to save Bilbao and he made contacts with all the basque tourist bureaus that were still in business. And for a moment Bilbao was saved and became the newest european destination. Everybody went or planned to go or said they were planning to go and everybody, in a funny kind of way, began talking about the Bilbao effect. Filip Noterdaeme did not as a matter of fact feel like going to Bilbao. He said he had had enough hearing about museums hiring star architects, he would content himself with adding a new wing to his own museum without the help of any architect. And so this was the story of the creation of the Chicken Wing and now for the story from the visitor's point of view as told some months after by Meow Meow. She happened to be in town for the unveiling of the Chicken Wing and so she came by with one of her fans, an australian lesbian with short brown hair who lived in Shanghai. I showed Meow Meow and her fan around the museum and it was very exciting to show one genius the work of another. Meow Meow instinctively understood everything about the Homeless Museum, its precariousness and its audacity. Her fan said that the Homeless Museum would be a big success in Shanghai even though no one would understand it. Then I led the two into the Staff and Security Department and there was Filip Noterdaeme sitting up in bed as always during openings and also this time a red ribbon on the floor leading towards the blinded window. Ah, Meow Meow, Filip Noterdaeme said with a radiant smile, with the body of a french ballerina and a voice like a russian belter, of course you must take a look at my museum's new extension. And he pulled up the blinds and there was the Chicken Wing, a perfectly cooked chicken wing attached to a wire hanger extending from the windowsill and bouncing in the wind. At that, Meow Meow did a developpé à la seconde to show Filip Noterdaeme her perfect ballerina extension. Before she and her fan left I asked Meow Meow to sign our guest book. She wrote, homeless (verité) Meow.

It was at about that time that the New Museum re-opened and broke new ground on the Bowery. We went to see it and all I remember from our visit is a large green-lit elevator that made very unpleasant loud bell tones every time its doors opened or closed onto the lobby and the galleries above and below. Also that everything at the New Museum even the elevator was named after a donor. This was not an entirely new thing to do but the New Museum was doing it more than even the Modern, as a matter of fact a year later Lisa Philips Philips the director of the New Museum renamed her directorial title after philanthropist auto insurance trustee Toby Devan Lewis, and Filip Noterdaeme upon hearing this promptly renamed his own directorial title after Jesus Christ.

Shortly after our first visit to the new New Museum Filip Noterdaeme began thinking of inventing a new museum of his own. He wanted it to be a complete reflection of the future, naturally concluding that it would have no art and be all façade, solely concerned with image and surface. He named it the Newest Museum and asked me to build an architectural model for it. The finished model looked very futuristic, all façade with digital projections and the illusion of a full house with dummies going up and down little electronic escalators. Many americans did not understand Filip Noterdaeme's idea of the Newest unless he mentioned the Wizard of Oz. Then they inevitably said, oh you mean to say it is all about that man behind the curtain.

Filip Noterdaeme called the offices of Creative Time to present the idea and model of the Newest to Director Anne Pasternak who was always on the lookout for new public art projects. We had once before had a meeting with her about the Homeless Museum but she, having an aversion to anything related to homelessness, had encouraged Filip Noterdaeme to come back another time with a more pleasing creative project.

We arrived at the offices and were asked to sit in the waiting area. It was there that I saw a leaflet that announced Creative Time's collaboration with the Modern to project Doug Aitken video clips onto the façade of the Museum of Modern Art. I remember saying to Filip Noterdaeme, I believe we have a problem. Just then we overheard somebody from the cubicle next to the waiting area calling out, hey does anybody know a black artist. Finally a young intern led us into the office of curator Peter Eleey. We had hoped to have our meeting with Ann Pasternak but it was Peter Eleey who received us, and like I said there was a problem. Peter Eleey was in fact quite offended about the idea of a museum that was all façade and solely concerned with image and surface and kept saying, do you really feel that this is what contemporary art museums do. It was a very short meeting. We left and Peter Eleey went back to working with Doug Aitken to project pleasing pleasant video clips of beautiful Tilda Swinton and other glamorous hip people onto the façade of the Modern. A little later we read a very funny article in The New York Times in which Doug Aitken claimed that in his search for a building façade for his projection he had picked the MoMA building by sheer coincidence, from afar.

I decided to sell the useless Wurlitzer piano. In all those years I had only once had a musical rehearsal at 172 Clinton Street. It was in preparation for a concert I was going to give at the Philadelphia Museum of Art with a trio and it was on that occasion that we painfully discovered that every single key of my Wurlitzer was about a quarter step lower than it ought to be and as can well be imagined the rehearsal was completely out of tune for sure. There had also been the occasion when I had hesitatingly tried to play Mozart's Fantasie in C minor and Filip Noterdaeme had insisted that it sounded more like a Gymnopédie by Satie. In any case I easily found an eager buyer for the useless Wurlitzer and once it was gone I put an affordable made-in-China Saarinen womb chair in its old spot and installed a shelf above it to display MoMA HMLSS, the new illuminated Goya con Goya, the very silly Flour Arrangement, etcetera. We called the new arrangement the Wurlitzer Atrium and had a plaque made for it. During openings, we hid a little device behind the Saarinen chair that softly played Wurlitzer music. The idea was that one would hear it but not be altogether aware of it.

Another addition to the HOMU Collection was the Broken Flavin Series. This I must explain.

One day, Filip Noterdaeme was giving a private tour at the Guggenheim museum, it might have been a group of rich ladies from California or maybe the british Chancellor and his son, I am not sure which, when suddenly there was a bang like a little explosion somewhere a few paces away. Everybody was bewildered but one of the museum guards said, oh surely someone must have stepped on the Dan Flavin again. Filip Noterdaeme went to take a look and it was true, there were broken shards of glass from one of Dan Flavin's fluorescent tubes. Someone rushed over to quickly sweep the shards away and Filip Noterdaeme said, may I please have these. He then found out that practically every week someone stepped on the Flavin because of the way the tubes were laid out on the floor and because museum visitors from out of town were always looking up, never looking down. Filip Noterdaeme asked Bowen Ames from the Art Services Preparations Department to save any shattered tubes for him in the future. To his delight Bowen was able to secure him two more broken sets in the following weeks. He brought them to 172 Clinton Street and I sealed each of them inside a large glass cylinder. We named them Broken Flavin 1, 2, and 3 and displayed them in the new Wurlitzer Atrium. Naturally we had to have another Sunday opening to show the Newest and the Broken Flavins and also a new and very expensive neon sign Filip Noterdaeme had ordered from the sign shop in Chinatown. It said Art is For Simple People and looked nice in the Café.

Many first-time visitors and several habitués came and I was very relieved when Erin McMonagle arrived and helped me keep everything in order. One of the visitors was a very tall man with a long beard and a soft voice. When Filip Noterdaeme asked him his name he said, a fluffy bunny. We thought this was a very peculiar joke but he showed us his ID card and there it was written, A. Fluffy Bunny and as it was now official we could then say nothing. It was A. Fluffy Bunny who later wrote a very moving testimony about what visiting the Homeless Muscum had been like.

Pablo Helguera came, ambitious Pablo Helguera, so capable of grand words and postures, full of sugary humble submissiveness in his eyes. He told Filip Noterdaeme, please don't stop this project ever. He had the ambition of the lowest, in other words the ambition to represent justice, love, wisdom, and superiority. This ambition made him very skilled at finding employment at the Modern and producing deeply earnest socially engaged art.

Another new visitor was Moby the techno pop star who came with a pretty blonde interior designer. He was very opinionated in the persistent shy way of geeks. He enjoyed his visit but did not touch any of the items at Café Broodthaers because he was a vegan. I told Moby all about Moby the dachshund that we had named not after him as some people had believed but after Moby Dick. Moby told us that he also had been named after Moby Dick because his father was a great grand nephew of Herman Melville. He then signed our guest book with a drawing of an alien that could have been a Matt Goering but wasn't. Years later he created a collage of three photographs called the three stages of life that included a photograph of Filip Noterdaeme lying supine in the Staff and Security Department.

Next came Sandi Dubowski the jewish filmmaker. He was a short bald man who lisped a little, always grinning and observing everything. He was not at that time a young man as filmmakers go, he had already had considerable recognition as a documentary filmmaker at the Chicago International Film Festival. When he presented his documentary, Trembling Before G-d, everybody could see the drama of being both an orthodox jew and gay. He told us of how the Homeless Museum had inspired him to give money to a homeless person on Purim and how good it had made him feel.

Writer curator artist Peter Scott was another regular who came that day. He had very long Mark Twain eyebrows that looked like spider legs pressing against his thick glasses which made it somewhat uncomfortable to look him in the eyes. He sometimes brought along his wife who was a carpenter and had beautiful white hair. On that particular occasion he had come alone and was standing next to a New York socialite, a certain Ms. Dumont who had come with her poodle and had sat down on a chair and simply would not leave. Downstairs her limousine driver grew impatient. Erin McMonagle came in to announce violently that the limo driver would not wait. And then after a violent knock the limo driver himself announced that he would not wait.

Then Yolanda Hawkins arrived with her partner William Niederkorn, a soft-spoken Shakespeare scholar. She had seen me perform in downtown cabarets and now she was curious about the Homeless Museum.

Yolanda Hawkins had a long history in downtown New York, not as long as Penny Arcade's but long nevertheless. She had acted in Richard Foreman plays and films and collaborated with John Jesurun. She understood perfectly the nature of the Homeless Museum and stayed for a long time talking to Filip Noterdaeme. It was a busy opening and we felt very tired after everybody had left.

And now I will tell you how a young american misfit made Weimar style cabaret of which he knew very little at the time he first met me into a popular attraction in downtown New York.

Earl Dax was an albuquerquian who had been living a little bit everywhere, in Los Angeles and Maryland and Philadelphia, and wherever he went he was always devoted to going out and meeting everybody and getting mixed up in all kinds of stories. He was always hard up and at the time I first met him living in Philadelphia and visiting New York quite frequently and in no time he got to know everybody in New York as well and made contacts everywhere. He once arranged for me to come to Philadelphia and perform in a small cabaret, which could have been marvelous except that he booked me on Oscar night and as everybody knows the only thing americans are interested in on Oscar night is the Oscars. This was my first experience of working for Earl Dax.

It was in those early days of our acquaintance that I invited Earl Dax to see one of my Weimar cabaret shows at Café Sabarsky and it affected him greatly in his vision but not in his imagination. It was only a little later that he moved to New York and began calling himself a curator and impresario. Then one day he called me and to my great surprise announced that he wanted to put together a variety show with a Weimar cabaret theme. He said, it will be called Weimar New York. Of course, he said, I do want you to be in it. I said, alright.

Weimar New York was completely a New York style show and there were no other german performers in it besides me and little great Sanda Weigl, so similar yet so different from her aunt Helene Weigl, the late wife of Bertolt Brecht. Neither did anybody but us two know anything about the Weimar cabaret history, but it did not matter, it was that kind of a show. In those early days I greatly enjoyed performing in Weimar New York.

I don't remember ever getting paid but it was interesting to once again meet and work with other performers. Because Earl Dax could never make up his mind as to who should be in the show, sooner or later everybody was in it, sometimes extraordinary, sometimes amateurish. There was Karen Kohler, a texan singer who dreamed of being a german cabaret singer and had been following me for years. She only once performed in Weimar New York, singing a Marlene Dietrich song, The Ruins of Berlin, and ever since then Filip Noterdaeme and I refer to her as the ruin of Berlin, Texas. It was not until a little later that she decided to form sweet-mannered innocent Kim Smith, a young australian Kylie Minogue fan, after my image for her directing debut. In any case Weimar New York shows always lasted many hours into the night and Earl Dax began calling them durational cabarets, which was very funny at first until it was not any more, not for the performers and not for the audience.

One day Earl Dax asked me if perhaps I would be interested in being the show's master of ceremonies. I demurred, telling him, not quite yet. He then asked Justin Bond, who was already at the time looking into ways to reinvent himself, having tired of his success as Kiki in Kiki and Herb the duo act he had created with Kenny Mellman. It was also at Weimar New York that the Pixie Harlots had their debut and everybody delighted in the way they celebrated sequins and high heels and amateurism. Another regular in the show was Taylor Mac whom I had first seen perform in little cabaret clubs wearing nothing but underwear and yodeling to a recording of Minnie the Moocher, which had made him look quite a bit like The Scream by Edvard Munch, it was a caricature but a rather wonderful one. He had in the meantime commenced wearing elaborate makeup and dressing up in very many layers of torn dresses and singing his own very wordy songs while plucking a ukulele. Nobody in those days knew how to be a freak better than Taylor Mac and of course everybody always loves a freak. A little later he began calling himself a theater person and to my astonishment publicly denied having had his beginnings in cabarets.

Another performer who took part in Weimar New York was Penny Arcade. I had of course seen her perform before, anyone living in New York in the Nineties with any interest in the theater had gone to see Penny Arcade's legendary shows that had broken so many boundaries but it was only at that time that I began to know her. There was a very profound feeling of life in Penny Arcade for anyone who knew her. All her life her hair had been raven black and now she had turned herself into a blonde. I always loved listening to Penny Arcade. We talked about the art of cabaret and she told me of her love of Vienna and Edith Piaf. Later, a year later I introduced her to Filip Noterdaeme and she instantly deeply understood his work and they became very devoted to one another.

Of course when Meow Meow was passing through New York on her way from there to there, she was forever passing through, never staying for long, I said to Earl Dax, you must have Meow Meow in Weimar New York.

Meow Meow appeared and she was possessed by the intellectual passion for artistry in her performance of glamour and madness. Justin Bond immediately announced after she left the stage that he had found a new enemy. He said she was an enemy but they became friends.

All Weimar New York shows usually ended with

sweet radical Tigger James entering the stage in high heel shoes, one higher than the other, and invariably ending his number naked and doing split jumps.

In those days I believed in Earl Dax and his future greatness even though, as I said, he always struggled with finances. He had a volatile temper and there were drinking problems. I remember one night after a show when Earl Dax seized a big glass and drank what was in it, then promptly went off his head, being completely drunk, and began to fight with the manager. How often did I tell Earl Dax, you must find a way to get wise about doing business. The situation got worse and worse the more successful Weimar New York became. A trip to present Weimar New York at the San Francisco Museum of Modern Art was alright but Los Angeles was a complete disaster, a complete and absolute disaster. Earl Dax once again blew his top and went off to Mexico. A few months later he returned with a suntan and I asked him to meet me for tea in the East Village. I always had my meetings in the East Village if I had bad news and in the West Village if I had good news. We sat down and I told Earl in no uncertain terms why I could and would not work for him any longer. But this was not until later.

It was Halloween and we invited Casimir and Rachid for a Halloween supper with Rami Ramirez and his partner Jason Arsenault. We were quite sure it would be entertaining. Casimir brought a bottle of excellent Amarone wine and what a pleasant dinner it was, Rachid full of life and gaiety, Casimir intense and talking of psychic games and insisting we dip apples into melted caramels and chopped peanuts to honor an all american Halloween tradition, and Jason Arsenault all quiet and looking like a handsome porn star. Rami Ramirez said to Casimir, did anyone ever tell you how much you resemble Shirley MacLaine. Well, Casimir did not like to hear that at all but Rami insisted, yes, yes, you do look and act quite a bit like her, and then everybody at the table agreed and I liked Rami Ramirez even more for saying things about anyone and anything, saying them about people, saying them to people, saying them when he pleases and how he pleases.

And now I must tell you how the Homeless Museum after having been one of New York's most exclusive museums for two years was suddenly reduced to being a museum for two.

It was in late 2006. Taylor Mac and his companion Pat the architect came to 172 Clinton Street for dinner one night and told us about their friend, reporter Dan Shaw from The New York Times who had a column in the real estate section in which he wrote about interesting apartments. Would we mind if they told him about 172 Clinton Street and the Homeless Museum. We hesitated. Why yes, Filip Noterdaeme finally said, I suppose we could invite him here. And sure enough a few weeks later Dan Shaw called and arranged for a visit.

He was a pleasant round-faced man. He looked at everything and listened attentively. Filip Noterdaeme told him, the museum is as much a part of us as we are a part of it. A few days later The New York Times sent photographer Chester Higgins Jr. to take photographs, rather wonderful photographs, of us and the apartment, and he told Filip Noterdaeme of his series of portraits of african tribesmen. He was very proud of his portraits of african tribesmen.

Casimir and Rachid had invited us to spend Christmas eve with them. They were living all the way up in Harlem and it was an intense dinner. Casimir was nervously exhausted from having spent the day in the kitchen preparing spätzle and roast duck for us. He talked with his characteristic brilliant violent emphasis that was his quality and that always made Rachid laugh. It made Filip Noterdaeme nervous, he has a wariness towards people who speak violently. Then it suddenly occurred to Casimir that he should call his twin brother who like I said was living in a mental institution in California. He placed the call immediately and talked to his brother and then handed Filip Noterdaeme the receiver and said, say something nice to my poor brother. Filip Noterdaeme said something nice. Then we sat down and ate duck and spätzle. There was an alarming strange noise coming from the bathroom and Casimir told us, oh do not worry it's just the children. He said the children but what he meant was the twelve stray cats he and Rachid had adopted over the years. He had locked them up in the bathroom so they would not disturb us but after dessert he opened the bathroom door and there was a cat avalanche coming into the room. We stayed late and early very early the next morning I had to get up and take a plane to the Dominican Republic to once again cook for Boykin Curry and his friends. This time Boykin Curry had also invited chef Gabrielle Hamilton who had once worked for him as a personal chef. She had since those days opened a restaurant in the East Village, Prune, and now Boykin Curry wanted her to see his utopian paradise and consider opening a restaurant there.

I immediately liked Gabrielle Hamilton and took great interest in her cooking. I said, of course you cook with thorough simplicity, all women chefs cook that way. But, said she, if I was a man chef would I not cook with thorough simplicity. No, said I firmly, only women chefs cook with thorough simplicity. As a matter of fact I also cook with thorough simplicity because I cook like a woman chef and it is this exception that has made my cooking a success with everybody.

And so Gabrielle and I did all the cooking at Playa Grande and everybody ate extremely well. Gabrielle insisted on brining and grilling gallinas, the local black chickens. The dominican cooks from the golf club thought that she was out of her mind, saying that only dominicans knew how to prepare gallinas. All I cared for was Gabrielle's recipe for anchovy butter. I planned to ask her for the recipe and then promptly forgot.

After four days I returned to New York and Filip Noterdaeme and I watched the New Year's Eve fireworks across the Hudson river from our bed. The next week Dan Shaw's New York Times article about 172 Clinton Street came out and we were very pleased with it. Seeing his work described in the Times gave Filip Noterdaeme a childish delight almost amounting to ecstasy. He remarked on how perfectly fitting it was to have an article about the Homeless Museum in the real estate section of the Times on the same day that the arts section of the paper had an article about the Museum of Modern Art's real estate deals.

The Homeless Museum having been written up in The New York Times had now become official and there was no denying of its existence. That week, landlords and museum directors all over New York City were talking about Dan Shaw's article and wondered what sort of artist had created such a defiant elaborate send-up of the contemporary museum world, a place so embarrassingly evocative of the museum world's obsession with real estate and yet so endearing in its candid depiction of insouciant domesticity.

Of course Paul the landlord like every landlord in New York always read the real estate section of the Times and it was only a short time after this that we received the letter from him that would change everything about our lives once again.

In the letter, it said that the apartment we lived in must be used as a private apartment to live in as the primary residence of the tenant and for no other reason, in other words Paul the landlord made it clear that he would not tolerate a museum, any museum in the attic of his townhouse. We wrote back explaining that the Homeless Museum was not really a public museum but a private art project that occasionally received visitors. Paul the landlord wouldn't have any of it and said, close the museum or else. War was upon us.

Igor Vander was a russian from Saint Petersburg who at age 20 had moved to New York to study fashion and now worked for the AEFFE fashion group where I sometimes borrowed Jean Paul Gaultier outfits for my cabaret shows. When the war with Paul the landlord was upon us he refused to believe it and explained that he could understand Thierry Mugler fighting Jean Paul Gaultier, in other words a fashion war, but not a serious war with one's landlord over an art project.

Not knowing what to do about it all I called Volunteer Lawyers for the Arts and talked to someone about the difficult situation. I was told in no uncertain terms that

230

there was no hope in winning an argument with Paul the landlord. How so, I asked. Because, said the voice on the phone, you are not entitled to receive such and such amount of people in a rental apartment without your landlord's consent and in an aggressive argument he might be trying to evict you and then, well I promise you then there will be a great deal of regret on your part.

Filip Noterdaeme and I discussed this at great length. Not wanting to risk eviction or look for another home we reluctantly gave in to Paul the landlord's demand and promised to not hold any more museum openings.

Filip Noterdaeme was very aggravated about this for some time. Then he finally said, it's quite alright. The Homeless Museum has existed at 172 Clinton Street for 2 years and it will continue to exist, we just won't show it to the public any longer, in other words the museum will be under house arrest and we will simply continue to live in it. To make a statement about the cultural climate of arrested development that the rules of real estate had forced upon us we kept the same hygrothermograph chart on rotation and the lines kept overwriting each other, week after week.

The other thing in connection with this, the barring of museum visitors from coming to 172 Clinton Street, was our acquisition of two tall muscular white male mannequins. Filip Noterdaeme called them our permanent visitors. I dressed them up in white shoes, white pants and white shirts and white basketball caps. Then I pinned HOMU buttons on their shirts and put audio tour headphones on their little heads. We placed one mannequin in the Main Hall and one in the Archives and Meteorology Department and there they stood, permanently looking and listening.

Ever since Filip Noterdaeme had named the Homeless Museum there had been much confusion about the name. Was it perhaps a museum about the homeless or a museum with art by the homeless. If I remember correctly it was Brady McDonald, the madly talented dancer from the Mark Morris Company who was very surprised and relieved to find that the Homeless Museum was not as he had assumed a dark place with repulsive piles of garbage bags. In any case, Filip Noterdaeme decided to change the name of his museum from the Homeless Museum to the Homeless Museum of Art and it was that little change that made the difference. Everything sounds better with of art after it, he said.

Now I must tell how Filip Noterdaeme conceived Fat Minimalism and what it had to do with a dinner at 172 Clinton Street with James Wagner and his companion Barry Hoggard.

James Wagner and Barry Hoggard were art collectors. They had come to one of the last openings at 172 Clinton Street and they had the distinct air of those who have seen everything but still feel the need to see more. One always saw them out and about at gallery openings and art events and then one could read about it online, both had their own little art blog. Indeed they had written nice things about their visit at the Homeless Museum and so we invited them to have dinner with us. There was to be a risotto with crayfish and chicken livers, a very strange and alluring dish I had once seen Daniel Boulud serve, and I had purposely prepared a homemade chicken stock to make it. The chicken stock was simmering and I as usual skimmed off the chicken fat and placed it in a shallow bowl in the freezer for later use.

James Wagner and Barry Hoggard arrived very much on time and we sat down and I served the crayfish and chicken liver risotto. James and Barry were very fond of talking about themselves and never asked any questions. They always seemed to be in perfect agreement with each other. It was a rather dull evening. I don't remember what I served for dessert, something acidic and colorful, possibly a pomegranate sorbet, in any case after James and Barry had left Filip Noterdaeme was quite a bit unnerved and said he needed a drink. I fixed him a whisky on the rocks and he saw the chicken fat in the freezer that in the meanwhile had hardened into a shiny yellow disc. Incidentally, he said, this would make a beautiful minimalist sculpture. We cut the fat into little squares and aligned them to make them look like a Donald Judd and Filip Noterdaeme simply said, Fat Minimalism.

It was a very funny coincidence that only a little later Filip Noterdaeme was commissioned to create an original art piece for a group show produced by Grand Arts called From the Fat of the Land. This was not only a very pleasant opportunity to travel once again to Kansas City but also to create a large scale Fat Minimalism.

We asked Grand Arts to arrange for 30 pounds of chicken fat and a tall refrigerator with a glass door and glass shelves. In the last minute Filip Noterdaeme decided to also ask for 12 dozen chicken eggs, he already had yet another idea on his mind.

We flew to Kansas City and as soon as we arrived we went to the Grand Arts workshop to look at the chicken fat and the eggs and the refrigerator. The chicken fat was beautifully yellow and smelled of fried onions. Stacy Switzer apologized for the smell and explained that this was because the chicken fat had been ordered from a kosher purveyor who very evidently followed the jewish tradition of rendering chicken fat with fried onions. Ah, you mean to say that Fat Minimalism will be made out of true schmaltz, I said.

I began by making plexiglas molds. Then the chicken fat had to be melted and poured and cooled, little by little. Finally Filip Noterdaeme and I assembled the solid fat sheets into sculptures. By the end of the day we had a Fat Morris, a Fat Judd, a Fat McCracken, and a Fat Andre and neither of them looked anything like a CD rack from Ikea. The smell of fried onions was in them and around them and on our hands. We set the refrigerator to its coldest setting, I believe it was 37 degrees Fahrenheit, and carefully placed the fat sculptures on the glass shelves. I will never forget how beautiful it looked, I was so very pleased.

Later in the Grand Arts guest loft Filip Noterdaeme did something amusing with the twelve dozen eggs. He stamped every egg with the HOMU logo and then, placing each egg on a tiny little metal ring, carefully neatly lined them up along the walls of the loft. Then he printed the names of the 144 most famous museums in the world on little place cards and put one place card in front of each egg.

The following month was a strange one. I returned to New York to cook once again in the Hamptons and Filip Noterdaeme, having been invited to teach a summer course at the Kansas City Art Institute, stayed in Kansas City as a guest of Grand Arts. The course he taught was The Undoing and Remaking of Museums. During all this time he largely lived on eggs like Piero Di Cosimo had in the 16th Century. Every morning and evening he chose three of the museum eggs and made a museum omelet or a scrambled museum. There were also poached museums and boiled museums and one stormy Saturday evening he made a soufflé out of the Louvre, the Alte Pinakothek and the Hermitage.

It was in Kansas City that he first heard mentioned and first saw a performance by Ssion, the postmodern pop group. Years later Grand Arts arranged for Ssion to perform at PS1 in New York City. It was on that occasion that Stacy Switzer told Filip Noterdaeme that the lead singer Cody Critcheloe on the subject of community had once simply remarked, community, community, gross.

During his stay in Kansas City Filip Noterdaeme also met artist Tavares Strachan from Barbados. Tavares had gained acclaim for once having measured the distance between what we have and what we want by traveling to the Arctic and returning with a 4.5 ton block of arctic ice. The two gave a joint presentation at Grand Arts. Tavares spoke about how ice was melting and Filip Noterdaeme spoke about how minimalism had gotten fat. After the talk the two played a game of horseshoe in Stacy Switzer's backyard. Filip Noterdaeme had never played horseshoe games before and it seemed perfectly natural that he would lose but he won, every time. Then he and Tavares went to a bar where the countertops were curiously made of ice blocks. What a strange coincidence, Filip Noterdaeme said, and how strange, how peculiar. Tavares soon got very drunk and kept shouting, power to the people.

One day in Kansas City Filip Noterdaeme went to a special event at the Nelson Atkins Museum of Art. It was a big to-do for invited guests to celebrate the opening of the new Bloch Building designed by star architect Stephen Hall and paid for by a Mister Henry W. Bloch.

Everybody was drinking champagne and Filip Noterdaeme went upstairs to look at the new offices. There he mischievously let himself into Director Marc Wilson's office and pocketed a brief he found on his desk. Then he returned to the party downstairs for more champagne.

The brief curiously read like a classified Pentagon document and was all about the museum having to adopt more aggressive marketing strategies. This prompted Filip Noterdaeme to write an open letter to Marc Wilson. Naturally, Director Wilson did not respond in any way but quotes from the letter ended up in an article in the Kansas City Star. It was written by Alice Thorson and titled The Art of Museum Critique. It was a very sympathetic and very understanding analysis of Filip Noterdaeme's work. Later on when he was discouraged by the lack of serious press coverage he had had over the years he would refer to it as having given him at that time great comfort. He says, in art and critique, when you create something, it is perfectly clear, and then you begin to be doubtful about it, but then you look at it again and you lose yourself in it again as when you created it.

Then From the Fat of the Land closed, Fat Minimalism became chicken fat again and Filip Noterdaeme returned to New York.

James Wagner and Barry Hoggard invited us for dinner at their apartment in Chelsea. There was nothing to do but say yes and so we went. The two showed us their apartment and their art collection and talked about real estate and how the value of the apartment had gone up and up since they had bought it for a pittance. Then we sat down and they talked of the artists they had discovered and collected before anybody else and of how many artists owed them their success. It was a long evening and when we walked home Filip Noterdaeme said to me, oh I hate them I really do, who do they think they are.

I had a few more weekends of cooking to do in the Hamptons before our summer vacation and Filip Noterdaeme as usual stayed behind in the hot city. It was always very strange coming back to 172 Clinton Street on Sunday evenings, returning from a world of abundance, air conditioning and sea breezes to a very hot Brooklyn attic apartment with stagnant air and a nearly as possible empty refrigerator. I was always tired from a long weekend of kitchen work in designed manicured surroundings overhearing the idle talk of the rich and Filip Noterdaeme was always manic from the city heat and no one but Florence and the two permanent visitors for company.

Then it was late July and we finally boarded a plane to Paris for our annual summer vacation. We stayed at Filip Noterdaeme's older brother's apartment on the boulevard Magenta for a few days and had a wonderful time. I can so well remember one mild sunny Paris afternoon when we took a walk down the rue St. Denis past the wholesale fashion boutiques and the seasoned prostitutes standing in doorways and overheard one prostitute say to another, moi quand je meure je veux être enterrée au Père Lachaîse parce que moi j'ai donnée ma chatte à c'pays, when I die I want to be buried at the Père Lachaise because I gave my pussy to this country.

It was during that stay in Paris that we visited the Musée des Arts et Métiers and saw a Dalida exhibit at the

Hotel de Ville. At the Musée des Arts et Métiers we attentively watched Foucault's Pendulum swing back and forth
and Filip Noterdaeme said that watching it made him recognize the difference between modern and contemporary
art, that modern art was fast and that contemporary art
was not. At the Hotel de Ville the Dalida exhibit was completely modern. There were people of all ages and Filip
Noterdaeme who had idolized Dalida in his youth was
very excited. How well I remember a video clip that was
shown in a little round booth whose walls were encrusted
with silver rhinestones. It was a clip of Dalida singing Je
suis malade, I am sick, at the Olympia, and it was impressive to watch how at the end of the song she held her final
pose for a very long time before taking a stylized sustained
deep bow. In short it was a very moving afternoon of grav-
ity and gravitas.

The next day we eagerly took the train and bus to
the coast to board a ferry that would finally take us to the
little french island we now both loved so much. While
we were waiting for the ferry I had a little chat with an old
retired fisherman who told me with a sigh and a smile how
fishing in the region had changed and that if one wanted
fresh sardines nowadays one had no choice but to buy
them imported from Sardinia. Then the ferry arrived and
he said to me, au revoir Madame. Ah, now we knew we
were in France.

The house we had arranged to rent for the summer was an old fisherman's house belonging to Anne-
Françoise, an eccentric woman painter from Brittany. She
had been living in the fisherman's house for several years
more or less comfortably in her solitary state but had
made it a profitable habit to rent out the house during the

summer season, making do with her little studio gallery in the harbor for a temporary home. She was one of those admirable artistes, in other words absolutely devoted, thoroughly occupied with capturing on canvas her love of nature, firmly convinced that everything photographed was far too banal. She had the loose lips and slightly swollen red nose that Filip Noterdaeme says come from disappointment and Dubonnet. She was also a most excellent translator of german texts and had once been hired by Miele to translate their product manuals into french.

We delighted staying at Anne-Françoise's house and grew accustomed to her colorful pasty paintings with very entertaining little price stickers in the corners. The one thing we were at first not all too pleased about was Anne-Françoise asking us to take care of her little black pussycat. Filip Noterdaeme did not want a cat in the house and I did not want to get attached to a pet again like I had with Moby the dachshund. I placed the cat's feeding bowl in the little storage house on the far side of the garden in hopes that this would keep her out of our way. It did not and little by little the little black cat seduced us and we became quite smitten with the kitten. I began cooking special meals for her and Filip Noterdaeme allowed her to sit on his lap, in fact it ended up with the cat sleeping on his crotch every night.

We spent our days riding bicycles around the island and swimming in the cold ocean. I still liked lying in the sun at noon but Filip Noterdaeme still preferred to stay in the shade. One evening, I imagine it must have been at the end of August he made me sit and watch the sunset in silence. Filip Noterdaeme is indefatigable with sunsets. But as he often says, one is always weary of natural spectacles and drawn to manmade spectacles. Nature is too mundane, it bores you, it needs to be properly framed. No sooner had the sun descended beyond the horizon that he began telling me about his idea for a theater that would be built for sunset watching only and be called the Solarplex Theater. Later in New York he told Bowen Ames about it and Bowen said, let's build it on my family's estate upstate.

After three weeks on the island we bade Anne Francoise's house and the little black pussycat goodbye and went on to Brussels. We did the usual things. To me Brussels was always strangely familiar yet different because, well because it was slow, fond of embroidery, heavy foods and beer, like Munich.

One night Filip Noterdaeme's mother invited us and everyone from the family to a traditional belgian restaurant and as we sat down I told everybody the story of how I had been mistaken for a madame by the old fisherman in the harbor and everybody laughed and said, this cannot possibly be true, how could he. Just at that moment the waiter appeared and said to me, et pour madame ce sera, and what will it be for madame.

We took a day trip to Antwerp where we walked all 527 meters of the Sint-Anna pedestrian tunnel to the other side of the Schelde River to eat belgian fries at a frietkot that Filip Noterdaeme's older brother had recommended. We walked and walked and when we got to the other side it turned out the frietkot was closed that day and we had to walk back through the tunnel again feeling rather hungry. Later we went to see the house that in 1969 had shown the 17th Century Section of Marcel Broodthaers's Musée d'Art Moderne for one week. We had gone on a whim and arrived unannounced and clearly there were new owners living in the house by now but Filip Noterdaeme had no qualms about ringing the doorbell. To our great surprise the owners were home and knew all about the 17th Century Section. They let us in and showed us the little garden in the back where Broodthaers had staged and filmed a performance in the rain. On the way back to the train station we found a frietkot that was open for business and we finally had our frites belges with mayonnaise. They were excellent but I would have preferred american mayonnaise to belgian mayonnaise, and Filip Noterdaeme asked me, just what is it that makes american mayonnaise so different, so appealing.

We took the train back to Brussels and were immensely pleased with our day in Antwerp, in other words we had once again and as always treated matters of great concern lightly and those of small concern seriously.

We were back in New York and heard that the venerable Barnes Foundation in Merion was going to be dismantled and moved to a new location in downtown Philadelphia. This meant that Mister Barnes's collection of Matisses, Picassos, Renoirs, Cézannes and Van Goghs and african sculptures and ornate wrought iron objects was now going to be presented in a new building and in the regular style of contemporary museums. This was not only a pity since the foundation's original style of display had been so singular that it had earned the foundation a unique place in the museum world, but, since Mister Barnes had decreed in his will that no changes be made to his foundation, it was treason.

Filip Noterdaeme went to visit the Barnes Foundation to see it one last time before the big makeover.

Cathleen Chaffee went with him. Filip Noterdaeme liked everything as it was but Cathleen Chaffee did not care for the Renoirs, she found something rather appalling in his drawing of women's bodies, something that repelled and shocked her. She and Filip Noterdaeme almost quarreled about the Renoirs. Looking at a late Renoir of an enormous nude that might have been a Rubens but was not, Filip Noterdaeme teasingly cheekily said to Cathleen Chaffee, but all the same Renoir paints better than Cézanne. Later he took a postcard of a Renoir nude and added Cézanne's signature below the image and mailed it to Cathleen Chaffee. This Renoir she liked quite a bit and she had it framed. The Cézanne Renoir was the beginning of Filip Noterdaeme's series of misattributions that little by little covered the Wall of Misnomers at 172 Clinton Street, next to the Egg on Schiele and the Francis Bacon with Extra Bacon.

Concluding that the Barnes Foundation needed not a full makeover but a cosmetic makeover Filip Noterdaeme asked me to create a special makeup line in four shades, Cézanne Brown, Van Gogh Yellow, Renoir Pink and Picasso Black. He called it the Barnes Makeup Foundation.

The story of making the makeup is a funny case of happenstance. First I bought mineral powders, natural pigments, floral essences and other necessary things. Then I found a used Cuisinart mixer on the street that was in perfect working condition and exactly what I needed to blend the ingredients together. I worked with careful cosmetic precision, mixing the ingredients and then filling the four blended makeup pastes into tubes, the kind usually used for oil paint, and putting together a little pamphlet to advertise the makeup line's qualities. I wrote, Renoir Pink, a base of soft clay blended with a touch of French primrose oil, this blush foundation will rejuvenate your skin and make it look like it did when you were a virgin, Cézanne Brown, feel strong with this robust foundation that shields skin from the elements with its unique essence of olive tree bark and sea breeze extracts, Van Gogh Yellow, add a touch of hysteria by applying this dense, lustrous foundation made with organic ammoniac and essential sunflower oil from southern France to your face, and Picasso Black, get in touch with your primal instincts by using this earthy foundation on your entire body, ingredients include mud from Seville's famed arena and hand-gathered bullfighter's musk.

Now that we had our own makeup line we had to tell everybody and invite members of the press for a sampling, there was no way around it, no matter what we had promised Paul the landlord. We sent out invitations and made it perfectly clear that everyone was to be very quiet when walking up the four flights leading to our apartment. If anyone in the building asks you where you are going, we wrote, you must not ever mention the Homeless Museum but simply say that you are visiting friends. This became the new formula for our clandestine openings.

It was just like the old days. The doorbell rang and I let everyone in and everybody got weighed and took the audio tour and I invited everyone to try on the Barnes Foundation Makeup. Lamar Clarkson from Art News was afraid of putting any on her face but she wrote about Filip Noterdaeme's cosmetic fix in her little column, Art Talk. Sheila McClear from Gawker was not afraid and looked very interesting with Renoir Pink eye shadow on her left eyelid and van Gogh Yellow on the right. Her article about us on Gawker was titled, Live like a crazy.

Young Juan Olivares came. We always liked Juan Olivares. He had the thin angular build of the medieval martyrs in the flemish primitives and spoke in a hesitant beautifully soft voice. Filip Noterdaeme was very fond of him, he has always had a fondness for boyish boys whose manhood is a promise not yet fulfilled, whereas I prefer manly men who fulfill their promise to a boy. When Juan Olivares had first come to the Homeless Museum, back in the days when our openings had not been clandestine yet, he was still underage, seventeen I believe, and about to graduate from High school. He had come with two girl-friends. They had sat around the bed in the Staff & Security Department and Filip Noterdaeme had invited pretty Juan Olivares to slip under the covers with him during an interview with a journalist. It was then that Filip Noterdaeme began penetrating young Juan Olivares's mind. The two became mentor and pupil and frequently met at a burger joint in Williamsburg where Filip Noterdaeme treated Juan to a burger and Juan treated Filip Noterdaeme to conversation about gossip and sex, sex and gossip. Regarding art, Filip Noterdaeme told Juan, always stick to form and forget about message. Message, he said, is for demagogues pedagogues and rogues and form is for geniuses lunatics and non-conformists.

Another young man who came to our first clandestine opening was Aaron Scott. He was a student from Portland, Oregon and said he wanted to become a journalist. He had been to 172 Clinton Street before and now he was back to interview and film everybody for a video portrait of Filip Noterdaeme. He was not very experienced and when he told Filip Noterdaeme of a teacher at Columbia University who had advised students to always treat their subjects like monkeys, Filip Noterdaeme refused to talk to him on camera and began slowly peeling and eating a banana while staring into the camera lens, just like Mario Montez in Andy Warhol's Harlot. Aaron Scott then tried his luck with everybody else and began interviewing visitors about the Homeless Museum. Sheila McClear said that she had expected to find many more art projects like the Homeless Museum when she moved to New York but that there really unfortunately was nothing like the Homeless Museum. Juan Olivares said he liked the director's penetrating intellect and Colby Chamberlain said that Filip Noterdaeme was being willfully ignored by the established art world and that eventually people would have to start thinking about his work and address it. When Filip Noterdaeme saw the video of Colby Chamberlain speaking of him and his work in such a way, he wrote to him, and are you going to put in writing what you have said on camera. Over the years there have been a few notable exceptions of people who have put their thoughts on Filip Noterdaeme's work in writing, Samantha Topol, Dan Shaw, Lily Koppel and Amy Whitaker.

A few months later Filip Noterdaeme decided to use the Barnes Makeup like paint and he made four beautiful little tiny makeup monochromes with it. They are now hanging in the Meteorology & Archives Department, next to the Guggenheim Monochromes. The Barnes Foundation is said to reopen in downtown Philadelphia in 2012 and Filip Noterdaeme now says with much amusement that when anyone asks him about the new Barnes Foundation he replies, oh you mean the Pottery Barnes Foundation.

It was at about that time that Colby Chamberlain was organizing the Dotted Line show at the Rotunda Gallery in Brooklyn Heights and asked Filip Noterdaeme to create a little HOMU membership desk to display our membership forms that we kept in the freezer at 172 Clinton Street. The opening was a lively one. Eric Doeringer was showing a series of museum employee identity cards for nonexistent museums, as a matter of fact he included two identity cards he had made for Filip Noterdaeme and myself that identified us as special event coordinators for the most improbable Thomas Kinkade Museum.

In the meanwhile the customary useless little gifts we had been given by dinner guests and museum visitors over the years had been accumulating and piling up in the closet in the Staff and Security Department and something had to be done about them. There was a fruitcake-scented candle, a black leather dominatrix tool with a white feather, a miniature disco ball, Dame Edna sunglasses, a can of smoked king salmon, two canadian flag pins, an expensive italian corkscrew and so much more. Rather than keeping them stashed away or throwing them out Filip Noterdaeme decided to turn them into a new exhibit. I built little wall shelves to display the useless gifts in the Archives and Meteorology Department and Filip Noterdaeme titled the exhibit the Oh Thank You Collection. From then on whenever someone brought us a useless gift, we said, oh thank you, and added it to the collection. There is a funny story about a little dainty crystal vase that Cathleen Chaffee had given us one day and that we felt belonged into the Oh Thank you Collection. However, not wanting to upset her feelings, we took it off the display every time she came to visit us and she was always very relieved that we had not included her dainty crystal vase in the collection.

It was at about this time that Thom Collins the director of the Neuberger Museum in Purchase invited me to perform at a gala at the Neuberger. It was a tribute to Kitty Carlisle and ninety-year-old Mister Neuberger himself was going to attend in a wheelchair. Thom and I discussed all the details, the train schedule, dinner and a limo ride back to New York after the show, my fee, and back-up dancers from the graduate class of nearby Suny Purchase. Finally I said, one more request. I would like to invite a very special kitty to be my guest in the show. Who are you thinking of, Thom asked. Meow Meow, I said, you will like her.

The day of the gala arrived and Meow Meow, her accompanist Lance Horne and I took the train to Purchase. It was always a pleasure to work with Lance Horne. He had an inner ear unlike anyone I had ever met. He always worked with calm concentration no matter if he played a Strauss aria or a Dresden Doll song or one of his own compositions. More than anything he liked to be in the moment and work from memory.

We arrived at the Neuberger and Thom Collins gave us a quick tour of the museum. Meow Meow marveled at a very large Calder and a tiny little Georgia O'Keefe and then it was showtime.

We had a success. I sang the Count Orlofsky aria from Die Fledermaus as an homage to Kitty Carlisle who had once famously sung it at the Met. The dance graduates from Suny Purchase did exactly as I had told them, executing a delightfully fast Ballet barre behind me while I sang a

Tom Waits song about madness and later lifting me high in the air during the dream sequence. Then Meow Meow made her entrance as usual from the back of the room, strolling through the audience nervously absentmindedly rummaging through her handbag, a living caricature of the restless diva. She intonated The Boulevard of Broken Dreams and stopping midway asked, where am I, this isn't the Louvre or is it. Then she stopped. She stopped right in front of Mister Neuberger in his wheelchair and continued singing, now to him. Mister Neuberger got very excited, more excited than he had been in a long time and to everyone's great surprise suddenly reached out and grabbed her breasts with both hands. Everybody gasped. The Neuberger family gasped and the guests gasped and the waiters gasped and Thom Collins got very white in the face. He later confessed to me that he had for a moment feared that Mister Neuberger might die of a heart attack right there and then and how this would have ruined his career. Mister Neuberger did not die of a heart attack, Meow Meow forgave him and Thom Collins's career was not ruined, as a matter of fact he became the director of the Miami Art Museum not much later.

There was a limousine waiting to drive us back to the city but before leaving we had a chat with little David Lewis. Small, quick-moving and always and still hungry for what might be or could have been, he was a well-known figure in the New York cabaret circuit and had a history of playing the piano for a great many long-forgotten chanteuses in long satin gloves. In fact Filip Noterdaeme insists that he had once seen him play for the incomparable Hildegarde at the Algonquin. Little David Lewis said to me, I must introduce you to my friend Tommy Tune, he would absolutely adore you, and I said, why don't you both come to my show at Café Sabarsky, and they did the next week and it was the beginning of our friendship with Tommy Tune.

It was a little later that Barbara Walters who prides herself on being eternally interested in everything and everybody was having a dinner party and asked little David Lewis to arrange for an entertainer. Little David Lewis suggested hiring me to do german cabaret songs and Miss Walters first agreed but then changed her mind and instead hired an american Broadway singer to sing american showtunes.

All this time Filip Noterdaeme had never stopped thinking about what was and had been happening in the museum world since the British Museum opened in 1753 and what it all meant for the museum visitor. Now that the Louvre and the Guggenheim were about to build satellite museums in the persian gulf to make their money as they could, Filip Noterdaeme decided that maybe it was time to declare the death of the museum visitor. He wrote an obituary that was the funniest saddest thing he had ever written. I ordered a condolence wreath, a beautiful large green wreath with a white ribbon, and we invited everyone to one of our clandestine openings to mourn the passing of the Museum Visitor.

Thom Collins came to the opening with his companion Matthew Goodrich. Thom Collins is a great gossip and as Filip Noterdaeme adores the beginning and middle and end of a story, Thom Collins was able to supply several missing parts of several stories. One story was about Richard Prince and Barbara Gladstone. Thom Collins said that Barbara Gladstone was pure evil. It was a complicated story but it had something to do with an exhibition of Richard Prince's early works at the Neuberger Museum and Barbara Gladstone not allowing any images of the works to be included in the catalogue. And then Filip Noterdaeme and Thom Collins talked about museum directors. Thom Collins said he had heard that Glenn Lowry had just had a facelift and was suffering from priapism. Priapism, said Filip Noterdaeme, what is that. Thom Collins explained that it meant having frequent erections without feeling aroused. Yes yes, Filip Noterdaeme said, it can be hard being a museum director.

Frank Smigiel of the San Francisco Museum of Modern Art came and also Mario Kramer of the Museum für Moderne Kunst Frankfurt am Main. Mario Kramer was more interested in sex parties than in the Homeless Museum and complained that New York did not have as many gay sex parties as Berlin.

There was also DJ photographer Lucien Samaha who always brought a great many young men from all over the world. They were very nice in the room, and they thought Filip Noterdaeme wonderful. They felt and indeed in a way it was true that he had a halo. There was wild-eyed James Leary of the Bruce High Quality Foundation, Matthew Lutz-Kinoy of the Freddy Mercury moustache, Holcombe Waller of Portland, Alexander Kauffman of the Philadelphia Museum of Art, and one woman, wide-eyed Marjorie Weinstein of the Whitney Museum. To Filip Noterdaeme's great delight Lucien thought of taking a photograph with everyone sitting on the director's bed.

It was only a few weeks later that we invited little David Lewis and tall Tommy Tune to have dinner with us at 172 Clinton Street. Tommy Tune brought as a gift a very fancy scented candle from Bergdorf Goodman. This candle did not end up in the Oh Thank You Collection, Filip Noterdaeme used it a few months later for his first self-portrait since he had created the Pussy Painting. He called it Scented Candle Descending a Staircase and it was a real meltdown. Tommy Tune told us how he had first learned about rhythm when his father had taught him horseback riding back in Texas. There was one particular horse step called kiss-your-papa kiss-your-papa and Tommy Tune stood up and showed it to us right in front of the Homeless Simulator. It was all very absorbing. Later Tommy Tune tried out our Corbusier chaiselongue and found it most comfortable. Of course it is, said Filip Noterdaeme, it feels like taking Jesus' place in Michelangelo's Pieta. We found Tommy Tune very charming and liked how he was interested in everything. Before parting he said, let's be friends forever. Ever since that dinner every time we run into little David Lewis he tells us, I cannot believe Tommy Tune really came with me all the way to Brooklyn that night to have dinner with you two, and don't you ever forget it was me who introduced you to him.

Another person we became acquainted with around that time was Rex Reed. He came to one of my Café Sabarsky shows and sat at the front table next to cabaret singer KT Sullivan. After the show he and I chatted about german singer and actress Hildegard Knef whom he had known when the world was young. I told him about a chapter in her third autobiographical volume, So Nicht, No Way, in which she had written about a New York evening where the two of them had painted the town. Yes, Rex Reed said, I remember that night very well and I heard about the book but it has never been translated into english. I promised him that one day I would translate and read the chapter to him.

Then it was December and Filip Noterdaeme went to see Cats on Broadway. It was not the long-running Broadway musical theater production in Manhattan but a very amusing amateurish Bruce High Quality Foundation production presented in a building that happened to be on Broadway in Brooklyn, in the rapidly changing neighborhood known as Bedford Stuyvesant. As everyone knows, every american city has a Broadway and Brooklyn and New York having once been two different cities both still have their own Broadway. Some insist they still are two different cities. Filip Noterdaeme arrived early and an usher in a cat costume showed him to his seat. The room was soon very full of people and who were they all. Mostly young Cooper Union students and an older, much older Francesco Clemente who had also come by himself and sat alone, looking a little bit forlorn. Then the show began and everybody was wearing cat costumes and cat makeup, not just the actors but also the musicians, stagehands and technicians.

In the meanwhile that same evening I was also performing in Brooklyn, at Earl Dax's first Tingel Tangel cabaret at a place called Glasslands in Williamsburg. This was in the days before but leading to the disastrous Los Angeles trip. When it was my turn to go onstage I made a terrible faux pas and mistakenly introduced the Pixie Harlots as their competitors, the Dazzle Dancers. One of the other performers that night was a girl singer named Lady Rizo. She was an indomitable force that made one think of a car with a powerful searchlight that could pierce the fog. Then the door opened and in walked a very stylish young couple. This was Shien Lee and Lucas Lanthier. She was a petite young woman with fine features and the most elegant small hands. He was an angelic young man with translucent white skin and curly hair. They had come all the way from Harlem to Williamsburg to see me because Mister Burton, a real dandy who had often come to see me at my Bar d'O shows had told them they ought to.

I soon learned more about Shien Lee. She was from Taiwan and had spent the last years in Los Angeles where she had made a name for herself by throwing elaborate costume parties and occasionally playing the erhu and singing chinese jazz songs from the time when Shanghai was known as the Paris of the East. She had since then moved to Harlem and had begun producing a monthly costume party named Dances of Vice. Ah, Dances of Vice, I said, the Rosa von Praunheim movie about Anita Berber the nude dancer of the Weimar Republic. Yes, she said, I am a big fan of everything Weimar and I have come here to ask you if you would consider performing german cabaret songs at my costume ball. I said to her, listen Shien. I have been doing Weimar cabaret in New York long before it became fashionable and do not mind doing more of it but now that everybody is producing Weimar-style cabarets in New York I think it is time for something different. What New York needs, I said, is something more international, possibly a Shanghai-style cabaret, and you could be the first one doing it. Shien Lee said she only needed Weimar cabaret. It was at about that time that I began to think of one day creating a cabaret of my own.

In the meanwhile in the art world everybody was talking about Damien Hirst cunningly buying back his own works to make a profit and the latest news was that his pickled shark had begun to disintegrate in its formaldehyde juice. Filip Noterdaeme could not help remarking on the irony in regards to the piece's title being The Physical Impossibility of Death in the Mind of Someone Living. He thought about it a little and then made fun of the whole situation by creating a sculpture he facetiously called The Physical Impossibility of Life in the Mind of Someone Dead. It was a steel bucket filled with bleached shinbones and a cow skull, very effective and guaranteed to last for a long time. One day Filip Noterdaeme played a terrible prank on me. We were having guests for tea, Gala the european disco pop star and her beautifully tall handsome surgeon boyfriend Andrew. I had met Gala through Lance Horne who had once accompanied her on the piano when she had given a cabaret performance in Shanghai. Gala and Andrew had just returned from a trip to Italy and brought us white italian torrone. Gala told us of her strange life of performing sold-out shows in stadiums in Europe and then returning to New York where she was reduced to personally handle all her business correspondence pretending to be her own assistant. After they left Filip Noterdaeme and I sat talking about the comedy and misery of stardom and suddenly he reached into the steel bucket of The Physical Impossibility of Life in the Mind of Someone Dead and pulling a tooth from the cow skull popped it into his mouth, cheerfully chewing on it, making loud crackling noises. Well, at that my hair just stood up. Then he burst out laughing and admitted it was not a cow's tooth he was chewing it was a piece of the white torrone he had sneakily fitted into the skull.

Cathleen Chaffee had begun working as an assistant curator at the Modern and arranged for us to attend an opening reception for members only. We arrived and were greeted by Cathleen Chaffee with the greatest delight. Everybody lingered by the open bar but Filip Noterdaeme wanted to look at the exhibition. We very much liked a sculpture by Martin Kippenberger called Martin, Stand in the Corner and Be Ashamed of Yourself. Then we saw Glenn Lowry showing a group of patrons around. We took a close look to see if it was true what Thom Collins had said about his facelift and indeed it did look like he had had a little nip and tuck as americans say, nip and tuck. We also remembered the rumor about his priapism and looked for a bulge in his pants but there was none.

We had another clandestine opening at 172 Clinton Street and Jonah Bokaer came with a handsome southern publishing agent named Bill Clegg. It was a new liaison for him and we thought it might be a good one but perhaps we did not know. Bill Clegg and Filip Noterdaeme talked at great length about peace activist Rachel Corrie whose journals Bill Clegg had published after she had died an absurd martyr's death in Palestine. It is, said Bill Clegg, of course the most important book of the year. He also said that his favorite book of all time was Jude the Obscure. He then told us that he was famous among his friends for his fried chicken and promised to cook it for us one day. Jonah Bokaer and Bill Clegg separated before Bill Clegg could make good on his promise and later, a good while later Bill Clegg published his own memoirs that exploited his absurd addiction to sex and crack cocaine.

Then came independent curator Nicholas Weist. He looked at everything and declared loudly that he was more fond of the Homeless Museum of Art than he was of any other museum. Filip Noterdaeme thought Nicholas

Weist witty and amusing and complimented him on his punk rocker hairdo, saying it was much more stylish than his beard. The two then talked at great length about hairdos and hair extensions. Filip Noterdaeme exclaimed, if only museums would hire hair stylists instead of star architects to create their extensions. The two talked happily and pleasantly for a long time and Filip Noterdaeme proposed a hair weave for the Modern and an afro for the Guggenheim. What about the Metropolitan Museum, said Nicholas Weist. An understated toupee will do, answered Filip Noterdaeme, no need to overdo it. Then the doorbell rang and it was a curator from Switzerland. He looked very swiss, with a rather round belly and a beard that wasn't stylish and in fact looked very much like Filip Noterdaeme's fake beard. I am sure he was not wearing lederhosen but in my mind as I look back he did, so complete was his swiss alpine image. He was also very much out of breath from walking up the stairs. This I found rather odd as everybody knows the swiss are usually so very well adapted to climbing high altitudes.

Then Gabrielle Giattino and Andrea Merkx came and Ellie Ga the petite explorer of cracks in the arctic ice and emotional young David Adamo. They all sat around the large bed in the Staff and Security Department and Filip Noterdaeme delighted in Andrea's quick wit and Gabrielle's ability to listen and understand. The conversation soon became lively. Everybody had something to say. Filip Noterdaeme said to David Adamo that feeling warm-felt feelings was always banal and futile and then he said to Ellie Ga that only the irritations and icy ecstasies of the artist's corrupted nervous system are artistic. Seth Cameron, one of the Bruces, as the members of the Bruce High Quality Foundation liked to call themselves, sat and listened attentively and then went down to the street to smoke one of his Gauloises as he was always wont to. He was from the South, Alabama or something but always posed as a blasé french intellectual which is why he smoked, and only Gauloises. Of course, any real french intellectual would have adamantly refused to leave the room for a smoke.

Filip Noterdaeme used to think that Seth Cameron had a purer intelligence than the other Bruces who he was quite sure had not created the collective, perhaps the idea had been originally his. Filip Noterdaeme once asked him had he originated the idea. He said with an intelligent inner smile that he thought he had. Filip Noterdaeme was not at all sure that he was not right. Seth Cameron said to Filip Noterdaeme, the Homeless Museum if it hasn't been perfectly obvious is a source of inspiration for us Bruces. We may be, he said, an amateur solution for professional problems but the Homeless Museum is an out-of-control solution for out-of-control problems. This at first pleased Filip Noterdaeme too much and then did not please him at all.

In the early days of the Bruce High Quality Foundation Filip Noterdaeme admitted that he had a weakness for the Bruces because they were such good pupils. They are rotten pupils, I protested. You don't understand, he said, it is so flattering to have pupils who do it without understanding it, in other words they take training and anybody who takes training is a favorite pupil. He admitted it was a weakness. Later when the Bruces became the new darlings of the art world Filip Noterdaeme lost interest in their work. They are having the success they are having because they look like contemporaries and they smell of the museums, he said. In the beginning, the Bruces had offered amateur solutions for professional problems but when things changed for them they began offering professional solutions for amateur problems. In short the adventure was over and they were doing what art world darlings were expected to do, they became divas slumming in the back of stretched limos.

Seth Cameron had brought along a young petite pretty woman with long straight black hair and fine features. Her name was Lena Imamura. She sat with me at the counter at Café Broodthaers and ate not one but two hard-boiled eggs and one mussel after another. This made me like her instantly. Lena Imamura had always been a New Yorker. She had grown up going to nightclub events with her father, a japanese american disc jockey of some renown, and this had taught her everything there was to know about New York nightlife. She told me of how she and two graffiti artist friends were running an art space in a Soho loft called the Canal Chapter. I told her that I was currently looking for a new venue for my cabaret performances. She was very interested. Maybe, she said, you should do your cabaret in our space. We have done art exhibits and fashion shows and film screenings and dance parties but never a cabaret, she said. Plus, she said, we are sponsored by Red Bull. I had heard of the swiss caffeine soda drink but had never tasted it. Oh, it's awfully sweet, Lena said, but the company is very generous with us. I said, I should very much like to see the space. We arranged to meet at the Canal Chapter. Before leaving, Lena said, when you come please do not mention Seth Cameron to anyone.

258

A few days later Filip Noterdaeme and I met with Lena Imamura and she showed us the Canal Chapter. It was a large loft on the fifth floor of a cast iron building on Canal Street, white, empty and beautiful with two very large blue velvet sofas in the front and a tiny disorderly office and storage space in the back. Then the two graffiti artists, Mike Sokovikov and Jason Wall arrived. Very evidently Jason Wall was Lena's boyfriend and that was the reason why we were not to mention Seth Cameron. He was a friendly lanky pale-faced bearded american who always walked with slightly bent knees and wore his dark hair long, all the way down to his hips. Mike Sokovikov, on the other hand, was a clever russian who looked very attractive in american jeans and knew how to get things done. Together the two were known as Mint and Serf. They felt themselves to be an important duo of the underground New York graffiti scene. They were very funny together. They had an impressive way to make up their minds very quickly and do things without hesitation. Filip Noterdaeme and I sat down on the empty blue velvet sofa and I began talking about the art of cabaret but Mike and Jason had already made up their minds and simply said, yes we would love to have a weekly cabaret night at the Canal Chapter, when can you start. I said, in April.

We left and on our way home Filip Noterdaeme said to me, Jason looks just like Jesus Christ in those old spanish paintings by Zurbaran. Later he showed me a Zurbaran painting of Christ Gathering His Clothes after the Flagellation and I had to agree. There was the hesitant bend in the knees, the dangling silken dark hair and the pleading eyes.

The next thing that happened was the dispute over

a very funny short story by Filip Noterdaeme called The Art Dealer. It had been commissioned by Annabel Daou, wife of MoMA curator Joachim Pissaro. Annabel was in the process of creating her so-called Disarmory Show as a critique of the official Armory Show of Contemporary Art and needed contributors for her planned Disarmory Show publication. She had heard about Filip Noterdaeme's bitingly satirical open letters and asked him to write something about art dealers. Filip Noterdaeme obligingly happily wrote a bitingly satirical short story about an art dealer and sent it to Annabel Daou. Much to his astonishment he did not hear back from her for a long time. Finally he called her and asked, is there something the matter with my story. Yes, she answered, I cannot possibly publish it, imagine the repercussions. The conversation soon became lively. Annabel Daou was all up in arms about the scandals that would or would not erupt if she published The Art Dealer in her Disarmory publication. And so Filip Noterdaeme learned that Annabel Daou was not in the least interested in disarming anybody or anything, she merely wanted publicity. The Art Dealer was eventually published, not in the alarmingly dishonest Disarmory Publication but in the delightfully dishonest first printed catalog of The Bruce High Quality Foundation.

I began thinking about the cabaret I was going to create at the Canal Chapter. For some reason or other, my recent acquaintance with Shien Lee in all probability, I had Shanghai on my mind, at any rate I wanted the cabaret to be as contemporary as the new Shanghai and as mysterious and international as Marlene Dietrich's Shanghai Lilly. It is a notable fact that I, one of the few real german cabaret performers in New York, decided to not create a Weimar cabaret but an international contemporary one. I named it the Shanghai Express Lounge. Everybody liked the name alright and Mike, Jason, Lena and I began transforming the Canal Chapter into a chinese speakeasy cabaret. I worked in those days with slow care and concentration and was very preoccupied with every detail. I wallpapered one entire wall of the loft with beautiful orange and gold chinese paper money and Mike and Jason, so adept at using power tools, built a small stage. The funny thing was that preparations for the Shanghai Express Lounge brought back memories of the cabaret events I had created when I was still in High school and then had as promptly forgotten.

Everything went as planned until one day a young woman with a lovely voice called me and said, my name is Juliette Campbell and I have heard that you are planning to open a speakeasy cabaret called Shanghai Express Lounge. Yes, I said. Well, she said in great distress, I happen to just have opened a speakeasy cabaret in Brooklyn named the Shanghai Mermaid, and I am calling to plead with you to reconsider the name for your cabaret. You see, she said, my Shanghai Mermaid has been years in the making and it would be detrimental for my business and confuse many people if suddenly there were to be two speakeasies in New York with a Shanghai connection. I said, I understand and let me think about it.

What to do. Shien Lee said, don't change the name, Juliette Campbell got it all wrong, there are no mermaids in chinese mythology, dragons yes but mermaids, not one. Filip Noterdaeme said, it should not be a problem at all for you to simply come up with another name, all you have to do is look up all titles of other Marlene Dietrich movies and surely you will find something. Not wanting there to be a war about Shanghai between Manhattan and Brooklyn, I followed Filip Noterdaeme's advice and renamed my cabaret Foreign Affairs. Ah, this name everybody liked even better and Juliette Campbell was very grateful. And then I came up with the wonderfully extravagant tagline, International Lounge, Postmodern Cabaret and Desperate Nostalgia Acts.

The Canal Chapter was fast beginning to look like a cabaret room. Lena Imamura made a beautifully large fluorescent Foreign Affairs sign to hang on the chinese paper money wall and I built a ticket booth out of a gilded antique picture frame I had found on the street. Mike and Jason convinced the managers at Red Bull to not only provide us with unlimited supplies of their caffeine soda but also with several cases of vodka for an open bar.

In the midst of all these eager preparations Boykin Curry called and said, governor Spitzer will be the guest of honor at a brunch I am hosting on my terrace, would you please prepare something fancy for us. It was going to be the Sunday after the Foreign Affairs opening so I said, yes, will do.

Juliette Campbell invited me to her Shanghai Mermaid speakeasy in Brooklyn. It was in the basement of a loft building close to the Manhattan Bridge and a very secretive affair. One had to walk along dark hallways and find a little door with a guard in a bowler hat with a red feather and once one had stepped through that door then, ah then one felt like one had dropped into another world. When I arrived the large festive room was already filled with people dressed in formal attire and there were candles and lampions everywhere and a jazz band playing and strippers dancing and Juliette Campbell, charming and nervous, welcoming everybody in a beautiful silk dress and peacock feathers in her hair. I had just ordered a cranberry juice at the bar and was talking to a young shorthaired woman and her handsome fiancé when suddenly Juliette Campbell rushed past us to quickly blow out all the candles in the room. Then the door opened and a large number of firemen in black fire suits and heavy boots walked in. The band nervously hesitatingly played on and I remember hearing two strippers pleading with the firemen, please don't shut us down, we will put on a really good show for you, promised. The firemen turned this way and that way and blushed and grinned and said ho ho ho. Then suddenly a group of police officers walked into the room followed by a very grim looking chief officer. Well there was nothing to do but make a fast exit through the back door. The next day Juliette Campbell told me that the police had in fact shut down her speakeasy soon after I had left but that neither she nor anybody else had gotten arrested. And, she said with a grin, I am already looking for a new venue, and the new Shanghai Mermaid will be even bigger and better. There was in her a fiery dedication to nightlife without rules that was curiously not in contradiction with her ladylike demeanor which I suppose made it that much easier for her to deal with the authorities.

The day before the opening of Foreign Affairs Governor Spitzer's picture was on the front page of all the dailies. Apparently he had been found frequenting illegal prostitutes and this discovery was the delight of all his critics. Everybody was talking about it and Boykin Curry very upset called and said, the brunch is off, naturally.

Opening night was an adventure. There was of course a guest list. The rule was, one had to be on the list to be let in, but it turned out that the door person Mike and Jason had hired was illiterate and this caused for a great deal of confusion for everybody who was lining up around the block waiting to be admitted. In the meanwhile I was pacing the floor upstairs in the loft frightfully nervous that the police might see the line of people and close Foreign Affairs even before it opened.

Little by little people began coming up on the elevator. I had hired alluring androgynous Matti of the Pixie Harlots to man the ticket booth and he did it in his usual charming way in high heels, sequins and glitter on his face. Everybody arrived and paid their admission and walked through a black curtain into the new cabaret room and who were they all. Filip Noterdaeme and I did not have the slightest idea but the loft soon got very crowded with young beautiful people and everybody was very excited to be there.

The program I had put together was an interesting one. I welcomed everyone and holding up the New York Post with governor Spitzer's face on the cover sang the Song of Sexual Dependency from The Threepenny Opera. Everybody laughed and applauded. Then the show continued with one performer after another. There was Nicole Renaud the french soprano with the accordion who always performs wearing a swim cap and beautiful long illuminated dresses. She sang a Serge Gainsbourg song about wanting to get off as quickly as possible. Then there was busty burlesque performer Amber Ray doing a delightfully sexy bebop black cat number with a very long cigarette holder that ended with her gingerly pulling a little white mouse out of her panties and swallowing it whole. Shien Lee demurely played the erhu and sang an acient chinese song about plum trees in bloom. And then came little great Sanda Weigl with a rumanian gypsy song that had everybody listen attentively, they just listened. Then it was intermission and DJ photographer Lucien Samaha played old records by Fairouz and Dalida and showed his colorful video montage of close-ups of Marlene Dietrich in Shanghai Express. The staircase behind the loft became the smoking lounge for those who smoked and those who wanted to get to know those who were smoking. I opened the second act with an old feminist anthem about women taking over politics and this everybody liked a great deal because many at the time were hoping that Hillary Clinton was going to be elected president of the United States. A week later Barack Obama decided to run against Hillary Clinton in the primaries and the political debate in America instantly shifted from the feminist to the racial. Perhaps at that time I did not feel that I was justified in continuing to present that song at Foreign Affairs, at any rate I replaced it with a new arrangement of Lili Marleen Rami Ramirez had written for me.

I do not remember who else performed on opening night, possibly Geo Wyeth, always fascinating on stage and elusive in person. Everybody who ever saw him perform usually went quite mad about him and wanted more and more of him no matter if they knew of his secret or not. In any case when the show was over everybody agreed that it had been a wonderful cabaret night and that they were going to tell everyone they knew about Foreign Affairs and come back the next week.

We hailed a taxi on Canal Street and as we were

crossing the Brooklyn Bridge Filip Noterdaeme said, well, you did it. Yes, I said, perhaps directing and hosting a cabaret is what I should be doing after all. Then I realized how nervously tired and hungry I was. I had not eaten all day, all I had had were Red Bull sodas, one can after another. When we got home I immediately made myself a bowl of what I call my vegetarian salami pasta, so very convenient to make on a whim late at night. As a matter of fact, cooking and eating vegetarian salami pasta late after a show has since then become a habit at 172 Clinton Street and I always keep all the necessary ingredients at hand in the refrigerator. One day, when I write the Daniel J. Isengart Cookbook I shall include the recipe.

It was only a few days later that we went to little David Lewis's birthday party at Celeste Holm's apartment on Central Park West. Naturally we were eager to go. David Lewis had told me that Rex Reed was going to be there so I brought along the Hildegard Knef autobiography that had the chapter about him he was so curious about.

We arrived and there were several lovely old ladies sitting in the living room. I was at first not quite sure which one of them was Celeste Holm, in fact I had a very pleasant conversation with one of them, saying nice flattering things to her thinking that it was Celeste Holm but I then found out it wasn't her at all. Michael Feinstein was there with his billionaire companion and said to me, my assistant Andy Brattain has told me such good things about Foreign Affairs. You should come by one night and see it for yourself, I said. At this his companion interrupted me and said, we are very busy and travel all the time, in short, we cannot be bothered.

Later that evening Michael Feinstein sat at the piano

singing love songs for the old ladies and batting his tinted eyelashes at them a great deal. Julie Wilson arrived late wearing a soft black velvet hat. Very evidently she was having a bad hair day. Celeste Holm asked her to sing a song and she obliged and sang one of Filip Noterdaeme's favorite songs, Down in the Depths of the Ninetieth Floor. It was very fitting and fetching. Then Celeste Holm's much younger husband insisted on singing, Who Wants to be a Millionaire. Celeste Holm reluctantly sarcastically chimed in every now and then, croaking I don't when prompted. Just then governor Cuomo walked into the room followed by a butler carrying a tray of little smoked salmon sandwiches. Filip Noterdaeme very amused by it all sat on the couch next to Rex Reed. Filip Noterdaeme delighted in his american cynicism and explanations of all things glamorous and catty. David Lewis played a few songs and then asked me to sing Marlene Dietrich's Falling in Love Again. I did and it went over rather well and then I joined Filip Noterdaeme and Rex Reed on the couch and showed Rex Reed the Hildegard Knef book. He got very excited and I translating read him the chapter in which she had written about their night on the town together. Rex Reed sat and listened like a little boy. It was a rather nice flattering portrait of him and New York in the early Seventies and he was very pleased. Then suddenly he got a little wistful. All these glamorous famous ladies, he said, I gave them the time of their lives but when the party was over they went home to their someones and I went home alone after doing all the work of showing them around and there was never anyone waiting for me in my bed.

Foreign Affairs continued to happen every week. I usually arrived at the loft early in the afternoon and most of the time it was in dreadful disorder with bottles on the floor and someone or other passed out on one of the blue velvet sofas from a party the night before. It was pure manual labor to throw out any hung-over graffiti artists out with the garbage and get everything clean and ready on time for the show. I never complained, I only thought of Marlene Dietrich who had famously scrubbed and mopped every concert stage on her hands and knees before making her glamorous white mink entrance. Then the musicians and guest performers arrived and settled in and Foreign Affairs was ready for showtime.

In the beginning it was mostly young artists and their friends who came to Foreign Affairs but after two weeks I started making out among the crowd some very serious-looking grown-ups in evening attire. They always arrived early and occupying all the seats sat silently politely waiting for the show to begin. Then there were special guests. Tommy Tune came with little David Lewis and he delighted in everything, the rawness of it all and the youth and erotic exotic energy. And then there was Yanna Avis.

I had heard much of Yanna Avis since I had moved to New York. She had for years had a charmed life as the glamorous young wife of car rental czar Warren Avis and made a name for herself as an international cabaret ingénue. Then Warren Avis had fallen ill and she had fallen on hard times. After his passing she had gone through a long period of silent mourning but now she was reawakening to the taste of cabaret and stage fever. We often saw her at my shows in those years and it was only a little later that she first mentioned to me that she was planning her cabaret come-back and that she had made up her mind that I should be her director.

Stefan Stzybel and his companion Philip Raia came every week. Stefan Stzybel was a large tall New Yorker of polish descent who always wore a comically tiny derby hat and tailored suits that in their way looked like they were not. When we first got to know him there was an ungainly wart on his right temple but he then had it removed. He liked to be called the tsar, Tsar Stefan. Filip Noterdaeme and Flotilla de Barge preferred to call him Steve. Ute Lemper the cabaret singer he adored above all others always called him Schteffan in the ordinary german way. Years later when he began to dabble in investing money in Broadway shows I took to calling him Broadway Baby.

All his life Stefan had been collecting vintage Mickey Mouse figurines and it was those figurines that had made his fortune. When we first met him he was just beginning to collect starving performers. Stefan loved to be entertained but what he loved even more was to do the entertaining and be at the center of it all. He often with simple recklessness held court at restaurants where the food was rich and his dinner guests and the waiters treated him like a tsar. Philip Raia gentle and calm always picked up the tab. Another thing that Stefan loved to do was giving gifts, highly useless gifts, and naturally every gift we ever received from him became part of our Oh Thank You Collection. I remember one evening he and Philip came to a dinner at 172 Clinton Street. We had utterly neglected to remove their many gifts from the Oh Thank You Collection wall and so there was no way to prevent them from seeing the ridiculous uselessness of their gifts, each and every one of them. Stefan took a sharp breath and then said, well well, what do we have here, a Tsar Stefan Wall. The next day we received a delightful thank you note from them. Thank you for a wonderful dinner, it said, the potted palm tree and stuffed giraffe are on the way.

Because of the success of Foreign Affairs every downtown cabaret performer now wanted to be considered for the show and I began my long apprenticeship of learning to say no to countless girls who fancied themselves burlesque performers. In those days every second girl one met wanted to be a burlesque performer and one had to be careful in dividing the talented from the desperate, in other words the ham from the spam. To me it was more satisfying to book bread and butter singers and songwriters like Rami Ramirez, Geo Wyeth and Todd Almond, talented rather wonderful singer songwriters. Todd Almond's songs were always strangely funny and beautifully tragic, in other words about life being too serious to be taken seriously. One if I remember rightly was about a handwritten note saying, love is mine at last, and he usually employed someone hidden in the wings to sing the last line with him in harmony. On the night he sang the song at Foreign Affairs Michael Slattery the opera singer was there to sing the last line with him. I remember watching Michael stand behind the curtain, eyes closed, and singing, love is mine at last, sounding like a beatific angel and looking like a pretty porky pig.

Then there was british La John Joseph who looked like a young Quentin Crisp and always performed in very elaborate fantasy costumes until I carefully gently urged him to give us the dandy not the diva. He did and made a large success of it.

I also remember the night Tine Kindermann performed with her musical saw. Little David Lewis and

Tommy Tune and Penny Arcade were sitting on the large blue velvet sofa and everybody else stood or sat on the floor and listened attentively. Tine Kindermann began playing the saw and sang a medieval german folk song about a little brother and sister dying of the black death. Evidently it was a serious poetic dark song but there was something not quite right about the musical saw that night. As Tommy Tune later put it, the saw was completely and utterly out of tune. The song went on and on, and I winced and Tine Kindermann too winced and her accordionist winced, and Tommy Tune and Filip Noterdaeme nearly exploded from trying not to laugh out loud. Everybody else sat with slightly vexed expressions on their faces wondering about the strange strained sound of medieval german music.

Then after five weeks Lena Imamura, Jason Wall and Mike Sokovikov lost their lease to the Canal street loft and Foreign Affairs closed. The Canal Chapter moved on to other things in a Lower East Side storefront but for all that the short Foreign Affairs run on Canal Street had changed my fortunes. I now had an established position as the creator of a successful downtown cabaret. People kept asking where and when Foreign Affairs would go on again, performers continued to contact me because they wanted to perform in it and venues contacted me because they wanted to host the show. It was not until the fall that Foreign Affairs reopened under very strenuous circumstances in a new venue, but more of that later.

The Whitney Biennial was a big to-do that year. Curator Shamim Momin had announced that there would be artists working in a kind of product-based nature where the work tended to be specific to the site of the exhibition or to the project they were working on. We went and I was furious, furious at the dull exhibits and furious that Shamim Momin in all those years had never bothered to accept our invitation to come to 172 Clinton Street where she would have witnessed an artist working in a completely product-free space where the work was already and completely one with its environment.

The Bruces, who had not yet become the darlings of the art world organized a sort of anti Whitney Biennial. They called it the Brucennial and announced that there would be disarming performances and art objects by over 100 artists. Filip Noterdaeme was going to be of it with his 1/2 Duchamp, a white kitchen stool with a perfect hole in the seat and no attached bicycle wheel.

We arrived at the Bruces' Bedford Stuyvesant storefront for the opening and it was quite a mad Brooklyn affair. There were young people standing everywhere drinking beer and to my surprise everybody was smoking cigarettes. We made sure that the 1/2 Duchamp was displayed correctly and then walked over to the far end of the gallery where Matthew Robert Lutz-Kinoy of the Freddy Mercury moustache was dancing and lip-synching to a recording of Freddy Mercury singing Love Kills. It was just mildly amusing until it suddenly became exciting when he ran over to a tall thin brunette in a purple tube top and without hesitation grabbed the beer can out of her hands and emptying the beer can over his head finished the song now looking utterly like sweaty manic Freddy Mercury at a Wimbledon Stadium concert. The only other thing I remember is a performance by three young men with a lot of facial hair doing strange things with suitcases and electrical saws and opening and closing a freestanding door they had set up in the middle of the space.

As I said the Bruces eventually became the darlings of the art world and it happened through their connections with the Schnabels. They continued to play at being bohemians but it was a pose. Creative Time gave them a building in Soho and they began selling their works through a swiss gallery and then later unavoidably they showed at the Whitney Biennale. The consequence of their success was that suddenly there was a great number of young New York artists forming collectives. It used to annoy Filip Noterdaeme dreadfully. He insisted that artist collectives had no identity, they had an output but no identity. Don't you understand the difference, he said angrily, any artist, any two artists, any hundreds of artists can have an identity and create something from this identity but artist collectives cannot have an identity in anything they do, they can have an output and this output can put them in the spotlight but that isn't an identity. The Bruces, he insisted, are not radical, they are careerists who have made a method of what we conceive as hip, can't you see. They cannot therefore possibly create anything meaningful because they are not radical.

It was only a little later that Cia Guo-Qiang the chinese gunpowder artist was given a retrospective at the Guggenheim Museum and he asked for submissions from artists for Everything Is Museum, a small side exhibit about the future of the art museum he was putting together for the Guggenheim's education department. Filip Noterdaeme submitted his model for the ISM, the Incredible Shrinking Museum, and it was included in the show. To Filip Noterdaeme's delight it was exhibited right next to a presentation of every museum project that Thomas Krens had proposed over the years and so everyone could with one look see and compare two completely differing visions by two completely differing museum directors. Thomas Krens's vision for the future of the art museum was expansion and Filip Noterdaeme's vision was implosion. Filip Noterdaeme immediately wrote an open letter to Thomas Krens, his fifth, a very funny letter in which he compared their two visions and called them the yin and yang of the museum world. Filip Noterdaeme put the letter in the mail and the next morning he read in the papers that Thomas Krens had resigned from the Guggenheim. It was quite a surprise and Paddy Johnson of Art Fag City wrote in her column, Who will HOMU's [The Homeless Museum of Art] Filip Noterdaeme address his letters to now that the man behind the Guggenheim franchise is leaving.

In those restless days Filip Noterdaeme often asked me, what can I do to keep the Homeless Museum alive. I cannot show it in our home and there seems to be no one wanting to show it somewhere else. In the meanwhile every day the papers published articles on other museums and it was all PR, praise and promotion. Filip Noterdaeme grew increasingly tired of reading about them and decided to facetiously pretend that art museums in New York were threatened by oblivion and that no one was laboring to make their existence known to the public. He carefully plotted an anti campaign called The Museum Awareness Campaign, MAC, and chuckled as he wrote little captions about each of New York City's top ten art museums for a little brochure, praising each museum's amenities such as their restaurants, shops and rooftop views and never once mentioning their art collections. He then took to the streets of Manhattan wearing his pink Paul Smith suit and fake beard and carrying a blackboard sign on which he wrote, Visit MoMA Today. He went to the Pulitzer Fountain on Fifth Avenue and began handing out his MAC brochures to passersby. When the time came for the annual Museum Mile Festival he went with Florence Coyote to take part, uninvited.

It was quite a scene around both of us that day. I was once again singing Brecht's radical socialist songs to everybody and anybody in front of billionaire Ronald Lauder's Neue Galerie, and Filip Noterdaeme was parading up and down Fifth Avenue with Florence Coyote in her pram and handing out his MAC brochures that urged everyone to please support New York's poor needy multimillion dollar museums. He was having a wonderful time and everybody was curious about his campaign. He ran into an old acquaintance from the old Bar d'O days, Lila Fontaine, a beautiful Rubenesque woman with perfect baby skin and the most charming smile. She immediately recognized him, took his arm and escorted him. Later they were joined by Eric Doeringer and Jason Wall and Mike Sokovikov. Then suddenly Robin Schatell the organizer of the Museum Mile Festival arrived on her razor scooter and barred the way. She had nervously followed, followed, followed Filip Noterdaeme up and down Fifth Avenue and now she had had enough. She was not going to have her festival spoiled by an artist. This was a serious festival, a serious event for museums and museum visitors only and not for artists, she would not tolerate such conduct and as a matter of fact was going to call the police to have Filip Noterdaeme immediately escorted off Fifth Avenue. Filip Noterdaeme did not budge and outraged

Jason Wall and Mike Sokovikov started arguing violently with Robin Schatell. Finally she departed on her razor scooter, sulking furiously. She stopped by the Neue Galerie where I, not knowing that any of this had happened, was still entertaining the crowd and just singing a german Brecht song about sweet revenge. We very much like what you do, she said to me after I finished, but we don't like this character over there with his pram and the stuffed dog. Oh I said, that is Filip Noterdaeme the Director of the Homeless Museum of Art, and it is not a dog it is a coyote. Do you mean to say, said she, that you know this man. Why yes, I replied, we belong together. At this she gave me a strange look and I remember thinking, surely I will never be asked to sing at the Museum Mile Festival again. And indeed I have not. A little while ago however I did have another opportunity to sing on Fifth Avenue, this time in the display windows of Bergdorf Goodman for a Fashion Week event. It was I and Joey Arias and Basil Twist and as the saying goes, we stopped traffic.

It was once again time for my summer cooking season in the Hamptons and I once again took the early train on Friday mornings sitting next to the same maids and cooks and nannies I had been seeing on the same train every summer for many years. They and I had aged a good deal but at least that year the train wagons were new, silver with blue vinyl seats and air-conditioning always on high, always too cold if you wore shorts and sandals. All of us regulars made it a habit of bringing scarves and blankets for the long Long Island train ride.

Filip Noterdaeme traveled to Copenhagen to give a presentation at a symposium. He decided to take along Florence Coyote and stage an interview with her. She will ask the questions and I will howl in reply, he said, and asked me to record questions in my best castrato cousin of Philippe de Montebello voice onto a CD.

On the day of his departure to Copenhagen he went to buy a large valise to pack up Florence for the plane. He went to an arab shopkeeper on Atlantic Avenue and came home with a very ugly burgundy-colored valise. I begged him to go back to the shop and exchange it for at least a black one. He flatly refused and we had a very violent argument about it. We fought and fought and finally we laughed and then it was time for him and Florence to go to the airport.

The next morning they landed in Copenhagen and Filip Noterdaeme presented a letter to danish customs that said, this taxidermy coyote is a work of art and needed for a presentation at such and such symposium. It was all very official and the authorities approved and Florence Coyote was welcomed into the Kingdom of Denmark.

Filip Noterdaeme remembers his trip to Copenhagen so well. When he returned a week later he said to me that perhaps one should live there. While in Copenhagen he met and spent time with many interesting people. There was Tony Chakar, a lebanese philosopher and also Elizabeth Streb of the John D. and Catherine T. MacArthur Foundation Genius Award. Elizabeth Streb was a real New Yorker and into extreme action dance. She once told Filip Noterdaeme that she did not believe in pathos. Then there was Pejk Malinovski, a great dane and poet. He told Filip Noterdaeme that he dreamed of traveling to Poetry, Texas. Filip Noterdaeme simply said to him, when in Poetry, read Poe to a tree. And in fact that is exactly what Pejk Malinovski did about a year later.

One day in Copenhagen Filip Noterdaeme visited the Gundtvigs church to look at its intricate brickwork. He had just entered the church when to his delight a young organist started playing Olivier Messiaen's Ascension on the church organ. Filip Noterdaeme has always had a fondness for organ music which may have something to do with his grandfather having been an organist. This story reminds me of an organ master class we once attended inside the Saint-Eustache church in Paris. It was given by a highly recognized master organist and it was perfectly enjoyable until one of the students, a young girl with wide hips and quite an accomplished organist as it were, began playing. We listened and looked and it was very unfortunate that she was wearing a lacy pink thong under low-cut jeans that day because no matter what she played and no matter how well she played it, once we had seen her thong, and there was no way to not see it as she sat with her back to the audience, every piece of music she played became The Thong Song.

On his last day in Copenhagen Filip Noterdaeme went to see an exhibit at the Kunshal Charlottenborg. He toured the museum and at one moment found himself alone in a gallery with a CD player playing a sound piece by Al Hansen. Without hesitation Filip Noterdaeme took the audio CD out of the little player and replaced it with the CD recording of Florence Coyote asking him questions. This little theft of his happened in the most casual spontaneous manner, a byproduct as it were of his happiness about being there and wanting to take along a little souvenir.

When he was back in New York Filip Noterdaeme insisted on causing a little more trouble, this time at the

Takashi Murakami retrospective at the Brooklyn Museum of Art. Murakami, having previously designed handbags and other things for the Louis Vuitton house had thought nothing of including a real Louis Vuitton boutique inside his museum retrospective. It was a very convenient way to sell more handbags. Filip Noterdaeme said, very well but a museum is not a real shopping mall until it has a sale. He asked Juan Olivares to help him design fliers that looked like discount fliers for the museum's Louis Vuitton boutique and distributed them in front of the museum entrance. Sheila McClear of Gawker wrote, that trouble-maker Filip Noterdaeme is at it again, and Tyler Green of Modern Art Notes wrote that the Homeless Museum of Art was the wittiest critique of big american museums. And then we left New York for the summer and boarded a plane to France.

We reached the little island in no time. It was the first time we were renting a charming little house that belonged to a retired french teacher. It had a lovely garden with a mulberry tree but it was astonishing how its insides with its french furniture and french paint and french carpets looked very much like every other french summer house. It was this house that inspired a very modern system I devised to hence make ourselves at home in any summer rental. It is a most efficient system. First one must take photographs, meticulous photographs of every detail in the house. Then one stores away all things that do not please the eye, such as seashell arrangements, embroidery, knick knacks, posters, paintings, framed photographs and calendars. If there are ticking clocks, televisions or radios, and there usually are, those must be put away as well. The final task is to go down on one's hands and knees and thoroughly clean the entire household. Only then may the real vacation begin.

As I said we radically made all those temporary changes to the little teacher's house and after that we truly had a marvelous time on the island just as usual. We got up early every morning and walked to Patisserie Mousnier to buy croissants. We never eat croissants anywhere else but on the little island and only those from Mousnier, and so naturally while we are there we must have them every day. At night, I always read to Filip Noterdaeme until he fell asleep. Then, as always, he preferred Nabokov to Thomas Mann and I preferred Thomas Mann to Nabokov. Filip Noterdaeme did not take to Thomas Mann until I read him his last book, Felix Krull, Confessions of a Con Man.

One afternoon, the tide was low, Filip Noterdaeme discovered little tiny black baby mussels growing on the rocks and said, I must have a miniature version of Marcel Broodthaers's Moules Casserole. We already had a miniature Broodthaers eggshell table as part of MoMA HMLSS and now he wanted a miniature Broodthaers Moules Casserole. He began harvesting and cleaning dozens of little tiny black baby mussels and insisted on taking them back to New York. There I painstakingly built a miniature version of Broodthaers's Moules Casserole using the little black mussels and a miniature casserole for dollhouses. Filip Noterdaeme liked the mini Moules Casserole alright but now he wanted me to install it inside a little music box like those twirling little ballerina dolls. It was a complicated project but I did everything as instructed and Filip Noterdaeme was very pleased with it and took to fondly calling it, Le Moulin Noir. On a whim, I made two pairs of earrings out of the leftover shells and then, two necklaces with rows of dried belgian fries. The earrings and necklaces became known as the Broodthaers Jewelry and we gave Cathleen Chaffee one set as a farewell gift when she left New York to spend a year in Brussels where she planned to work on her Marcel Broodthaers thesis.

We were happy to be back at 172 Clinton Street and there was excitement in the air. Over the summer, Bowen Ames had been at his family's farm estate upstate, close to the canadian border, and with the help of several artist friends had realized the Solarplex, Filip Noterdaeme's idea for an open air theater intended for sunset watching only. The premiere screening of The Sunset was going to happen on Labor Day. Naturally Filip Noterdaeme wanted to be there and agreed to travel there on a Greyhound bus. It left on a rainy midnight from Port Authority. It left but it never made it, there was a problem with the motor and the bus returned to New York and so Filip Noterdaeme, more than a little unnerved, found himself back in New York after 6 hours of travel without having gotten anywhere. Anyway, on Labor Day the sun set upstate without the director and Bowen Ames later told us that when the sun had finally completely set everybody who had come, there were quite a few, rose to their feet and enthusiastically applauded the star.

For quite some time, Filip Noterdaeme had dreamed of creating a collection of DNA samples from artists he held in high esteem. If they weren't alive anymore, he decided, a hair from a blood relative would do. He called the project the CPRA, the Center for the Preservation and Resurrection of Artists.

His first target was Dimitri Nabokov, the son of

Vladimir. After much combing through his contacts to find someone who might have a way to contact Dimitri to ask for a strand of hair, Lila Aza Zanganeh volunteered. Unfortunately Dimitri was balding and as it turned out not at all willing to give up even a single hair for anybody, not for Filip Noterdaeme or anybody else. Next was Anna Reinhardt, daughter of Ad. Filip Noterdaeme met her at a symposium and boldly asked her for a strand of hair for his project. Anna Reinhardt without batting an eye plucked a long grey hair from her head and gave it to him. Filip Noterdaeme was delighted.

The CPRA collection grew very slowly. Justin Bond flatly refused, saying that a witch did not give away her hair. Penny Arcade obliged and plucked a hair from her right eyebrow. Lady Rizo gave Filip Noterdaeme a hair of her left nipple. Each hair was stored in its own little vial and kept for posterity and possible cloning. I have not yet asked Evee Lynn for a hair sample but one day I will.

The Homeless Museum had by now been under house arrest for close to two years. They had been very productive very hectic years. However it all finally came to an end. How. Filip Noterdaeme found a solution to bring the Homeless Museum into the outside world. He asked me to build a new HOMU Booth, similar to the one he had used at the Armory Show but lighter and portable so he could transport it with ease and set it up wherever he pleased. From now on, he said, the museum will be wherever I am.

I built the booth and painted it Richard Meier White and wrote, THE HOMELESS MUSEUM OF ART and, THE DIRECTOR IS IN onto it in Donald Judd green.

And this is how Filip Noterdaeme finally found his

essence. Once he started performing on the street with the new booth what had begun in the Staff and Security Department now became refined, picky, special, he became allergic to banality and extremely intuitive in regards to the inner lives of his visitors. He was, in short, more interested in their lives than in art. The first spot Filip Noterdaeme picked to set up the new HOMU Booth was a machiavellian choice. It was on the Bowery, in front of a vacant building between the New Museum and the Bowery Mission. People wandered past the booth and people sat down at the booth and the house arrest was over and the dread of not being able to show his museum to the public disappeared and peace was upon him.

VII
On the Street
2008-2010

We were, in these days as I look back at them, constantly on the run.

I was eager to find a new home for Foreign Affairs and Filip Noterdaeme was about to bring the Homeless Museum to the streets of Manhattan.

After Foreign Affairs closed at the Canal Chapter Neke Carson invited me to present the cabaret revue at the Gershwin Hotel Lounge. Mike Sokovikov and Jason Wall were going to produce and promote it again and at first it looked as if it was going to be just like before. Then little by little they let me down and I had to produce Foreign Affairs all by myself. I believed I could achieve this.

The Gershwin Hotel lounge had a grand piano on a dais and several sofas but little else. Preparations began and I was, as I said, constantly on the run, here and everywhere, in other words really nowhere. It was the beginning of a long series of mishaps and collapse.

It began with the large black curtain I made for the stage. I sewed it by hand and added nickel grommets to hang it up. It looked very beautiful in the lounge but then a manager from the Gershwin hotel appeared and said, this curtain must be treated with fireproofing liquid. Well I did that too and it was laborious and expensive and I hung it up again and then the manager reappeared and said, no no, it must be done by someone with a certificate. Well at that I gave up on the idea of the curtain altogether and gave it to Shien Lee to use for her costume balls. Then another thing that used to preoccupy me terribly was the fact that the Gershwin Hotel did not have a liquor license and that I did not have a sponsor for an open bar like I had had at the Canal Chapter.

Raven O had left Las Vegas and everybody was talking about his show at a new downtown nightclub called The Box. I went to see it for myself with Yanna Avis and her friend Yanou Collart, a belgian press agent for french chefs. Yanou was very impressed with Raven O's platinum hair and tight white jeans and assertive authoritative way to play cat and mouse with the audience. I said, yes indeed Raven O has always been as sharp as a tiger in a cage but since his return from Las Vegas he has become a white tiger on the run. The show was a vigorous one and when Raven O sang Love for Sale Yanou all excited called out, I'm buying. Later I introduced her to Raven O and to Yanna Avis's great amusement she promised to try to get him invited to perform at the Crazy Horse in Paris. Yanou had a very assertive way to be helpful and when I told her of my worries about not having a liquor sponsor for Foreign Affairs she immediately arranged for the delivery of four cases of french wine.

Opening night came and there were more problems. Yanou Collart was furious because I, having been awfully preoccupied with too many things had nearly forgotten to send out a VIP invitation to her friend Gael Greene. Mike Sokovikov and Jason Wall complained because they wanted priority seating and bottle service and there was neither, and Yanna Avis and Rex Reed were in a bad mood because they were seated next to loud imposing Stefan Stzybel. Meanwhile backstage there was tension in the air because I had unwittingly booked both Justin Bond's newly former musical director Kenny Mellman and Justin Bond's formally new musical director Our Lady J. The show began and everything was going particularly wrong. Kenny Mellman not all too pleased of having to share the stage with his successor got into quite a state and his performance was a sinister one. Meanwhile Our Lady J had cancelled her back-up singers and instead of the rousing gospel-song I had requested perfomed a strangely demure song about a gun inside a pink Prada purse. Then there was Coco, a young protégé of Stefan Stzybel. She was a pretty thin girl, alive with big pools of eyes and a charming way about her. I had agreed to let her perform after Stefan had again and again assured me that she was the new Josephine Baker but hers was a half-baked performance, in other words it had a certain yeast but it did not rise. I have since then vehemently refused to take on any of Stefan Stzybel's protégés.

It was on that same night that I reinterpreted Marlene Dietrich's famous gorilla number from Blonde Venus for the first time. Everyone agreed that the gorilla suit and mask I had bought were a marvel but in fact it was nearly impossible to see anything through the mask's tiny eye slits and so it was quite an arduous process to make my way through the audience and onto the stage. Filip Noterdaeme was handling the follow spot and I groped and stumbled and did my best to grope and stumble in a very gorilla-like way. Overall I believe the impression I gave was a dramatic one. Having finally reached the stage

I stripped out of the gorilla costume and then sang about Hot Voodoo wearing nothing but sequined hot pants. These were the delight of Rex Reed who later wrote to me, well that was not a very good evening but you looked pretty good in those hot pants. I wrote back, well I am glad that my ass has saved my ass.

I stubbornly continued to produce Foreign Affairs on my own for several weeks. Before each show I bought liquor for an open bar and after each show I paid out the musicians the dancers, the singers and the bartender. Neke Carson having simply sat at the ticket booth all night collecting money kept two thirds of the ticket sales walking away with full pockets after each show while I went home broke and depressed. Filip Noterdaeme to amuse me put on my gorilla mask and jumping up and down with a kind of high monkey squeal screeched Henry James' famous words, We work in the dark, we do what we can, we give what we have, our doubt is our passion and passion is our task, the rest is the madness of art. No, I said, the rest is silence.

The most exciting guest performer I booked for Foreign Affairs at the Gershwin Hotel was Lady Rizo. She was at that time still a bratty girl singer getting her act together which is to say that she had not yet fully mastered the technique of stealing every show and still be a lady but everybody already liked her a great deal. She looked very nice in the room and everybody commented on her dramatic vibrato.

Then one night Lee Chappell came to Foreign Affairs. I had first known Lee Chappell in the early Nineties when he was still holding court on Saturday nights at the Roxy where he produced events that were all glamour and glitz in a charmingly provincial way. Things had suddenly changed for him when nobody cared for glamour and glitz any longer and muscular go-go boys in combat boots became the new thing. In short, he had fallen on hard times and was reduced to working as a receptionist at a hair salon.

So now Lee Chappell had come to see Foreign Affairs at the Gershwin. He usually seemed to be feeling a great deal of excitement and always showed and expressed it. After the show he said to me, Daniel, I just made a little inheritance and this will finally get me back into the business of nightlife. I want to help you out, he said, as a matter of fact we can help each other out. Let me, he said, produce Foreign Affairs and together we can take it to the next level. This was a favorite expression of Lee Chappell's, to take it to the next level, and he used it an awful lot. I did not realize then how completely and entirely an opportunist Lee Chappell was. He promised he would take care of everything and find a better venue to restart Foreign Affairs in the spring. And so we agreed that I would continue to star and direct and he would produce and one week later I closed Foreign Affairs at the Gershwin.

The next thing that happened was Sarah Bodinson calling and saying, I have told everyone at the Modern about Foreign Affairs and they want you to put together a cabaret night for the current exhibit, Kirchner and the Berlin Street. Naturally I was all for it. I created a cabaret named The Boulevard of Berlin Dreams, and it was completely modern. The performers I invited to take part were little Sanda Weigl, Lady Rizo, Amber Ray, and Rami Ramirez. I also hired a group of preppy proper young musicians from the Manhattan School of Music called Grandpa Musselman and his Syncopators. Years later Filip Noterdaeme arranged for them to play at the Guggenheim Museum's annual staff party but to our great regret the acoustics in the rotunda being rather appalling one could barely hear their preppy proper New Orleans jazz syncopations.

The Boulevard of Berlin Dreams was a big success in every way. However the highlight was a runway show I commissioned from Machine Dazzle who was at the time beginning to make a name for himself as a cut and paste costume designer working in the ways of dada and trash rather than Prada and cash like everybody else. I staged the runway show to a grand chorale from a Philip Glass opera and it was one Kirchner painting after another come to life in the downtown New York style. Then the show was over and everybody received a Modern paycheck.

It was at about the same time that Mashinka Firunts, a petite curatorial student who liked to dress in dainty vintage black and white hats dresses and gloves and sometimes worked at the front desk of the Neue Galerie asked me for an interview. It seems, she began, that you are often presenting cabaret shows inside museums. Yes, I said. Do you, asked she, consider your work a part of what we call relational aesthetics. I told her in no uncertain terms that I have and had nothing to do with relational aesthetics. I am an aesthete and I always relate to my audience but no matter where I perform, I am always I, an entertainer. In other words thai food is always just thai food no matter where you eat it and entertainment is always just entertainment no matter where you find it. The question is, I said, is it good thai food and is it good entertainment.

It was only a little later that month that Filip Noter-daeme brought the new HOMU Booth to the original Boulevard of Broken Dreams, the Bowery on the Lower East Side. Here I must explain why he went to the Bowery and how it had everything to do with homelessness and the New Museum.

Filip Noterdaeme remembered the old New Museum well. He had often gone to see exhibits there during the Nineties and once we had gone there together to meet and greet Pierre et Gilles. As I said things had changed since then. Marcia Tucker was dead and the New Museum had broken new ground on the Bowery where over the years the old flophouses had been shut down and replaced by boutique hotels and fancy restaurants. There was then only one flophouse and one homeless shelter left, the Sunshine Hotel and the Bowery Mission. The Sunshine Hotel was on the New Museum's right and the Bowery Mission on its left. Filip Noterdaeme set up his booth between the New Museum and the Bowery Mission and began his long apprenticeship of sitting on the chair of solitude and listening to strangers. The street performance, his first of that kind, became known as Mission on the Bowery and it was the beginning of the Homeless Museum changing from being a museum for insiders to being a museum for outsiders. It was not much later that it became a museum for everybody.

Mission on the Bowery lasted 4 weeks. During that time Filip Noterdaeme wrote two new open letters every week and in these were each time expressed two juxtaposed perspectives by addressing two juxtaposed types of characters such as the artist and the amateur. He always brought along a stack of copies of the latest set of letters to his Sunday afternoon performances and handed them out to everyone passing by. Reading the letters was like observing an exercise in counterpoint. They were most amusing in a greek way and many who read them were bewildered.

One person who understood everything about the letters was Penny Arcade. She came and quite simply and directly as is her way told Filip Noterdaeme what she thought of his presence on the street and what it meant to her. Ah the letters, she said, they are so brilliant, so incredible. She said Filip Noterdaeme and Jack Smith were the only people she knew who dared to openly critique the politics of art. She said it and then she wrote about it to everybody she knew.

One day a young reporter from the Metro Section of The New York Times approached Filip Noterdaeme at his booth. She had that curious attitude of a good reporter and was very interested to learn more about Filip Noterdaeme and his Homeless Museum. Her name was Lily Koppel. Many homeless men from the Bowery Mission had also become curious about Filip Noterdaeme and his strange booth. Some of them thought that perhaps the Homeless Museum was all about them. They came one at a time and sat down. Some asked questions but most of them simply sat and told Filip Noterdaeme their tale of woe. One of them was a soft-spoken sad man named Albert who lived at the Sunshine Hotel and got all his meals at the Mission and so there was a great deal of him walking past the HOMU Booth in either direction. He often paused to talk to Filip Noterdaeme and his life story floated out of him like corpses from the past.

It was rather remarkable that no one from the New

Museum ever stopped by the booth or sat down to talk to Filip Noterdaeme. He had at least expected Amy Mackie to come and sit down. She was a distant acquaintance and worked as an associate curator at the New Museum. At first when he had told her about it she had seemed curious about Mission on the Bowery. Every week he waited for Amy Mackie or someone, anyone from the New Museum to visit the HOMU Booth and when it became clear that nobody would come he decided to write one of his sets of open letters to Albert and Amy. The letter to Albert included a statement by Marcia Tucker, Act first, think later, that way you have something to think about. The letter to Amy Mackie referred to the reasons why Marcia Tucker had created the New Museum after having been fired from the Whitney Museum and urged Amy to defect from the New Museum that in the meanwhile had begun to resemble the old Whitney an awful lot and start a museum of her own.

Amy Mackie did not reply to the letter and declined to talk to Lily Koppel. Later we found out that as a matter of fact the public relations department of the New Museum had warned staff members to not talk to Lily Koppel about Filip Noterdaeme and his street performance. In any case, her New York Times article came out only a little later and it was titled A Museum With No Exhibits, but Plenty of Ideas. Filip Noterdaeme said, better than being a museum with no ideas and plenty of exhibits.

That same week, we went to a Creative Time party at the Mason Dixon Line, an East Village bar with a mechanical bull. Amy Mackie was there with her Gucci handbag and when she saw Filip Noterdaeme I am quite sure there was suddenly an expression of panic on her face. Filip

Noterdaeme slowly moved in her direction to talk to her and she hurriedly made a very fast exit anxiously clutching her Gucci handbag. This irritated Filip Noterdaeme a great deal. I said to him, look you must understand that between you and the Gucci handbag she naturally chose the Gucci handbag. The New Museum, I explained, gives nice salaries, nice for living in gentrified New York City and nice for buying handbags but they do not like their assistant curators interacting with outside artists not even in a bar with a mechanical bull and so Amy Mackie not wanting there to be any terrible repercussions naturally is now avoiding you à tout prix. I believe the handbag was cream colored but it might also have been a light brown crocodile affair, I cannot say. How can it be, Filip Noterdaeme said, that the New Museum, a once radical institution is becoming even more guarded than the Museum of Modern Art. Even Director Glenn Lowry, he exclaimed, had listened and talked to me in the days of the Penny Campaign.

The following Sunday Filip Noterdaeme went to the Bowery for the last time and handed out copies of his final set of open letters. They were addressed to Jesus Christ and to Lisa Phillips the director of the New Museum, and they summed up his experience of the last four weeks. At the end of the day he folded up his booth and left the Bowery never to return.

After Mission on the Bowery, Filip Noterdaeme could never inhabit his own self quite the same way again, which is to say that he had changed. For weeks he dreamt and talked about what had happened, about the homeless who had come and talked to him and the art world insiders who had not. He went into a period of mourning and hibernation and began reading Tristes Tropiques by Lévi-Strauss. The first sentence is an interesting one, Je hais les voyages et les explorateurs, I hate traveling and explorers. The rest of the book is all tropical travels and sad explorations.

Then it was Christmas time and Boykin Curry and Celerie Kemble asked me to come cook for them in the Dominican Republic for the third time. This time it was going to be a family affair. I boarded an early plane to Santa Domingo and when I arrived in the late morning there was again the Botero driver waiting for me. His name was Miguel and he still spoke only a few words of English. Once again, it was a long car ride to the hotel but this time it was daytime and it was hot. The car radio was loudly playing Salsa and Merengue music and I remember Miguel turning around and looking at me in the back seat and shouting, Daniel you like Dominican Republic. Si senor, es muy lindo, I said. We first drove to my hotel and then to the villa were I was going to cook for Boykin and Celerie and there were security guards and maids and a pretty round swimming pool. Then we drove to the market. Miguel was involved in all kinds of businesses and had special arrangements with every store he took me to. He always carried a gun in a halter under his jacket. He was very proud of his gun. He said it was necessario for my protection and because of the dinero he was carrying to pay for all the groceries I was buying. The most important thing I had to buy was a special chlorine solution for treating fruits and vegetables against parasites. Then there was the question of the tap water at the villa. The security guards and the maids said, no hay peligro, no te preoccupes, there is no danger don't worry, but no one was quite sure if the villa had a water filter system. I say no one was quite sure but perhaps they knew that there wasn't.

I stayed in the Dominican Republic for four days. Every morning Miguel picked me up and drove me to the markets. One day we went to a chicken farm where I had to point at live chickens. They all looked the same to me and I remember how strange it was to sit in the car with four still warm deplumed eviscerated chickens on my lap. I also remember that the local fish stores carried mostly frozen seafood, and even when it appeared fresh at first it was often not. In short, one never knew.

I found cooking in the Dominican Republic decidedly more strenuous than in New York or anywhere else. I never stopped worrying about the famously contaminated water of the island and even though I only used bottled water for cooking there still was the question of the dishwater.

The last dinner I served before returning to New York I remember very well. It was a very elaborate indian rice feast. The guests arrived and sat down and began eating prawn curry and rice and other things and suddenly the doorbell rang again and it was Mark Colodny one of Boykin Curry's New York friends. I was beside myself because Mark Colodny was famously allergic to all kinds of spices and I had used all kinds of spices for every single dish of the indian rice feast. He told me not to worry and helped himself to a bag of potato chips. I believe that may very well have been all he had to eat that night.

The next morning I flew back to New York and once I arrived I immediately had to call our house doctor for an appointment. He said, caribbean traveler's diarrhea, don't you know the rule, boil it, peel it, cook it, or forget it. I said I did boil, peel and cook it and I still got it. When Boykin Curry asked me to come once again to the Dominican Republic the next year I told him in the nicest way possible, your paradise is not for me, in other words I would prefer not to. You see, said I, I love culinary explorations but I hate traveling to the sad tropics.

It was during that same winter that the Cleveland Museum in Ohio hired me to come and perform at the opening of a Lalique Jewelry show. It was all about diamonds are a girl's best friend and life is a cabaret. I went with three musicians. I asked Todd Almond with whom I had had much success at Café Sabarsky and also Patrick Farrell a charming young accordion player from New Orleans and then there was Mike Jackson on bass.

Mike Jackson had been the bass player in the band of the old Weimar New York shows and he and I had once represented the show on a very hot July day at Jeffrey Deitch's Art Parade in Soho. I did not know the connection at the time but I later found out that Weimar New York had been invited to take part in the parade mostly because Mike Jackson's girlfriend Suzanne Geiss was the managing director of Deitch Projects. In any case the carpenters of Deitch Projects had built a Weimar New York float for us that was going to be pulled by four muscular boys in sequined shorts. We started out just fine but after just a few paces one of the wheels of the float broke and so there was nothing else to do for us than walk the parade. I sang the theme song of Weimar New York over and over again and Mike Jackson as may well be imagined had a difficult time walking with his upright bass while playing it. It was during that afternoon that he confessed to me that he much preferred playing the guitar.

So now we were going to perform at the Cleveland Museum. When we arrived I heard that the local Cleveland press had already amusingly announced that I was a performer from New York who had once transformed his Brooklyn apartment into a museum for the homeless. The other performer booked for the event was Baby Dee who once had been an East Village fixture playing the harp atop a high-rise tricycle. That evening at the Cleveland Museum she played the harp sitting on a stool not on a tricycle and I delighted in her performance, so strange as a museum performance in Cleveland and yet so reminiscent of a New York of the past.

After the show Baby Dee and I had a chat in the green room. She said, I mostly moved to Cleveland to avoid becoming homeless. I thought that perhaps she could use a hair stylist but she insisted on what she called her cowboy hat hairstyle. We talked about Joey Arias and Antony of Antony and the Johnsons who was having his big break at around that time. Baby Dee said in regards to Antony, well he used to be obsessed with Joey Arias and one day he should acknowledge Joey's influence on his style.

While I was in Cleveland Filip Noterdaeme took a daytrip with Penny Arcade to Montclair University in New Jersey to see a Jan Fabre production called Orgy of Tolerance. Filip Noterdaeme delighted in Penny Arcade. The two talked a great deal during the bus ride and when Filip Noterdaeme told Penny that he had been feeling very self-absorbed lately she said, oh Filip an artist can never be self-absorbed enough. She then told him of something Quentin Crisp used to say to her and which she loved to quote in Quentin Crisp's voice, Miss Arcade, time is kind to us nonconformists. Penny Arcade knew many interesting lines by other artists she had known and worked with and when she quoted them she always gave them credit and turned it into a performance by imitating their voices, sometimes funny sometimes tragic and sometimes both at the same time, whenever she quoted Jack Smith, which was often.

When they arrived at the Montclair University auditorium there were already quite a number of art world insiders who had come all the way from New York City to see Jan Fabre. There was Mathew Barney and his diminutive little wife Björk and also Antony of Antony and the Johnsons, big and shy.

Then the lights dimmed and the orgy of tolerance began, a big to-do with plenty of musicians actors and dancers. And then the tolerant orgy ended and Jan Fabre spoke to the audience explaining that the piece referred to the orgy of consumption and revealed the decay of the human race.

Back in New York one early morning Juan Olivares came to 172 Clinton Street to take photographs of Filip Noterdaeme in bed for his new series called, Men I Want to Sleep With. He was at the time working for Terence Koh and apparently sleeping with many men and photographing more.

Lee Chappell in all this time had been looking for a new venue for Foreign Affairs. I was very anxious that he should find one. Finally he found the lounge in the back of the Night Hotel on 45th Street near Times Square. As it turned out the manager of the hotel had tried to get some business going in the lounge on weeknights but had not succeeded. The way in which Lee Chappell explained to him how hosting Foreign Affairs on Mondays would be a win-win situation for everybody impressed him immediately. The manager said he would talk to the owners and convince them to let us have the lounge on Monday nights. He did and preparations for the new Foreign Affairs began. Not wanting to host the show by myself again I asked Lady Rizo to be my co-hostess. It was going to be her first New York residency and she was excited, evidently even more excited and amused than I. It was for this occasion that Liz Liguori shot the very fine double portrait of the two of us on the white leather sofa. Lady Rizo leaned over me and asked solemnly, do you like my mascara. I hesitated, why yes, I am wearing the same.

During these early months of the Foreign Affairs revival Lee Chappell worked a great deal. Not as in the old Roxy days, night after night, but once a week. He was particularly fond of decorating the Night Hotel lounge with glitz and glitter. He also had a little foldable stage with metal hinges built for the show, just large enough for one person to stand on, and it was from that stage, the smallest stage in all of New York City, that I fell off during the show one night and broke a rib but that was not until many months later.

Across from the Night Hotel was the Grace Hotel. It had a heated indoor pool in its lounge and Lee Chappell convinced the hotel owners to let him produce a late night pool party on the same night as Foreign Affairs at the Night Hotel. It was I who told him to name the party DR!P. The pool party was hosted by Shequida and very quickly became popular with boys who liked boys and men who liked boys who looked like girls. I had first known Shequida when she used to perform at a nightclub called Fez, now closed. Shequida sang beautiful Italian soprano arias, some lapses into baritone pop songs that I cared for less, but she had been trained at Juilliard, her voice was lovely and she was very very beautiful with a marvelous café au lait complexion. She was a gender illusionist not a drag queen as she liked to point out and she had the long thin legs that give the characteristic beauty to all gender illusionists.

One of the nice things about the new Foreign Affairs was that there was going to be a house band. Mike Jackson was finally going to play the guitar and then there was Dave Berger on drums and Patrick Farrell on accordion and sometimes a young trombone or trumpet player from Granpa Musselman's band or handsome little Yair Evnine who played every instrument, be it the cello or the guitar, with a purer intelligence than most and who liked to talk about food. An ardent californian of israeli descent, Yair Evnine was more serious about food than jewish customs and in fact routinely prepared home-cured bacon. I also remember how one Christmas season he went wild about my Jamaican Black Cake.

We usually rehearsed on Sunday mornings at the loft where Mike Jackson was living with Suzanne Geiss. The loft had a lot of strange modern art and a room full of expensive clothes. Suzanne Geiss and Mike Jackson had always adored fashion, they had spent fortunes on fashion, more than anybody they understood the importance of being dressed appropriately fashionable in the world of contemporary art.

I usually arrived at the loft with pastries and Mike Jackson served tea or coffee. Lady Rizo always arrived late and it was the only time one ever saw her without makeup and her hair undone and wearing glasses and it was always a bit of a shock to see her like that, so different yet so much herself. I always liked working with Lady Rizo. She was comfortably fearless onstage and comfortably fearless off stage and singing a duet with her was always a walk on the wild side.

The new Foreign Affairs opened.

In the beginning the Night Hotel manager let us use a hotel room for our dressing room but when the hotel maids began complaining about glitter on the floor and glitter on the bed and makeup on the towels we were downgraded to a locker room in the basement, behind the kitchen where one could see a tired cook prepare frozen mini burgers and other hotel foods.

Over the next months I invited everybody who was anybody to perform at Foreign Affairs. There was Sherry Vine and Nicole Renaud and Flotilla de Barge appeared and Julie Atlas Muz and Amber Ray and Worldfamous Bob and Sade Pendarvis and of course Dirty Martini and Ms. Tickle and Lance Horne and also Spencer Day who somehow always made me think of fresh country apples. There were many more. How well I remember pretty magician Michael Carbonaro doing the shaving cream pantomime that later made his success on television. He was still pleasantly smelling of shaving cream when he came up to me after the show one night in great distress and said, I am not feeling all that well. He was very pale and very anxious and so I took him to a hotel room and made him lie down on one of the queen-size beds with the pretty black and white satin sheets. I was still trying to cheer him up when Lady Rizo and Brady McDonald the madly talented Mark Morris dancer came into the room.

301

Naturally they were more experienced than I with these sorts of things and began discussing breathing exercises and meditation. Then Filip Noterdaeme walked into the room. I was still sitting next to Michael, holding his hand and saying soothing things. Filip Noterdaeme laughed and I looked sheepish. Later he teased me and said, naturally you felt all al dente about pretty Michael Carbonaro lying in bed like a bowl of spaghetti.

Joey Arias was finally back in New York after six long years in Las Vegas. He for sure was not going to go back to performing in small clubs but he promised me to one day do a guest appearance at Foreign Affairs as a favor.

We were in those days all very hopeful that Foreign Affairs could become a real enterprise. Lee Chappell insisted that he could make it happen with the help of public relations agent Jeanine Pepler. Yet there was tension in the air before every show because not a great many people came and it made me wonder about Jeanine Pepler. I kept telling Lee Chappell that he needed not a public relations agent but a promoter with New York City nightlife connections. Lee Chappell insisted that he only needed Jeanine Pepler.

After the show everybody usually went across the street to DR!P to look at pretty boys dipping and dripping. It was a lively scene. Shequida ran a tight ship and it was always amusing to talk to her. She was surprisingly in boy drag on those occasions and this made her look not like an opera diva as usual but like Grace Jones trying to pass as a homeboy.

Tommy Tune came to the new Foreign Affairs. He sat next to Filip Noterdaeme and leaning over whispered to him, I have just been named a New York Landmark.

Julie Wilson was also in the audience that night but for some reason she refused to be introduced to Tommy Tune. This did not mean that she was coming to think that he was to blame for her not having been cast in his Broadway musical Nine, it proved nothing, but on the other hand it did possibly indicate something. Having had not a Broadway career but having become the doyenne of cabaret instead Julie Wilson had never been declared a landmark but Filip Noterdaeme thought she was if not a landmark then at least a milestone. Then there was the time when little great Sanda Weigl brought Rosa von Praunheim the queer german film director. We talked after the show and he invited me to assist him with a reading at the Gay Center on 13th Street the next day. I do not remember the reading but remember Rosa and I waltzing down the aisle as I sang La Vie en Rosa at the end.

The next week we invited Rosa and his young blond boyfriend to have dinner with us at 172 Clinton Street. It was a Monday and naturally I spent the whole day cooking and then we sat and waited for Rosa and his boyfriend to arrive. The food was already getting cold when the telephone rang. It was Rosa saying I am not feeling well from a lunch we had earlier today at the cafeteria at the Metropolitan Museum, apologies but we are not coming. I wished him all the best and hung up and told Filip Noterdaeme, dinner is off, and Filip Noterdaeme remarked that the Metropolitan Museum was closed on Mondays and that Rosa should stand in the corner and be ashamed of himself like Martin Kippenberger. Then he asked me to reheat the dinner, he always likes his food hot. We never invited Rosa again and that was that.

Candace Bushnell came to Foreign Affairs with her

little entourage and a camera crew from CNN International who filmed a little of the show but mostly her and her friends eating caviar and blinis and applauding. It was a few months later that I received a call from Tony Lauria who told me he had seen a glimpse of me singing on CNN in his hotel room in Greece.

Then one night opera diva Measha Brueggergosman came with young conductor Edwin Outwater. It was a great pleasure to know Measha. She was very fond of everything german and knew german cabaret. Her agent Bill Palant had once invited us to attend her Ravel recital at the home of an important art collector whose name I do not remember. Jean-Yves Thibaudet had accompanied her on the piano and we had delighted in her voice and presence. However I had wondered a little about her floor length dress with trail and the way she moved. Is she perhaps wearing flats, I asked Bill Palant. No, said he, Measha always performs barefoot.

And so now Measha had come to see me perform. Together with Edwin Outwater we discussed ideas to collaborate in the future and then Filip Noterdaeme and I invited them to have a drink at DR!P. Measha delighted in the excitable voluble crowd of pretty young boys in skimpy swimsuits and there was no way to prevent her from gingerly wading into the pool with a martini in her hand. The next night, Bill Palant took me to see Measha perform John Cage's Aria at Carnegie Hall. After the concert, Measha and I went to a burger joint where she insisted on feeding me half her burger. It was a delightful evening. Later, much later, I had a chance to perform in The Seven Deadly Sins with her and Edwin Outwater in Waterloo, Canada. This time I was Anna II, Measha was

Anna I. She sang barefoot as always and wore a modern crumpled dress with trail that she kept in a plastic bag in the back of her car. After the show we drove through a snowstorm to her home in Toronto where she cooked a late night meal of sausages for us. But as I said that was not until later.

In the meanwhile we had been getting many inquiries regarding a viewing of the Homeless Museum and agreed to hold another clandestine opening. It was to be our last.

Many came, familiar visitors and friendly visitors and new visitors and friends of familiar visitors. Jonah Bokaer came with Turid Meeker, a beautiful scandinavian curator who was friends with Laurence Wiener and told me she had idolized Marlene Dietrich in her youth. Veronica Roberts from MoMA came and wrote in our guest book that the Homeless Museum was genius creativity. Then Lena Imamura arrived with her friend Ruby McNeil, daughter of Marcia Tucker. In short it was once again an opening for art insiders. They weighed in at a record 2,137 pounds and I had a wardrobe malfunction when the bun of my geisha wig fell off during a conversation with a young museum administrator from North Carolina.

After everybody had left Filip Noterdaeme looking at the new signatures in the guest book said to me, why should I, an eternal outsider eternally invite insiders inside. In short he decided to change HOMU BKLYN from being a part of the present to being a part of history and said, no more openings. One day, he said, a museum will build a facsimile of my live-in museum and it will be just like a period room at the Metropolitan Museum. He greatly relished that thought and asked me to build an architectural model of HOMU BKLYN. It is only by such tools that we can secure that the facsimile will be accurate, he said. When Luis Crocker, the director of the Museum of Contemporary Art Detroit came to visit us a few weeks later we made a point of showing him the finished model. Luis Crocker politely looked at it but he was more interested in the recipe for the plum tart I had prepared for his visit.

It was at about that time that Filip Noterdaeme found a little article on the internet that named the Homeless Museum one of the five most insane museums ever. The other four were the Museum of Quackery, the International Museum of Toilets, the Museum of Bad Art, and the Icelandic Phallological Museum. The article amusingly referred to me as a real woman dressed up as Madame Butterfly. Filip Noterdaeme was very pleased to find his museum on that list but argued that the list was not quite accurate, surely the five most insane museums ever were the Museum of Modern Art, the Metropolitan Museum of Art, the Guggenheim, the Louvre, and the Prado.

It was at about that time that Adam Lerner, the director of the Museum of Contemporary Art in Denver, asked me to give a lecture on cabaret at an experimental event at the Museum of Modern Art. It was called Mixed Taste: Tag Team Lectures on Unrelated Topics, and my lecture was going to be paired with a lecture on art preservation by spectroscopy specialist Chris McGlinchey. It was good experience.

After our lectures Adam Lerner asked the audience to find similarities between the art of cabaret and the science of art conservation and Filip Noterdaeme remarked upon the passion of the scientist and the precision of the artist. I remarked on the chemistry of the audience. Then a cocktail was served in the lobby and Filip Noterdaeme and I were introduced to Sergio Bessa, the director of the education department of the Bronx Museum. He and Filip Noterdaeme talked about the late Marcia Tucker and when Filip Noterdaeme mentioned that her daughter Ruby McNeil had been to our last opening Sergio Bessa told us a strange story. It had happened not too long after Marcia Tucker's death, he said. He had by chance come upon a stoop sale on Sullivan Street in Soho. There were the usual knickknacks and women's clothes but also art, a lot of it. Not feeling all that interested at first he had looked a little and suddenly realized that much of the art was important and valuable. The sale was attended by a young girl and a man who kept bringing more and more things onto the stoop and Sergio Bessa says it took him a little while before he recognized them as being Marcia Tucker's daughter Ruby and late husband Dean McNeal. Sergio Bessa said he had been quite appalled to see husband and daughter so carelessly getting rid of Marcia's personal belongings and private art collection but that he could not resist buying a painting for $50 that he knew was worth much more.

Once again it was summer and I once again took the train to the Hamptons every Friday morning. Eric Ellenbogen had in the meanwhile sold his mansion and Cary Davis and John McGinn had begun renting summer houses of their own. Earlier that year they had fallen in love with an old house by the bay and arranged to rent it for their weekend leisure. There I once again cooked breakfasts, lunches and dinners but it was not at all like the busy old days at Eric Ellenbogen's open house, as a matter of fact it was rather pleasant and quiet. The kitchen window had a view of the bay. I always prefer an ocean view to a bay view, I find it so much more engaging. At first the bay view reminded me of the lakes of Germany and I wished it weren't so. Then I made it a habit of crossing the bay in a little blue kayak during my afternoon breaks and it was the swift motion of the kayak in the water that each time assured me that I was fully and completely in America.

Filip Noterdaeme as usual looked for interesting things to do in the hot city while I was away and one evening went to see a performance at the Bowery Poetry Club by eighty-four year old Bingo Gazingo, king of the street poets. Filip Noterdaeme was the only person in the audience. Bingo Gazingo recited poems and rants for half an hour. When he was finished Filip Noterdaeme applauded and Bingo Gazingo said, I seldom get any applause but thank you anyway. Recently Filip Noterdaeme made me listen to a recording of Bingo Gazingo singing, The More I Love You The More I Love You More. It was a very sad recording and I said to him, you see loneliness in age is different for men and women, men become sad and women become mad.

After Bingo Gazingo left the stage at the Bowery Poetry Club that evening Filip Noterdaeme simply remained seated and stayed for the next performer, Taylor Mead, the old Any Warhol Superstar. He had a bit more of a following than Bingo Gazingo. Somebody from the club had to help him onto the stage because he was too weak to get up the steps. Taylor Mead read some of his x-rated poems interlacing them with sound bites from a little transistor radio. He also rambled about modern life and joked about his recent stroke, how he was waiting to be kicked out of this life and that all he would have to do is fall one more time. Then his performance was over and the club filled with young East Village people arriving for the next attraction, Bingo Night with drag queen Linda Simpson and drag king Murray Hill.

Having witnessed two ailing marginal poets perform back to back on the Bowery Filip Noterdaeme reflected once again about Mission on the Bowery and how it had ended in disillusion. Maybe, he said, I ought to continue performing with my booth and not mind such things as the art world. Consider, he said, Bingo Gazingo and Taylor Mead, they have kept at it no matter if there was any interest or applause and surely you admit that if they can so can I. I concurred. He made up his mind to do a new series of outings and, not wanting to return to the Bowery, decided to bring the HOMU Booth to Union Square. He picked a spot close to the Gandhi statue.

There were no open letters this time, only a ticket dispenser and a clapboard saying, Visit the Homeless Museum of Art Today. The idea was that anybody who took a seat in the visitor's chair would get a ticket to enter the museum. This version of the HOMU Booth used to confuse a lot of people because it was never exactly clear to anyone what and where the art of the museum was. Filip Noterdaeme thought it was the homeless everywhere and said so, sometimes calling them living art. This people found unacceptable. They found the homeless difficult to look at, they did not hold their attention.

In the following weeks Filip Noterdaeme spent every Saturday afternoon on Union Square. There were animal rights activists and their homeless dogs and cats on his left and a lone saxophonist on his right who played the same song, Somewhere over the Rainbow, all day, and Filip Noterdaeme cursed his compatriot Adolphe Sax, inventor of the saxophone. His pink Paul Smith suit began to fade in the sunlight and the fake beard was itching his face. People rushed past him carrying shopping bags and he experienced one moment of disinterestedness in his HOMU Booth after another and began to wonder a great deal about the future of his outsider art that felt beyond outside outside with much turmoil inside. One exception was that discussion about Léopold Sédar Senghor he had with a street sweeper from Senegal. And then there was the time when Yolanda Hawkins and William Niederkorn came by the booth. Yolanda sitting and William first bending down then crouching next to her told Filip Noterdaeme about their late friend Stuart Sherman who had also performed on the streets of Manhattan. William Niederkorn said that Stuart Sherman had performed everywhere for nothing, with or without an audience, and that he had then died of AIDS and was promptly forgotten. Now Yolanda Hawkins and William Niederkorn were beginning to put together a retrospective of his work for a gallery show. Reflecting upon this story Filip Noterdaeme began to think gloomy thoughts. When he came home that evening he said to me, perhaps I also will not be recognized until after I die, just like Stuart Sherman.

Joey Arias made good on his promise and came to perform at Foreign Affairs. He had not done any live shows in New York since his return from Las Vegas and everybody came. Lee Chappell was pleased because for once it was standing room only at the Night Hotel.

It was an exciting evening. The musicians were excited and the audience was excited and I was excited.

Joey opened the show with his signature song, You've Changed. He looked remarkably beautiful illuminated by our little spotlight, wearing a new Patti Labelle wig and chewing gum. Then as always he liked to irreverently play with the audience and the chewing gum, pulling both in many directions and sometimes sticking the gum onto the microphone where it quite naturally looked like one of Hannah Wilke's chewing-gum vaginas. Later he sang Why Don't You Do Right, and it was during that song that he ordered a handsome young man who sat in the corner to come onto the stage. Once there the young man did not know quite what to do with himself and before he knew it Joey went down on his knees and with facetious furtiveness unzipped the young man's fly, put the microphone down his pants and back out through the fly and finished the song singing into it. Everybody squealed with delight and the young man squirmed with delight. At the end of his set, Joey spat his gum on the floor and made an exit. Filip Noterdaeme picked it up and saved it for his Center for the Preservation and Resurrection of Artists.

It was at this time that Peter Scott of the Mark Twain eyebrows was putting together a group show called Market Forces. He invited Dan Graham and Filip Noterdaeme and many others to be of it and it was the first time that MoMA HMLSS was exhibited in a gallery. The show then traveled to the Erna Hecey Galerie in Brussels and naturally we had to go see it there on our way to the little french island. It looked very nice in the gallery and we were very pleased.

During our short stay in Brussels we also paid a visit to Marie-Puck Broodthaers. Since those old days when Filip Noterdaeme knew Marie-Puck she had moved her little storefront gallery to a large townhouse in the rue General Patton. Filip Noterdaeme said she had not changed at all. There was a gleam on her lower eyelid and on her full dark lips. The expression seemed to me a strange mixture of dreaminess and cunning. She showed us around the gallery on the ground floor and Filip Noterdaeme immediately recognized La Souris Écrit Rat, a print by her father showing a shadowgraph of a cat. Marie-Puck went upstairs to pour some prosecco for us. Suddenly a little black cat appeared and leaned against Filip Noterdaeme's leg. Without delay he picked her up and posed with her in front of the print in perfect imitation of the shadowgraph. I took a picture of the two and then we went upstairs to drink prosecco with Marie-Puck. She and Filip Noterdaeme reminisced and Marie-Puck talked about James Lee Byars whom she described as half angel and half devil. Oh, how I miss him, she said. She also told us that when she worked at Michael Werner's gallery in Düsseldorf she had to sign a contract clause that forbade her to have sex with artists who were represented by the gallery. I came to like Marie-Puck and thought she was half devil and half angel just like James Lee Byars. While we sat and listened to her wild stories the phone rang many times but Marie-Puck did not pick it up, saying that she recognized that ring, that it was her mother Maria Gilissen calling and that she absolutely did not feel like talking to her. Then we got up and thanked Marie-Puck and promised her to visit again.

We went on to the little french island for our summer vacation. There nothing had changed and we often remarked that if there were any changes we would not be returning every year.

The first thing we did back in New York was paint the shelves of the Morgue & Library Richard Meier white. When the paint was dry Filip Noterdaeme decided to shelve all the books facing the other way, that is with the spines facing backward. He found that they were much more pleasing to look at this way. But how do you find a book, our friends said. You don't find a book, Filip Noterdaeme said, the book finds you. And it is true, whether it is by Thomas Mann or Paul de Man, the book always finds you. Emmanuel Levinas finds you and Jacques Lacan and Hannah Arendt find you and they all find you in their own tongue and their own time, and Twain and Thoreau find you, and so it is with every book and author at 172 Clinton Street.

It was indian summer season and Boykin Curry and Celerie Kemble asked me to come out to the Hamptons and cook for a family weekend. The house they were renting was a famous one. It was called Grey Gardens.

Everybody in those days was fascinated with the legend of Grey Gardens, even those who had not seen the notorious Maysles brothers' 1975 documentary or the Broadway musical or the television adaptation. In short everybody had an opinion about Big Edie and Little Edie and their countless stray cats, even the columbian lady I sometimes hired in East Hampton to help me with the groceries said, ah si, la casa de los Kennedys. The house now belonged to Sally Quinn and Ben Bradlee and allegedly Little Edie when they bought it had told them that all the house needed was a fresh coat of paint. In any case when I arrived at Grey Gardens for the first time I am sure I cannot deny that there still seemed to be a faint smell of cat pee in the parlor.

Grey Gardens is close to a pond and the thing about the pond at this time of the year was the gnats. They were everywhere and every time someone entered the kitchen from the garden there were gnats coming in and they all gravitated to the baby blue kitchen ceiling. This put me in quite a state and at one moment I locked the kitchen door in a red rage and furiously vacuumed the ceiling. It was on that occasion that I invented the red beet and blue cheese gratin.

It was only a little later that year that Filip Noterdaeme and Cathleen Chaffee went to the Peter Freeman Gallery to see a Décor by Marcel Broodthears. It was called Ne dites pas que je ne l'ai pas dit – Le Perroquet, Do not say I didn't say it – The Parrot. Never shown in the United States before, it had a live african grey parrot in a cage set between two potted palm trees and there was an audio recording of Marcel Broodthaers reading one of his poems, Me I say me I say I. It is a rather ironic coincidence that the Décor had been created in 1975, at around the same that the Maysles brothers had filmed Big Edie and Little Edie fighting and yelling, me I say me I say I at each other.

It was during that same season that we had a very strange adventure at the Waldorf Astoria. We were staying there to assist Winni Hohman, a german waiter I had known in my catering days and who was now in charge of overseeing the several days of non-stop wining and dining of eight hundred Allianz insurance agents flown in from Germany. Winni had been rather desperate to find german speakers for the job and as we were at this time without any money at all I had agreed to be there on the condition that he agreed to also hire Filip Noterdaeme who speaks and understands german alright.

And so one morning Filip Noterdaeme and I checked into the Waldorf Astoria and waited for the german insurance contingent to arrive. You know how germans are, Winni said to us by way of explaining, naturally I had to organize and plan every single minute of their stay. The first thing he asked us to do was to inspect the numbers of towels and slippers in every one of the reserved hotel rooms. It had to be the exact right number of towels and slippers for each room and Winni was very adamant about it. Being a good german I was bent on following Winni's orders but Filip Noterdaeme thought that Winni had to, in a way, be kidding, and began referring to him as Winni the Pooh. And so instead of counting towels and slippers he simply sat down in one of the hotel rooms and read for a while and then promptly returned to the lobby telling Winni that all was in perfect order. Then the eight hundred Allianz people arrived and everybody had to be at attention. Everybody was at attention but the Allianz people were not happy because their hotel rooms were either not ready or not in perfect german order and naturally there were not enough towels and slippers at the ready and so there was a lot of confusion everywhere on every floor of the Waldorf Astoria. Later there was a Begrüssungsabend, a big welcoming event at the Museum of Modern Art. Winni wanted it to be a surprise and nobody was supposed to tell the eight hundred germans where it was going to be. Instead, the eight hundred germans would have to, as Winni said, follow the music. He had arranged for saxophone players to stand on every other city block along the short route from the Waldorf Astoria to the Museum of Modern Art and play New York, New York, and only New York, New York. Having concerns about the germans getting lost along the way Winni also arranged for us german-speaking helpers to stand at attention on every other corner and hold up Allianz Begrüssungsabend signposts. So there we were, Filip Noterdaeme standing close to the Seagram Building and tiredly leaning against his signpost and I on the Lever House Plaza two blocks away, next to two enormous Hello Kitty sculptures by Tom Sachs and a text installation by Barbara Kruger that said, Another Day, Another Dollar. The hired tired saxophone players were playing New York, New York without pause but not in sync and Filip Noterdaeme once again cursed his compatriot Adolphe Sax. The germans arrived in droves and I commented on how good they were at waiting for the green light before crossing the street and scolded them in german when they were not. When I saw Filip Noterdaeme, the director of the Homeless Museum of Art, an as yet insufficiently known institution of which he is the founder, stand outside in the cold for two hours in a cheap rented tuxedo and holding up a signpost pointing towards the Museum of Modern Art, I must confess I began to cry.

After a long day of doing more mindless things and having been served stale sandwiches from the Waldorf Astoria kitchen we were finally released to our hotel room and there Filip Noterdaeme and I had a serious talk. I have not, he said, survived in New York for 20 years to become a human signpost. We discussed for a long time all the different angles of the situation, the rent to be paid and the dignity to be saved, and in the end we decided the only thing left for us to do was to simply leave. When, I said. Now, said he, I am ready. By that time it was three o'clock in the morning and we had to escape the Waldorf Astoria through the back door like thieves. Just a few months ago I ran into one of the german-speaking girls who had worked with us at the Waldorf. We laughed about Winnie de Pooh and she said, those five days with Allianz were the worst days in my New York life, and that we had been her heroes for having left.

It was in those days that I began directing Yanna Avis. She had booked several nights at Feinstein's cabaret at the Regency for her comeback. It was a very arduous and absorbing process. We usually met at her Fifth Avenue apartment. Yanna Avis had always strongly believed in the importance of being representatively seductive in the international cabaret ingénue style. This did not interest me. You must, I said, learn to express the eternal lightness of being with a grain of salt. Under my direction Yanna Avis and I together worked out a series of experiments in minutely detailed performance. Upon these ideas I based some of my most permanent distinctions in types of performers and it was the beginning of my work as a director and performance coach.

On opening night surprisingly it was I who was the most nervous. We had a dress rehearsal and the thing that mattered most to Yanna Avis was that every light spot should have a pink gel on it. Satisfied she then went up to a hotel suite on the third floor to calmly have her hair and makeup done for two hours. In the meanwhile I sat in the lobby and watched as Yanna's wealthy international friends little by little trailed in to see the show. Suddenly a striking tall woman with a large head and long dark hair dressed all in black walked into the lobby. I looked and looked but could not figure out who she was. I was quite sure I ought to. Then Yanna Avis's friend Raphael Castoriano, a flamboyant international man about town arrived and immediately ran up to the woman in black and kissed her hello. He always seemed to wave at something and when he saw me he waved me over and said, Daniel, meet Marina Abramovic. This made me chuckle. I said to her, of course it is you, I did not recognize you. She insouciantly shook her hair and said, but I am always the same. She had the manic charm and languid hunger for attention of all performance artists. We talked and I mentioned the Eau d'Abramovic and she said, oh yes my perfume, I heard all about it, I absolutely must have one. I was about to explain that the Eau was not actually a perfume when the maître d' interrupted us saying, ladies and gentlemen the show is about to begin please find your seats. Everybody went into the cabaret room and then Filip Noterdaeme arrived and was seated next to Marina Abramovic at a front row table. Marina Abramovic instantly began talking to him about having just been awarded her third honorary doctorate of arts in Plymouth and also about her aversion to wine and how she had just returned from Rhinebeck where she had drunk the essence of her guru who called himself John of God. Filip Noterdaeme listened, leaning back a little. Then Marina, leaning forward a little, told him that she had begun working with a personal trainer every morning to get ready for her upcoming retrospective at the Modern where she was going to perform for 596 hours. But this, she said before leaning back in her chair, is top secret.

Then Yanna Avis made her entrance and she was all glamour with a few cracks at the seams like a beautiful chipped porcelain plate with a lonely olive on it. And so

I had kept my promise to make Yanna Avis's comeback a success and she was very pleased. Mein Herr, she gallantly said, she always called me Mein Herr, je vous tire mon chapeau.

The next morning Filip Noterdaeme put a drop of witch hazel into one of the flacons of Eau d'Abramovic and mailed it to Marina. She never thanked him for it but later Raphael Castoriano told us that she kept it on her desk.

It was only a few weeks later that I fell off the little Foreign Affairs stage while singing a Grace Jones song, I'm Not Perfect. Something happened and I lost my footing and fell dangerously, landing painfully on my back. Naturally I instantly jumped up again and went on with the show. Sweet manic Amber Martin was our guest singer that night. I seem to remember her wearing a completely see-through pantsuit made of lace with nothing underneath. She vigorously took to the tiny stage and belted out an aggressive Janis Joplin song with Mike Jackson happily playing the guitar. Everybody cheered.

After Lady Rizo and I closed the show as usual with Lou Reed's Walk on the Wild Side we all stood around in the locker room downstairs and I said, I believe I broke a rib. No darling you have not, Amber Martin said to me sweetly, all you need is a nice hot bath and some herbal tea. It was an interesting case of the kind of denial one can observe in America where optimism all too often has to stand in for a health insurance. Sweetheart, I said, what I need is not a hot bath, what I need is an x-ray.

The next morning I went to the hospital and the head nurse examined me and took an x-ray of my ribcage. Is it broken, I said. She said it was. Well there was nothing to do but follow her advice, to take deep breaths every 15 minutes for a month or so. It will hurt, she said, but breathe deeply every 15 minutes you must or your could catch pneumonia. She then prescribed very strong painkillers.

It was only a couple days later that I went to see Taylor Mac's new play. It was a big to-do in five acts and everyone was in it. Filip Noterdaeme thought he had already seen the best and the beast of Taylor Mac when Taylor was still an underground cabaret performer looking and acting like an angry escapee from a mental institution, and so I went by myself, alone and still on painkillers. The show began and there was Taylor Mac as a potty-mouthed potted lily flower wanting to get married. Lady Rizo was the dreaming bride and Tigger James the theater curtain, somehow. It was the only time I ever saw him not do naked split jumps in a show. Or perhaps he did, I am not sure. Being in a painkiller-induced haze I felt reasonably entertained for all of the five hours it took to sit through the show.

It was at about that time that Time Out Magazine wrote about the Homeless Museum in its home design issue. Ashley Halpern the senior editor had sent reporter Sophie Harris to 172 Clinton Street and Filip Noterdaeme had explained to her everything about the Homeless Museum. Above all, he said, you must understand that this is not just two faggots decorating their apartment. When the home design issue came out the next week Filip Noterdaeme was very pleased to find his remark included in the article. Everybody read it and commented on it and we went on with our lives.

In the meanwhile Evee Lynn had all but given up

on leaving her apartment for even short periods of time. Not wanting to face the outside world any longer, she preferred sitting at home watching television and calling for home deliveries. She used to say, all my life I have presented myself to the world wearing a mask and now that I am over eighty I simply don't want to bother with it any longer. Going to the dentist was the only exception, and it was always I who helped her to get there, there being no one else she could ask. We always took a cab across town and she always tipped the drivers very generously. Her dentist was a sensitive depressed chinese-american man who had known her since the days she used to date his father and, as may be imagined, for Evee these visits were then also an intimately complicated trip into her jagged past.

Evee Lynn never complained about her current life and insisted that she was not altogether discontent. Am I miserable, she asked. No. Am I happy. No. But there you go she said in closing, I am a very very complicated person. Her depression had been in fact the only faithful partner she had ever had in her life. In this way she was never truly completely lonely.

It was at about that time that Filip Noterdaeme and I went to attend an event called Kreemart. It was organized by Raphael Castoriano and all about art and cakes, seriously. When we arrived the room was full of people and cameramen and there were thin pouting half-naked models walking around the room holding silver trays with little pieces of red velvet cake. If you wanted a piece of that, you had to say, oh Mickey you're so fine you blow my mind and open your mouth. We passed. It was on that occasion that we were served silver cake by the three spoiled artist daughters who called themselves The Delirious Downtown Divas. Then we passed by a little room with a brown leather chaise longue, the kind modernist therapists like to use in their practice and next to it a chair with someone looking like a Richard Prince pulp fiction nurse silently sitting on it. We did not realize it just at first but it turned out that the chaise longue was a cake, too. Someone should lie down on it, Filip Noterdaeme said. If Julie Atlas Muz was here, said I, she would. And indeed, a week later, Julie Atlas Muz performed at Foreign Affairs and there she did sit on a cake. It was a birthday affair for Lee Chappell and she brought out a little red velvet cake and did a cakewalk dance around it and then simply sat on it. And then we ate the cake.

In any case at Kreemart after the Mickey cake and the silver cake and the chaise longue cake there was the Experiment by Marina Abramovic. It was held in a separate room and everybody who took part in it had to first put on a white lab coat. This of course had already been done years earlier by genius Barry Humphries when he once had demanded of his audience members to wear white lab coats during his Dame Edna Show but now Marina insisted that we had to wear white lab coats before we could have her cake and eat it too. Raphael Castoriano nearly blew his top when it looked like there were not enough white lab coats available. Then everybody lined up and Marina applied sticky squares of gold leaf over everybody's lips and a french pastry chef gave everyone a little miniature cake to hold in the palm of their hands. It was a little french affair topped with raspberry-syrup-flavored tapioca that he insisted on calling caviar de framboise. Then Marina arranged everyone on a tiered platform for a group photograph. She showed us how we were to hold the tapioca cakes and warned us to not eat them until she told us to. Then she stepped back and said solemnly, you are now human cake. At this some of us giggled and this was a problem. Marina insisted that this was a serious experiment about serious art and she would not have her photo op spoiled by silliness. Then the group photo was taken. And then we ate the cake.

Filip Noterdaeme never wished Marina Abramovic away. Once when he and Sara Bodinson were talking about Marina's retrospective at the Modern he said, yes, Abramovic and Sarah Palin, they are the incomprehensibles whom anybody can understand. He also said that the Museum of Modern Art could be renamed the Museum of Marina Abramovic and still be MoMA, that way there would be a wax museum on 42nd Street and a quack museum on 53rd Street.

It was only a little later that I decided to close Foreign Affairs. It had been running at the Night Hotel for 9 months but with Jeanine Pepler not knowing how to promote it with the right people and nobody wanting to travel to gentrified Times Square to see a downtown cabaret show and Lee Chappell losing money every week it had fallen on hard times. We had of course always invited Adam Feldman the cabaret critic of Time Out Magazine but he had told Lee Chappell, oh I never go out on Mondays. Finally I said to Lee Chappell, it's no use, let's close it and find another venue downtown. We had one last performance. That night Adam Feldman finally came. He came and wrote nice things about it in his column but it was too little too late.

Having experienced much solitude during his outings on Union Square Filip Noterdaeme admitted not yet having conquered the public realm where one could excel and distinguish oneself from all others but excel and distinguish himself he was about to. I said to Filip Noterdaeme, the time has now come when you must be made known to a larger public. I myself believe in a larger public. Filip Noterdaeme too believes in a larger public but the way has always been barred. No, I said, the way can be opened. Let us think.

I said it must come from your performance, your way of interacting with everybody in character, the way you used to at our openings at 172 Clinton Street. Filip Noterdaeme suggested bringing along Florence Coyote as a psychic sidekick. That will do exactly, I said. And decided upon more changes. We agreed that to lure people in it had to be made to appear like a perfectly likable contemporary museum, in short, a museum without ideas but plenty of exhibits.

In the following weeks we refurbished the HOMU Booth entirely to become a distilled mobile version of HOMU BKLYN. It was going to have a couple of miniature exhibits, a very short audio tour, a weathervane extension and a chicken wing extension. Making the Chicken Wing for the booth was an interesting process. Filip Noterdaeme did not want to have to use a fresh wing every week and so I prepared a chicken wing that would last and last. It was a process similar to making Peking Duck. Above all, I said, you must be comfortably heard by all, and furbished the booth with a microphone and two little Honeytone speakers. Finally Filip Noterdaeme decided to have not one but two kindergarten chairs for visitors, one for friendship and one for society.

Filip Noterdaeme refused to continue wearing the cumbersome fake beard from Bob Kelley's and so we replaced it with a much more comfortable thin little fake mustache. A few months later he also dispensed with the fake mustache and used a pencil to draw a little Hercule Poirot mustache instead. I also bought him a new suit and a pair of horn-rimmed glasses to wear. In short, his new look along with the new version of the HOMU Booth represented a dandified version of HOMU BKLYN and Filip Noterdaeme was very pleased that it should be so. As a spot for his newest outings he chose a place under the High Line in Chelsea. Here I must explain a little about the High Line.

Once there was a meatpacking district on the far west side of the Village in Manhattan. The meat was brought all the way down from 34th Street on an elevated railroad track called the High Line. Then trucks had become more convenient than tracks and the rail was shut down and grass grew on the tracks.

The meatpacking district was then a strange area where nobody wanted to live. By day it was all about the meat and at night it was about the flesh. There were tranny hookers in pumps standing and waiting on bloodstained cobblestones and gay men looking for sex in dark alleys and finding it in sex clubs. In short, it was an area for anybody who did not want to be seen by just anybody. Then Florent Morellet, the son of François Morellet, the father of french minimalism, opened his twenty-four seven bistro on Gansevoort Street and gradually things began to change.

Florent then having attracted a clientele of tranny hookers drag queens and other nightlife creatures had a very fast steak frites success. Soon everybody who was somebody wanted to be there, naturally followed by the nobodies who wanted to see and be seen with the somebodies. No sooner had Rudolph Giuliani the mayor of New York shut down the sex clubs and chased away the tranny hookers that the neighborhood was suddenly no longer about meat and sex but about fashion and Sex in the City. The meatpacking plants moved to the Bronx, Florent sold his business and there were plans to demolish the High Line to make room for real estate developers. It was at that time that Robert Hammond the most charmingly sincere of all idealists had the idea to save the High Line and turn it into a public park. This greatly pleased Diane von Fuerstenberg the richest of Filip Noterdaeme's compatriots in New York and the High Line was then reinvented as a playground where one could do two things, walk and sit, as long as one stayed off the grass, alas. The park became the new new thing and Filip Noterdaeme opportunistically strategically set up his booth underneath the park's north entrance on 20th Street and announced to everyone who cared to listen, here I sit and can do no other. The spot under the High Line became the new home of the Homeless Museum for all of five hours on Saturday afternoons, weather permitting.

Once at Grey Gardens when I was discussing the High Line with Boykin Curry and Deborah Needleman, Boykin Curry said, it's all fine and well but I wished they had kept it a bit more gritty, the way it used to be when we were young and used to amuse ourselves by having illegal barbecues on the decaying tracks. I said I thought the design of the new High Line was very gay. Not possibly, Deborah Needleman said, it is quite pleasantly wild, is it not. No, I said, it is a highly controlled design look pretending to be wild which is the way gay urbanites seem to like their environment nowadays. They like it that way in their life style magazines and they like it that way in their cluttered decorated homes and they like it that way in their favorite expensive hotel destinations and they like it that way in their pornography. Filip Noterdaeme likes to say that the High Line had once been a rail for steer carcasses and now it was a boardwalk for bovine tourists. As a matter of fact he has taken to calling it the Bovine Memorial Walk.

Not wanting to transport the booth and Florence all the way from Brooklyn to Chelsea every week he rented a small storage cell at a place called Manhattan Mini Storage on 21st Street. From there he walked with Florence and the foldable booth to the north entrance of the High Line on 20th Street and set up his street museum which to this day remains the only functioning museum in the neighborhood, the Chelsea Art Museum having recently closed and the Whitney Museum planning to open in 2015. He had returned to the street because he wished to live deliberately and front the essence of the other. More than anything he wanted to find out what people meant by what they said. He used to be interested in what they were, he was now interested in what they said, he said. Having Florence at his side helped him a great deal. He used to say, she is the one who listens and I am the one who does all the talking. Hello, he would say into his microphone to no one in particular, my name is Filip Noterdaeme and I am legendary, and he said it with that inscrutable air he sometimes had that let one guess whether he expressed sarcasm or ecstasy, or parody of one or the other.

I sometimes visited Filip Noterdaeme during these outings. He was usually surrounded by a great many people. He was very pleased that this should be so. Of course everybody was always taking pictures.

It is difficult to describe just what it was that Filip Noterdaeme was doing to his visitors. He often says that it was the presence of Florence that made all the difference. She helps me navigate the flow from one visitor to another, he said. And it is true, no matter if it was Flotilla de Barge or a banker from Florida dressed in black, Filip Noterdaeme put words in Florence's mouth that instantly shockingly revealed everything about them. This often caused for great waves of emotion among his visitors and Filip Noterdaeme himself was sometimes overcome with wonderment at his own ease at having caused such strange Oprah moments. It was Shuki Cohen who often said in this regard, Filip Noterdaeme is the most brilliant therapist I know. Beppe Lovoi once asked me, how does Filip suffer fools so gladly. You see Beppe, I said, when he listens he tends to enjoy hearing the difference between what people say and what they mean but when they mean what they say he gets bored. Of course nobody ever really means what they say and so he never gets bored. And everything else followed from that. It isn't that he began to believe in himself so much as that he was inhabited by a sublime indifference. He had become interchangeable with his creation, and he accepted that creation on its own terms now. Most importantly he never allowed himself to feel too much during his street performances. Nobody but a beginner, said he, imagines he who creates must feel. He used to say, if you care too much for what you have to say, you can be sure of totally disastrous results.

He returned to the High Line every Saturday and listened and talked to one visitor after another all afternoon without ever stopping. When the time came to wrap up the day's performance, he'd say to his last visitor, that is finished now. It was a pleasure. Now this is a pleasure.

And so Filip Noterdaeme having found his place in the world distinguished himself from all others and peace was upon him once again.

It was during one of his weekly outings that Filip Noterdaeme first met Pia Frankenberg. Pia Frankenberg was from Germany. She had a mullet and wore only Berlin black which is so different from New York black. Filip Noterdaeme delighted in the directness and completeness of her understanding of his performance. She and Filip Noterdaeme became friends at once and it was only a little later that she invited us to watch the Thanksgiving Parade from the windows of her home on Central Park West. In all those years neither Filip Noterdaeme nor I had ever cared to watch the Thanksgiving parade and so we accepted gladly.

We arrived and I had barely set down a platter of home-baked vanillekipferl I had brought as a gift when I heard a clicking noise behind me. I turned and it was Elliot Erwitt, Pia's husband, taking snapshots of his grandchildren. Pia led us to the large windows facing the park just as a giant inflated smurf was being paraded down Central Park West. We marveled at the smurf and Pia told us of how one year the arm of an inflated Donald Duck had broken one of their windows. Later we watched a live broadcast of the parade's special musical performances on Herald Square and to my great surprise there was Lance Horne playing the keyboard for Alan Cumming. I marveled at Alan singing so well in the cold morning air. When I ran into Lance Horne a few months later I told him how impressed I had been and he laughed. But Daniel, he said, Alan was of course lip-synching.

We invited Pia Frankenberg and Elliot Erwitt to have tea with us at 172 Clinton Street. Elliot and I talked about the grey cushions I had cut from Beuysian felt for our Eames chairs and Pia told Filip Noterdaeme that the Metropolitan Museum had commissioned Elliott once again to photograph the museum's famous Christmas tree for yet another book about its 18th Century Neapolitan crèche figures. Another, said Filip Noterdaeme, how so. It will, said she laughing, be the third time Elliot is photographing the tree, he did it first in 1985 and then again in 1993. We thought this was highly amusing because as everyone knows the Met's Christmas tree is always the same, every year. Before leaving, Elliott signed our guest book with André S. Solidor aka Elliott Erwitt. One week later we received a Christmas card from Pia and Elliott in the mail. It had a very amusing picture of the two and their dog Sammy posing amidst pine trees covered in soapsuds and empty champagne and whisky bottles and a rack of dishes at their feet.

It was at about that time that we went to Saint Marks Church for a Memorial for Stefan Brecht. There was a lot of downtown royalty in the room when we arrived. Wallace Shawn was there and Robert Wilson was there and in the back we saw Yolanda Hawkins and William Niederkorn and little great Sanda Weigl. It was a very strange memorial. There were shy family members reading eulogies and haitian musicians playing the drums. Sanda of course knew everything about the Brechts, knew of their wealth and knew of their tormented history. She was appalled when she saw the cheap buffet in the corner. Do you know, she said to me, how rich these people are.

In those days we kept hearing about Klaus Biesenbach looking to buy and preserve performance art for the Modern. When we heard that he had walked out of a panel discussion at the Arts Directors Club in a hissy fit because someone was videotaping the panel against his demands Filip Noterdaeme sent him a flacon of Eau d'Abramovic with an open letter in which he urged him to perform an act of baptism with the Eau to fully induct himself into the world of performance art. Penny Arcade, having read and reread the open letter immediately responded by writing a letter to Filip Noterdaeme that moved him deeply. She wrote, Oh how Jack Smith would have fallen at your feet in tears to see your bravery, your insouciance, your lance of intelligence piercing the spectacle in its non-heart. How Guy Debord would have praised you and delayed his suicide. A thousand roses at your feet. I rise again, like Lazarus touched by your grace.

And so, performance art, the last discipline not yet incorporated into the mainstream became the new thing. Suddenly everybody wanted to be doing it and every museum was looking into ways of presenting it. Tino Sehgal had a solo show at the Guggenheim Museum that was all about walking, talking and progress. This I disliked almost as much as Martin Creed's performance at the Abrons Arts Center where to my great regret the elite of the art world wildly applauded his loud monotone fuck songs and videos of people vomiting. In the midst of it all the Museum of Modern Art hired Filip Noterdaeme to teach a course on the history of performance art. It was there that he introduced his distinction between dandies and divas in performance art. Performance artists, he said, can only be one or the other. The diva will always fashion a cult around her persona while the dandy will be more solitary and independent and bask in his own light. In other words, he told his students, the dandy is committed to the artifice of his creation and the diva is committed to the adulation of her self. Marcel Duchamp was a dandy, Hannah Wilke was a dandy, Ray Johnson was a dandy, Andy Warhol was a dandy, and Jesus Christ, Joseph Beuys, Marina Abramovic and Oprah Winfrey were divas. This used to confuse everybody a great deal and the fans of Marina and Oprah in the class were not pleased.

When December came, Filip Noterdaeme did one last outing under the High Line and then locked Florence and the booth into his rented storage compartment for the winter.

I decided we should have a Christmas party and spent many days baking german Christmas cookies, all kinds of them. Filip Noterdaeme was astonished at the patience with which I made them but he was rather mistrustful of my german gingerbreads, saying that they were not as thin or crisp as belgian gingerbreads. They are not refined, he said. And it is quite true. Belgian gingerbreads whatever else they may be are refined. They are very thin, they are very crisp, and sooner or later they are all eaten. German gingerbreads are not crisp, they are not thin and inevitably there are always some left that nobody wants.

On the day of our Christmas party the first snow of the season fell and it was incredibly beautiful. Everybody came. Jonah Bokaer came first and said that we were precious. Lady Rizo came with her husband Andres Rizo and

Machine Dazzle came by himself with glitter on his face. Then there was Aaron Scott and Julie Atlas Muz and Jo Boobs the director of the New York School of Burlesque and many more. Filip Noterdaeme served Glühwein to everyone and everybody ate borscht and flamekuchen with sauerkraut and speck and german cookies and talked about everything and nothing. It was a lively party. And then just as we thought the party was going to unwind the doorbell rang again and I opened the door and there was Meow Meow running up the stairs in a beautiful red coat. She had had a show at Joe's Pub that night and Dave Berger had driven her all the way to Brooklyn to join us. Then more latecomers arrived and the party started all over again. I made more flamekuchen for hungry Meow Meow, Machine Dazzle started fondling one of our permanent visitors and Jo Boobs and Lady Rizo crawled into the Homeless Simulator and struck cat poses. Everybody took pictures and Dave Berger looked on with a wide grin and said, boobies. Filip Noterdaeme said to Meow Meow, can I have a hair from your wig for my Center for the Preservation and Resurrection of Artists. Wig, what wig, she said. Then she pulled several strands of hair from it and gave them to him. All in all the party lasted nine hours.

The next day we took Tommy Tune to see Meow Meow's show at Joe's Pub. We sat down at our reserved table and perused the full room. Lady Rizo was there and Bill Palant was there and in the corner sat a tall white-haired man all by himself and it was David Byrne. Earl Dax nervously paced the room trying to look like he was in charge. Penny Arcade did not have a seat and we invited her to join us at our table. We introduced her to Tommy Tune who stood up and she said, oh you are not that tall.

Then Meow Meow made her entrance as usual with a cigarette clasped between her gloved fingers. It was one of her signature props and she never let it go for the entire show, even when she took off the glove there was another glove and another cigarette underneath. The show had a beautiful long dream sequence and everyone held their breath. Tommy Tune and I sighed in unison when she wistfully announced that the dream sequence was now over. At the end of the show Meow Meow crowd-surfed as she always does, all the way through the club to get herself a drink from the bar and Penny Arcade leaning over whispered to me, I used to do that in my shows but they always dropped me.

Having once again witnessed the genius of Meow Meow I began to think a great deal about talent and genius and the difference between the two.

I have always believed in talent and I have always believed in genius. Talent is always and totally characteristic and genius is always and totally impersonal. In this way talent will always succumb to character and genius will always overcome personality. Evee Lynn laments that her talent failed to make her a star, Tommy Tune wonders where there is a place for his talent in today's changed Broadway world. Joey Arias continues to mix the frivolous with the profound, Filip Noterdaeme continues to live in a state of permanent creation, and Meow Meow continues to perform her kamikaze cabaret around the world. Penny Arcade is fighting cultural amnesia and Lady Rizo wonders when the bells will ring for her. And so they all work every day and every day and every day and they work and work terribly hard. I have sometimes preferred brilliance over talent or genius. Brilliance is talent fulfilled without being only characteristic or becoming impersonal.

The rest of the year seemed to be one party after another.

There was a supper of butternut squash soup and a very dry homemade persimmon cake at Pia Frankenberg's and a potluck party at the Lower East Side home of Julie Atlas Muz and Jo Boobs where everybody who was anybody of the New York burlesque scene was present and in the middle of it all little Jeffrey Deitch looking very much out of place in a three-piece suit. Then Penny Arcade invited us to a holiday supper at her apartment on Stanton Street. We arrived and Penny greeted us in her pajamas, having just gotten out of bed. She told us she had slept through the day after a long restless night of smoking and preparing pizza rustica for the party. In the kitchen Penny's houseguests, two charming young women from Valencia were busily cooking spanish tapas. At the table sat two quiet pale-looking New York lesbians dressed in black and looking rather like two cats waiting to be fed. Penny showed us her art collection and introduced us to her old neighbor friend, Roland KC. KC was a purist painter and when Filip Noterdaeme kindly politely asked him about his practice he began talking first about his teacher Amédée Ozenfant and then of the artistic and gay life in New York in the Forties and Fifties and Sixties. The stories were endless and Filip Noterdaeme listened to him a long time and then all of a sudden he could not listen any more.

After the party Filip Noterdaeme said to me, purists like Roland KC can never become part of this world, they come and go, leaving no trace behind. Maybe, he added wistfully, all that's left of a life that's lived are its stories.

I said yes, but who will tell them and who will remember the stories after they have been told. One mustn't tell them, Filip Noterdaeme said, one must write them down.

The big event of the season was Marina Abramovic marinating at the Modern. It was called, The Artist is Present. Everybody was writing about it and talking about it and writing and talking about it.

We went with Penny Arcade and Shuki Cohen and there was Marina in a long blue dress, surrounded by cameras and floodlights and sitting motionless at a table facing a single chair that everybody was eagerly waiting to occupy. It was a big to-do and there was a long waiting line when we arrived and special security guards kept reminding everyone of what was allowed and what was not going to be tolerated. There were to be no photographs, no talking, no discussion, no touching, no elbows on the table, no standing, no laughing. Marina sat and sat and sat and we waited and talked about the spectacle of Marina. Finally it was Penny's turn to sit across from her. Filip Noterdaeme and I watched from afar and he said, look, the antidiva is facing the diva but the diva is not really looking, her eyes are turned in on herself. Real looking, he said, is aiming again and again, always back to the beginning, always aiming again. After a while Penny got up and came back to us saying, this show should be called The Artists is THERE. Marina is there alright she said but she is definitely not present. You see, she went on explaining, I am an artist and Marina is a careerist. Shuki Cohen went next and completely tuned into Marina's mind and came back saying, I really feel sorry for her. Then we went upstairs to look at the Abramovic retrospective. There were videos of Marina brushing her hair,

Marina running around a meadow in the rain and Marina standing still holding a bowl of milk. The part everybody was talking about were the many nude performers that had been placed throughout the exhibit restaging some of the various poses of martyred discomfort Marina had assumed in the past. I did not like any of it, I found something rather appalling in the incessant depiction of ritual and pain that reminded me of torture chambers in medieval castles. Well, Penny said, obviously, Marina is a pain junkie. Filip Noterdaeme compared the retrospective to Sarah Palin dressing a moose in Alaska, great for comedy but tragic for politics or art.

It was only a little later that Penny Arcade had an event at Le Poisson Rouge to celebrate the publication of Bad Reputation, a book of her collected plays. There were staged readings of excerpts from La Miseria and Bitch! Dyke! Faghag! Whore! and dance breaks for everyone with Lady Miss Kier deejaying and Tigger James and Julie Atlas Muz dancing like in the old days when they had been in the original cast of Penny Arcade's show New York Stories. Judith Malina read the part of the italian mamma and she was so convincing that Filip Noterdaeme refused to believe that she was not really an italian. Then Debbie Harry read the phone girl monologue Penny had written about the time she had been working as a phone operator in an illegal bordello and everybody remarked on Debbie's comic timing. Taylor Mead sat at our table and when Penny called out to him from the stage he got up and Filip Noterdaeme carefully slowly walked him onto the stage. As may be imagined it took a very long time. Taylor Mead then having reached the microphone began reciting one of his poems but he could not remember the lines and laughed and cursed and everyone applauded. Filip Noterdaeme said later that Taylor Mead had had the distinct smell of a homeless man.

One person who played an important role in the next months of my life was Dave Berger. He had been playing drums for Meow Meow and for Justin Bond and now he deeply cared for the art of Isengart. It was my conception of exactitude in performance at Foreign Affairs that had made the close understanding between us. I believe, he said, there is something in you that no one has seen yet. Filip Noterdaeme agreed and said, do something that nobody would expect you to do. Why don't you, he said, sing Elvis Presley songs. I thought about it and the more I thought it and the more I liked it more. Finally I said, I'll do it, and I will call the show The Importance of Being Elvis. It was a sincerely insincere title. I used my distorted interpretation of Rock 'n' Roll simply as irony had been used in Weimar Cabaret. I did inevitably take my comparisons from my cabaret repertoire because I liked cabaret and knew something about it. However this was the idea. I had come to this distortion and reinvention of the King of Rock 'n' Roll by intuition.

I began rehearsing with Dave Berger. More than anything, he said, you must now learn about the backbeat of the blues. Singing on the backbeat as everybody knows is especially difficult for europeans. Tommy Tune once explained to me, not only do europeans not know how to sing on the backbeat, but they think they know how to and all they do is slowing everything down. This, he said, is what we call metering and the french are notorious for doing it all the time.

I spent the winter tirelessly rehearsing, listening to

338

Elvis Presley records and little by little learning about the backbeat of the blues. Filip Noterdaeme suggested that I apply to Julie Atlas Muz who could help me. She agreed to direct the show and it was she who explained to me the deep deeper meaning of Poke Salad Annie.

Then it was spring, Filip Noterdaeme returned to the High Line with the HOMU Booth and Florence, my fortieth birthday came and went and the next day was the premiere of The Importance of Being Elvis at Joe's Pub. Dave Berger had put together a band of six musicians and to my great delight the show was sold out and who came. Tommy Tune came and Joey Arias and Penny Arcade and Sherry Vine came and Raven O and Flotilla de Barge came and also Pia Frankenberg and Yanna Avis with her international entourage.

I opened the show as silver Elvis quickly transforming into black leather Elvis and naturally concluding the show as white polyester Elvis. In the front row sat an elegant petite blonde woman in a black jacket anxiously looking up at me. It was after the fourth song that she suddenly jumped up and grabbing my arm called out, what about Heartbreak Hotel. Lady, I said, the show is not over yet. But will you sing it already, she lamented, I have come from far away to see this show and I am the founding president of the very first Elvis Presley fan club. Everybody laughed and cheered. I kissed the woman's hand and she sat down and then I sang Heartbreak Hotel. I say I sang it but I sang it in german. For years I had translated foreign songs into english for my american audiences and now I was making the most known american song foreign for them so they could once again hear it as if for the first time.

Something funny happened when I sang Tomorrow is a Long Time. I was leaning against a column in the middle of the room, standing high up on the balustrade, when I suddenly felt a pair of hands fondling my legs from below. They belonged to a very cat like woman with black hair and emerald green eyes whom nobody knew. Later everybody's favorite moment came when I sang Love me Tender and walked into the audience to kiss everybody on the lips like Elvis Presley always had, with the notable difference that I kissed both women and men. The woman with the emerald green eyes positioned herself strategically in my way like a cat on a hot tin roof. I kissed her on the lips and she purred and went back to her seat. Joey Arias later said, you should have wildly made out with her. I said, I couldn't possibly. He laughed and said, it's called acting, dear. Filip Noterdaeme said his favorite song had been Long Lonely Highway.

The Importance of Being Elvis had a success and little by little I was beginning to amusingly being referred to as the Weimar Elvis. Even straight Ed Schmidt later admitted that he had regretted sitting too far in the back to get an Elvis kiss like everybody else.

In the meanwhile Saturday afternoons under the High Line had become anything but lonely for Filip Noterdaeme where he was fast becoming a local sensation. The two visitors' chairs, one for friendship and one for society, were almost always occupied and Filip Noterdaeme always found something to say. Whenever a dog came near Florence and sniffed her tail he relished in announcing into his microphone, oh I see we have an art critic among us. One delightful story was of the young parents who had come with their young son Sammy. Sammy was proudly wearing blue nail polish and when Filip Noterdaeme asked him about it Sammy said that blue was his dad's favorite color and that it was his mom who had painted his nails. Oh, I see, Filip Noterdaeme said, you know how to keep your parents at your fingertips.

One day a visitor gave Filip Noterdaeme a sample bag of Rachel Ray dog food treats. It was meant as a facetious gift for Florence but from that moment on Filip Noterdaeme told every visitor that Rachel Ray was his official sponsor and made a point of showing the sample to everybody who sat down and sometimes offering the dog treats as a snack. Of all his visitors since then Filip Noterdaeme says only one was curious enough to actually taste them, Jaron Tager from Ohio, an eager student of Zen with a beginner's mind.

Another visitor Filip Noterdaeme remembers clearly from this, his second season of outings under the High Line, is Alec Hall. He was a young Canadian composer who sat and sat and to this day no one sat longer at the booth than he. The two talked about many things, important things and not so important things, for example problems of infinity eternity identity and so forth. And then there was the swedish woman who said she was a lifeguard and whose mother had passed away long ago but Filip Noterdaeme with the help of Florence conjured her mother's spirit to sit on the chair of society and at that, well at that the swedish lifeguard nearly drowned in tears.

As with the Sunday openings at 172 Clinton Street, there soon were regulars. Patty Heffley was one of them. She lived across the High Line and often came by to tell Filip Noterdaeme about her latest S&M adventures or her newest diet and one day she brought him a slice of delicious home-made Zwetschgendatschi, german plum cake. Filip Noterdaeme's unremitting undivided attention to everybody who sat down of course attracted many narcissists who delighted in their own emotions and purposes. Filip Noterdaeme welcomed them all. He used to say, there are really only two kinds of visitors at my booth, the curious and the needy, and they are both equally entertaining. In short, he learned the art of losing oneself without getting lost. It was Robert Hammond who surprisingly told Filip Noterdaeme, what you do is what makes me like the High Line.

Baseera Khan was someone we got to know fairly well during this period. She was technically a texan but her parents were observing muslims from India. We had first met Baseera at the Rotunda Gallery at the time of Colby Chamberlain's Dotted Line show. She was at that time about to get engaged to her boyfriend Jason Fox or the white male as she liked to call him. This had been cause for a very big scandal in her family until Jason, sweet loving Jason had agreed to convert to Islam. In any case now Baseera was putting together a group show at the Hosfelt Gallery in midtown. She called it Moonlighting and invited Filip Noterdaeme to be part of it. Filip Noterdaeme decided to show the 90 charts from the Homeless Museum's hygrothermograph. Everybody had noticed our little arrangement of them hanging side by side in the Archives and Meteorology Department, and Filip Noterdaeme said they were proof that the museum had indeed been active day and night during those two years even as he had been moonlighting as a gallery lecturer and adjunct professor to make a living. It took me several hours to neatly hang up all the charts at the Hosfelt gallery and when I was done I stepped back and marveled at them. The history of the Homeless Museum at 172 Clinton Street, it was all there, the creative heat and the cold rejection, the ups and downs, and one could also detect the conflict of arrested development in the dense labyrinth of red and blue lines of the 90th chart, the one we had kept in rotation since Paul the landlord had demanded we close the museum.

The opening was a lively affair and afterwards we went to celebrate at a korean restaurant near the gallery. I asked Bazeera about her favorite indian restaurants in New York and she said, such and such. A few weeks later Filip Noterdaeme and I passed by an indian restaurant on 33rd Street and I said, isn't this one of the indian restaurants Bazeera recommended. We went inside and ordered all kinds of things, samosas and curries and rice and other such things. The food was excellent, delicious and fresh, and we felt very proud to have an indian friend who could tell us where exactly to get the best indian food in New York. The next day we wrote to Bazeera about how much we had enjoyed the food from the indian restaurant on 33rd Street. She wrote back, I am glad you did but I have never heard of the place you are talking about.

Then came a most memorable evening that Filip Noterdaeme spent with Maria Gilissen Broodthaers and Cathleen Chaffee at Marian Goodman's penthouse on Central Park West. It was a supper in celebration of the opening of the Broodthaers show at Marian Goodman Gallery, Section Cinéma, and all the Broodthaers scholars, old and new, were there, Benjamin Buchloh, Manuel Borja-Villel, Cathleen Chaffee and Rachel Haidu. Filip Noterdaeme sat next to Maria Gilissen and she recognized him for what he was and adopted him as her son for the night. Commenting upon the madness of the politics of art around them, Filip Noterdaeme whispered to Maria, L'invention du cinéma continue. This made a big impression on Maria and she autographed the catalogue of the show for him, ignoring the flemish spelling of his name but writing, fittingly, L'invention du Cinéma continue, c'est la phrase de Marcel et de Philippe, N.Y. Sept. 9 – 2010 Maria.

Joey Arias was the most cheerful person we knew that fall. For many years filmmaker Bobby Sheehan had been following and filming him for a Bar d'O documentary. Bobby Sheehan being a perfectionist needed additional concert footage to complete the film and arranged for a special concert with Joey, Raven O and Sherry Vine at the nightclub where I had first seen Joey Arias and Raven O perform the Strange Fruit show in the mid-Nineties. Naturally we went. There was a little area with a golden backdrop set aside for interviews and Bobby Sheehan asked Filip Noterdaeme and I to talk about how we had met at Bar d'O. Earl Dax was next and he talked about how scandalous the nights at Bar d'O had been. We thought this was rather strange because we had never seen him there, as a matter of fact Earl Dax had not moved to New York until years after Bar d'O had already closed.

The show began. Raven O sang about night and day and talked of his love for Joey and Sherry and about not feeling the need to wear stilettos any longer. Then Joey Arias made a beautiful slow entrance with a transparent black mantilla over his face and sang You've Changed, as usual ending with, but there's one thing that's happening to me right now: sex change. Then Sherry Vine joined him onstage for a duet and when the music started, I believe

the song was Witchcraft, something got into Joey, he just
stood frozen in time for a moment with a beatific expression on his face. Sherry Vine gave him a comic sideway
glance and said, girl, you just missed your cue. Everybody
laughed and cheered and Joey all startled said, oh I am
so sorry, I was just thinking of you, Sherry, and of what a
beautiful cocksucker you are. Well at that we all laughed
even more and then Joey began laughing uncontrollably.
Then he recovered and once more the music started and
as he was about to sing he started laughing again but this
time the music continued and he and Sherry somehow
made it through the song. It was a wonderful night, easy to
remember but so hard to forget.

Meow Meow was back in town. It had been almost
a year since we had last seen her. Since then she had performed in London, she had had the parisians go mad for
her, she had been seen in Melbourne down under and
she had become part of the avant-garde all over. We invited her to have dinner with us at 172 Clinton Street. She
was late and sent us a text message:

Kill Meow.

Meow equals late.

She has nice wine but she is late.

Unheimlich unhöflich for a gorgeous Daniel date.

She sits on the platform and waits and waits.

It always takes longer than expected.

Here endeth the rude Haiku.

Please start eating!

Naturally we waited and finally Meow Meow arrived
with a bottle of red wine and we sat down. She told us that
she was going to star in a stage adaptation of Les Para-
pluies de Cherbourg in the West End and that Michel

Legrand was going to write a new song for her to sing in the show. Then Filip Noterdaeme and Meow Meow compared notes about the needy and the curious who always seemed to come to his and her performances, how the needy are always interested and the curious always interesting.

Sean Metzger was a young professor of cultural studies who had been fascinated by the first Foreign Affairs at the Canal Chapter. It was he who arranged for me to give a guest lecture at Duke University in North Carolina that winter. I flew down to Durham and spoke to the students of the cabaret life of Paris, Vienna, Munich and Berlin in the past and the cabaret life of New York in the present. You must understand, I said to the students, that the more things changed the more they stayed the same. And then I surprised everyone by saying, above all you must understand that the next step down from cabaret is the street.

The next thing that happened was Sofranie Trencia a french canadian circus artist I had met in Berlin flying me to Cancun to be the conférencier at the opening of the Playboy Casino. It was a very festive affair with a long red carpet and klieg lights and limousines. There were two parkour dancers performing dangerous vigorous moves and jumps outside by the entrance and both, first one then the other, injured themselves because they were blinded by the flashes from the paparazzi's cameras. They had to be carefully carried backstage where they sat with ashen faces and their feet deep in ice-filled buckets. Then I had to get onto the casino floor and start the show. It was a very strange experience to perform in such an exotic place and find myself entangled in these eccentric circumstances. I had expected an audience of american business men in the company of mexican Playboy Bunnies but it turned out to be mostly mexican business men in the company of american Playboy Bunnies. The show had several dancers and acrobats and a french canadian duo doing an aerial pas-de-deux around a rotating pole. Then I sang Whatever Lola Wants in spanish and then the casino showed a very brief video message of Hugh Heffner in his signature burgundy velvet bathrobe.

After the show I was driven back to my hotel in a limousine and there on the desk in my suite was my paycheck and a playboy watch. As may be imagined, the watch became part of the Oh Thank You Collection.

Lee Chappell and I had been looking everywhere for a suitable downtown venue for Foreign Affairs and agreeing less and less about many things. Lee Chappell was in those days working under such a state of tension that explosions were frequent. Finally he convinced me that we should reopen Foreign Affairs in a nightclub in the meatpacking district called The Griffin. No sooner were preparations for the opening night under way that it became apparent that Lee Chappell not satisfied any longer with being a producer wanted to also direct the show and possibly perform in it. Under the plea of financial pressure he was denying to hire the musicians I had asked for and then was found to have negotiated with the club owner about perhaps selling him the show. This was not only unfair, because it was I who had created Foreign Affairs, but, since he had not invited me to be present at the negotiations, it was treason.

And so Foreign Affairs reopened under rather strenuous circumstances. Lee Chappell had insisted on booking several acts I had not approved of and kept making long unnecessary announcements between numbers and this evidence of lack of stagecraft had an awful effect upon the audience. I was furious and refused to deal any further with Lee Chappell until Shequida stepped in and told Lee that he had to apologize properly. He did, however I left the show and forbade him to continue using the name Foreign Affairs for his productions. Lee Chappell renamed the show Café Panache and produced and directed it for a little while until it folded without anyone taking much notice.

The year drew to a close. I baked Christmas cookies as usual and we invited some friends to join us for tea. Harry Heissmann came with Samson his little french bulldog. Samson sat obediently at Harry's feet and Harry talked about chairs as he always does, in fact Filip Noterdaeme always refers to him as Harry of the chairs. This story reminds me of a chair Harry had built back in the days when we were studying together at the academy in Munich. We had been given the task to design a new chair and Harry had fabricated a chair that looked like a very big jellyfish atop of a rock. It looked somewhat awfully phallic and the design professor full of indignation flatly refused to sit on it.

Harry and Samson stayed only a little and just after they left we had another visitor with a dog, Joey Arias arrived with his new french bulldog puppy, Rumbles. He brought as a gift a box of herbal tea called Three Ballerina's Tea. There was a drawing of three ballerinas with very tiny waists on the box and I was not quite sure what it all meant until Joey explained, this tea is my secret remedy for when I have to wear a tight corset.

More friends came and the little party soon became

lively. Joey fed some cookies to little Rumbles and Rumbles promptly started pumping, as Joey said the scots like to call it. Filip Noterdaeme discreetly opened first the skylight and then every other window. Later that evening little Rumbles did a little more than just pump, leaving a gift on the dining room floor just as Bazeera Khan and Jason Fox walked in.

The cozy afternoon soon turned into evening. Joey told us that he was going to bring his new solo show to Le Poisson Rouge in early January. Lady Rizo said, oh I am bringing my solo show there in mid-January. And then, leaning forward, she said to him, warm it up for me.

Tommy Tune invited us for a Christmas Eve supper at his loft on Union Square. There we met Carmen Dell'Orefice who kept taking pictures of everyone until Filip Noterdaeme who did not know that she was one of the most photographed women alive said to her innocently charmingly, now someone really ought to take a picture of you. We all had a toast and Tommy Tune said, bless you all. Carmen Dell'Orefice told us of how it did not matter much to her that Bernie Madoff had betrayed her and squandered all her life savings because she was perfectly content to continue working and in any case had never lived beyond her means, after all, she said, she was a child of the Depression era and had grown up on Roosevelt Island when it was still called Welfare Island. The only problem now, she said, is that my daughter will have to learn how to work because there won't be anything there for her when I am gone. We marveled at her beauty and natural grace. Another guest we marveled at was Liliane Montevecchi. She introduced us to her italian beau of whom she said, when I met him he was a little boy and now he is an old man. How can I forget seeing Liliane Montevecchi and Carmen Dell'Orefice sitting side by side looking like fire and ice, demure ladylike Carmen dressed all in white and silver on the right and Liliane with the rough edge and highly expressive wild eyes of a real parisienne dressed in a red Halston jersey suit on the left. Then Tommy Tune's sister served possibly the best turkey I have ever eaten. It was filled with a tamale stuffing she had brought all the way from Texas. She told us the security at the airport had been very suspicious about the tamales but she had stood up for her tamales and we were the better for it. It was a delightful dinner and when it got late Carmen Dell'Orefice said, I better be off. I offered to escort her downstairs and hail a cab for her but she said, no darling, one of the things I am very good at is hailing a cab.

For some time now many friends, and strangers, have been asking Filip Noterdaeme to write his autobiography and he has always replied, not possibly.

He began to tease me and said that I should write my autobiography to tell the story of our lives. Just think, he would say, what a lot of money you would make. He then began to invent titles for my autobiography. My Life With The Director, Boyfriends of Bankers I Have Cooked For, My First Twelve Years With Filip Noterdaeme. Then he began to get serious and say, but really seriously you ought to write your autobiography. I said, isn't it a bit early at forty. No, said he, now is the time you still remember things as they truly happened. Once again we talked about Roland KC the purist painter who had been so anxious to tell us his life stories at Penny Arcade's holiday party. Finally I promised that if during the summer I could find time I would write my autobiography.

Once when Tommy Tune was talking to Filip Noterdaeme about his solo show he said, I am a pretty good performer and a pretty good director and a pretty good producer but I find it very difficult to be all three at once.

I am a pretty good housekeeper and a pretty good cook and a pretty good handyman and a pretty good creative director and a pretty good singer and a pretty good translator for songs and I have to do them all at once and I found it difficult to add being a pretty good author.

About six weeks ago, Filip Noterdaeme said it does not look to me as if you were ever going to write that autobiography. You know what I am going to do. I am going to write it for you. I am going to write it as simply as Gertrude Stein did the autobiography of Alice B. Toklas. And he has and this is it.

CPSIA information can be obtained at www.ICGtesting.com
Printed in the USA
BVOW040726190613

323661BV00001B/1/P